DESIGN BEYOND DEVICES
CREATING MULTIMODAL, CROSS-DEVICE EXPERIENCES

Cheryl Platz

NEW YORK   2020

"The future is multimodal because we are multimodal. Here is an essential guide to unleashing the potential within that symmetry."

—Bill Buxton,
Partner Researcher at Microsoft Research and
Author of *Sketching User Experiences*

"This book harnesses our very selfish desire to make cool things into the ability to benefit clients, stakeholders, customers, and society itself. Chock-full of insightful conceptual models and practical applications, designers will be both inspired and prepared."

—Sam Ladner, PhD,
Author of *Practical Ethnography: A Guide to Doing Ethnography in the Private Sector* and *Mixed Methods: A Short Guide to Applied Mixed Methods*

"Using simple frameworks and questions, Platz creates a practical playbook that challenges teams to understand the problem, reflect on the design constraints, focus on people, and avoid the traps of exclusion in a multimodal world."

—Jose Coronado,
Vice President of Global Design Operations, JPMorgan

Design Beyond Devices
Creating Multimodal, Cross-Device Experiences
By Cheryl Platz

Rosenfeld Media LLC

125 Maiden Lane

New York, New York 10038

USA

On the Web: www.rosenfeldmedia.com

Please send errors to: errata@rosenfeldmedia.com

Publisher: Louis Rosenfeld

Managing Editor: Marta Justak

Interior Layout: Danielle Foster

Cover Design: The Heads of State

Indexer: Marilyn Augst

Proofreader: Sue Boshers

ISBN: 1-933820-78-0

ISBN 13: 978-1933820-78-1

LCCN: 2020939920

Printed and bound in the United States of America

Dedicated to the memory of two educators
whose influence set me on this path:

Nancy Tickel, who encouraged my writing
while modeling an inclusive spirit

and

Dr. Randy Pausch, whose teaching and mentorship
helped me make my childhood dreams come true

HOW TO USE THIS BOOK

Who Should Read This Book?

If you've ever wondered what comes after websites, you should read this book. If you're struggling to integrate your mobile app with a website and a smart speaker app, you should read this book. If you're intimidated but intrigued by future tech like VR and AI and don't know whether you should care, you should read this book.

If you're frustrated with futurists and are looking for actionable content to help you move your product forward, you should read this book. If you feel lost in a world of unethical tech and need some guidance on how to keep customers at the center of your work, you should read this book.

And for all of the designers, program managers, developers, and engineers who want to understand how to create the ambitious, expansive interfaces of their science fiction dreams? You should *definitely* read this book.

What's in This Book?

This book is structured to emulate the best-case, end-to-end design journey for multimodal experiences.

In this book, you'll find:

Chapter 1, "Creating the World We Want to Live In," provides a definition for multimodality and other foundational concepts you'll need in order to create worthwhile experiences using the content in this book.

Chapter 2, "Capturing Customer Context," and Chapter 3, "Understanding Busy Humans," provide a framework for querying and representing the human context in which your products will reside.

Chapter 4, "Activity, Interrupted," and Chapter 10, "Let's Get Proactive," explore the implications of proactive engagement with customers, and provide design frameworks for exploring that space.

Chapter 5, "The Language of Devices," and Chapter 6, "Expressing Intent," explore the full scope of input and output technologies that can be combined to build multimodal experiences, organized by the human senses each of these technologies engage.

Chapter 7, "The Spectrum of Multimodality," lays out a spectrum of different multimodal interaction models that balance tangible and intangible interactions.

Chapter 8, "It's a (Multimodal) Trap! and Chapter 9, "Lost in Transition," dive into the most difficult design challenges facing multimodal designers: synchronization, context, discoverability, ergonomics, identity, and transitions.

Chapter 11, "Breathe Life into the Unknown," describes some of the ideation techniques and mental models that multimodal designers have been using to explore and ideate within uncharted territory.

Chapter 12, "From Envisioning to Execution," covers specific types of design deliverables you'll need to provide a shared understanding of your multimodal experience across all of your team members.

Chapter 13, "Beyond Devices: Human + AI Collaboration," and Chapter 14, "Beyond Reality: XR, VR, AR, and MR," cover the most future-looking topics in the space today: the role of AI, digital assistants, and extended reality in multimodal and cross-device experiences.

Chapter 15, "Should You Build It?" explores the impact of this work, and offers an ethical framework for evaluating proposed solutions to ensure that you're standing on morally and conceptually solid ground.

Advice on leading with inclusion and concrete questions for exploration of each topic in your own work are included throughout this book.

You'll find a variety of perspectives in 10 featured interviews with accomplished industry veterans and scholars, including:

- Mozilla R&D researcher Janice Y. Tsai, PhD
- Computational linguist Syed Sameer Arshad
- Conversational design pioneer Cathy Pearl
- Google Nest staff designer Jen Cotton
- Multimodal innovator and speaker Anna Abovyan

- Mixed reality leader Craig Fox
- Atomic design author Brad Frost
- Creative Director and IDEO alumnus Ovetta Sampson
- Virtual reality pioneer Jesse Schell
- Social computing researcher Casey Fiesler, PhD

This book does *not* provide:

- Design deep dives for any one specific modality. Plenty of books already exist on these topics.
- Comprehensive user research techniques. This book provides frameworks for generating research questions, but there are plenty of resources about ethnographic research and user testing.
- A comprehensive exploration of ethical frameworks. While this book provides prompts and structures for evaluating potential impact and minimizing harm proactively, I encourage you to conduct your own research about the various ethical frameworks to determine which aligns with your beliefs.

What This Means for You

Before you panic, rest assured—the skills you may have now as a designer, engineer, or project manager generally won't fade into obscurity. You'll still need to design for multimodal devices, and we'll talk about that, too. You'll learn how to adapt your existing skills for individual devices that support multiple input and output modalities. But that singular focus falls short of being truly human-centered in a world where technology is capable of so much more.

But beyond the frame of a single device is where the real magic happens. You need to explore the invisible systems and affordances that allow your customers to move seamlessly from device to device, location to location, when appropriate, without losing key context. Beyond exploring, you need to find ways to express those systems in concise, broadly understandable deliverables.

Even if you're not attempting to bring anything as grandiose as the bridge of the Starship Enterprise into existence, the models presented in this book should help you grapple with your most complex cross-device scenarios, and will help you identify what benefits you'll see—both now and in the future—by investing in true multimodal, device-agnostic system and service design.

Make no mistake—this is a long road to walk, but the journey is worth the effort. You'll inevitably get overwhelmed at times, as you're really attempting nothing less than codifying the whole of human interaction into systems that your devices can interpret across a dizzying array of inputs and sensors. Just like your customers, you'll shift modalities of mind frequently along this path. You'll need different frameworks at different times to make informed decisions. Be kind to yourself. Rome wasn't built in a day.

It's time for you to stop asking your customers to adapt to their technology, instead of the other way around. It's time for you to learn to design *beyond* devices.

Let's get started.

What Comes with This Book?

This book's companion website (rosenfeldmedia.com/books/design-beyond-devices) contains additional content. The book's diagrams and other illustrations are available under a Creative Commons license (when possible) for you to download and include in your own presentations. You can find these on Flickr at www.flickr.com/photos/rosenfeldmedia/sets/.

FREQUENTLY ASKED QUESTIONS

What exactly is multimodal design, anyway?

We define it in Chapter 1, "Creating the World We Want to Live In," but think of it this way: multimodal experiences are experiences that can engage multiple human senses. Devices that let you speak *or* touch to make a selection. Twenty years ago, your PC (generally) only engaged you visually, and you only engaged your PC with touch. You have many more options today (see Chapter 7, "The Spectrum of Multimodality," to fully understand all those options), but those options bring a lot more complexity to the design party [see Chapter 8, "It's a (Multimodal) Trap!"].

What's so hard about multimodal design?

One of the biggest challenges is the introduction of invisible inputs like voice and gesture, which complicate both the delivery of designs and the interactions themselves. Many of the existing deliverable standards don't scale to systems with multiple inputs and outputs, but in Chapter 12, "From Envisioning to Execution," you'll see concrete examples of how to transform your complex ideas into tangible designs. As these devices become ubiquitous, interruptions are also a growing challenge. Chapter 4, "Activity, Interrupted," and Chapter 10, "Let's Get Proactive," will help you design predictable, responsible proactive systems.

Is this book about artificial intelligence?

This book is not *solely* about artificial intelligence (AI). But modes of interaction like speech and gesture are inherently driven by artificial intelligence, so the topic is unavoidable, even for designers. You'll learn about specific types of artificial intelligence driven input and output in Chapter 5, "The Language of Devices," and Chapter 6, "Expressing Intent." Chapter 13, "Beyond Devices: Human + AI Collaboration," is entirely devoted to artificial intelligence as a concept—how it works, the potential biases, and the ways in which it can most effectively be deployed in your experiences.

Does this book cover accessibility and inclusive design?

Rather than lock accessibility into its own chapter, inclusion has been woven into the fabric of this book. In Chapter 1, you'll learn more about some of the concerns that have been raised in recent years about the design community's relationship with the disability community and new ways of thinking to address those concerns. You'll find content about the potential risks of exclusion—as well as opportunities for inclusion—all throughout Chapter 5 and Chapter 6. And where appropriate, additional content is included throughout the rest of the book. Finally, Chapter 15, "Should You Build It," introduces a new lightweight framework for querying the potential impact of your work, good or bad.

CONTENTS

FOREWORD

Humans are—as far as we know—the only creatures on Earth capable of communicating the same message in multiple modalities, switching at will depending on context and abilities. Other animals sing, snarl, and stridulate (that thing crickets do), but each species has its set of modes, and each of those is constrained to a range of meanings. A blue-footed booby can't hum its way into the heart of a mate unable to see the kinetic output of its distinctive dance. Vervet monkeys emit a different warning call for each of their four major predators, but lack the same options for a silent signal when danger approaches.

We, however, hit the multimodal jackpot. To convey the deeply human message of your love for someone, you may choose to speak aloud, mouth the words, sign the phrase with a single hand, send a GIF, or nudge an arm, based on what's most comfortable for you and intelligible to your intended audience. In a slightly different situation, you might choose a different way.

But wow, this gets complicated once we bring digital systems into the mix. No wonder we've tried to put off dealing with the full implications, hoping partial solutions like "mobile first" and "conversational UI" could stand in for fully human-centered design. The truth is that focusing on a single device or mode at a time actually leaves a lot of humans behind.

Fortunately, Cheryl is here, not only as an expert and compassionate guide through this new territory, but also to hold us to task. She reminds us that in order to include everyone, we need to question everything. She shares her enthusiasm for technology grounded in the recognition that we all remain people with bodies—a fact that can appear either awkward or inconvenient to designers and technologists.

This book represents the essential next evolution of design for digital systems, integrating everything that has come before and making the principles and process clear, regardless of the reader's previous area of practice. Even if you aren't going fully device-independent and multimodal in your work immediately, you will come away better equipped to accommodate the incessant interruptions and device switching that are just a part of daily life with technology now. Your work will be more gracious and humane.

As Cheryl explains in one of several case studies, simply offering a single additional input modality can offer an individual agency over their environment that they lacked before. We toss the word "empowerment" around a lot, but this is it.

Humanity is shared, but each of us is unique in our current context and our capabilities. Read this book. Rise to the challenge issued within. And you can help ensure that everyone can fully participate in the promise of our future. If only we could also wag our tails.

—Erika Hall, Director of Strategy,
Mule Design Studio

INTRODUCTION

News of the website's death has been greatly exaggerated, but you can no longer assume that your customers will sit down at a single device to complete tasks. Reality is more complicated: a single experience might span a website, a mobile app, a smart speaker, and a car. The future is multimodal and multidevice.

It's time for us as an industry to abandon our preoccupation with being "mobile first" or "voice first." Your customers are savvy enough to choose for themselves, in the moment, the manner of interaction most suitable to their needs. When you focus on the tasks that customers want to complete, the way they complete them, and enable that way of working uniquely across multiple input and output choices, everyone wins.

Cortana, Alexa, and ... Stitch?

While I've always been fascinated by technology, my path toward this book was launched in earnest by ... Pikachu. *Hey You, Pikachu!* to be exact.

During my undergraduate studies on my road to a computer science and human-computer interaction bachelor's degree at Carnegie Mellon University, I had the opportunity to play with some cutting-edge technology like robotics, artificial intelligence, and virtual reality.

But in the year 2000, a few years after I'd fallen permanently down the *Pokémon* rabbit hole (What? It's a great RPG), Nintendo released *Hey You, Pikachu!* (Figure I.1) for the Nintendo 64. This game was astonishingly multimodal: it came with a special microphone attachment (Figure I.2) that allowed you to speak to Pikachu. I knew it was a gimmick. The game was developed for elementary school kids, and I was old enough to vote. But when I experimented with it and spoke to Pikachu for the first time, I *felt* something. When he ignored me (either due to a bad mood or the limited capabilities of early millennium microphones), it cut me to my core. I ended up writing a graduate school paper about the Hero's Journey in *Hey You, Pikachu!*— but the voice technology cast a longer shadow in my life.

FIGURE I.1
Small *Pokémon*, big impact: the game *Hey You, Pikachu!* helped shaped my career.

FIGURE I.2
The author (in full 90's velour) uses a microphone peripheral to experience her first voice-controlled video game experience, *Hey You, Pikachu!*, in her brother Kyle's bedroom.

My first professional experience with multimodality came when I worked as the assistant producer for Electronic Arts on one of the seven launch titles for the Nintendo DS, *The Urbz: Sims in the City*. (I know. The name. It's a long story.) The multimodality on that title was primarily haptic (buttons) and kinesthetic (touch/gesture).

A few years later, I was back on the Nintendo DS as lead producer for the Nintendo DS exclusive *Disney Friends* (2007). Inspired heavily by *Nintendogs*, *Animal Crossing*, and (yes) *Hey You, Pikachu!*, *Disney Friends* was my first personal experience shipping voice user interfaces. The insights I gained about touch UI design, automatic speech recognition, localization, and the emotional impact of voice interfaces were invaluable (see Figure I.3). I also logged quite a bit of time talking to Stitch about his badness levels.

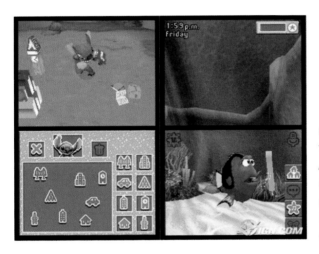

FIGURE I.3
While developing *Disney Friends*, we used multimodal design to push the envelope of immersive experiences on the Nintendo DS.

My winding path again took me into the multimodal forest when I joined the Windows Automotive team from 2012–2014. The (never-released) experiences we designed felt like science fiction: we were working on seamlessly switching from voice to haptic controls to touchscreens and back again, not unlike the bridge of the Starship Enterprise.

From there, it was a short hop to Cortana to work on productivity scenarios like scheduling meetings with voice and touch on desktop. That final step prepared me for what became my Amazon Echo adventure. During my two years at Amazon on Echo products, I worked on everything from computer vision projects like the Echo Look (rest in peace, old friend) to the Fire TV integration, the Echo Show, Alexa automotive, and smart home scenarios.

NOTE WHO'S CORTANA?

While Amazon's Alexa platform of voice driven devices is well-known, Cortana has been on the scene even longer in one form or another. Cortana is Microsoft's intelligent assistant. While currently restricted to the desktop, Cortana was originally the assistant built into the fabric of the now-defunct Windows Phone platform (RIP).

But the biggest part of my attention on Alexa was directed at systems-level design. How could we adapt the Echo platform, built for voice-only interaction, to support the addition of the Echo Show and its screen? My time driving the design of Alexa Notifications, Do Not Disturb, and our interruption model were some of the most exciting design problems I'll ever tackle in my career.

By transforming your design framing from device-bound experiences to device-agnostic systems, you can open up a world of opportunity for your customers to just be human. They can finally begin to express themselves as they do in the "real" world: fluidly adapting their expressions based on their instinct and needs in the moment.

Years after my own multimodal design adventure began, I see the rest of the industry still grappling with the next steps in this space. I wrote this book to bridge that gap, and to encourage us all to apply a systems thinking approach to this incredibly rich set of opportunities for human-computer interaction.

The Need for New Foundations

Because technology companies often operate at breakneck speed and jealously guard their potential intellectual property, new concepts are rarely considered as part of a broader context of use before launch. Those minimum viable products have become the inadequate infrastructure in which new websites, new apps, and new devices must operate.

The cost of this tunnel vision used to be fairly limited, as you could at least assume a customer was providing full focus to an experience in the moment. Sure, you might not understand a customer's home setup, but at least you knew that when they used your shopping cart, they were on a standard PC with a keyboard and pointer. What happened elsewhere? Not your problem! Desktop or die.

That assumption is no longer true. Design for a single environment or scenario simply perpetuates an outdated, device-centered philosophy. A philosophy borne out of a world littered with physical and functional constraints. A philosophy that has long excluded many people who are facing disabilities or situational obstacles that were considered "too costly an edge case" for anything but the most minimal accommodations.

But those aging minimum-viable systems can't bear the weight of more complex, human-centered interactions without some serious new scaffolding. This book is your blueprint for building that scaffolding into your own work.

The World Turned Upside Down

When I began writing this book, it was September 2019. As I complete the process, I'm nearing the sixth month of my home sequestration due to the COVID-19 pandemic. This is not the world into which I thought I'd be releasing this work. So much tragedy and pain and loss squeezed into such a short period of time. At first, I was gripped with a sense of book-related doom against the backdrop of everything else. Surely, I'd have to rework everything! But in the end, little has changed except the urgency of the approach.

More than ever, we need to question everything, because the world we were trained for no longer exists.

More than ever, we need to keep our customers and their context vividly present at the center of everything that we do.

More than ever, we need to be energetically inclusive and anti-racist in our work because neutrality is causing harm to those around us.

More than ever, the industry must be vigilant and ensure that we do not let good intent blind us to the potentially harmful nature of our actions.

More than ever, we need to take the time to question whether what we're doing is worth doing, because human resources are so precious, and the need is so great.

There are still plenty of things worth doing. So many exciting challenges. So many opportunities to bring people along, to increase equity and justice, to decrease suffering, to increase joy. These are epic challenges beyond the boundaries of any one device, and they are the future of design.

And it is this very moment, when the world is trying to define a new path forward, when opportunity for positive change is at its greatest. I hope this book finds you safe and healthy, and I humbly hope it helps provide our industry a foundation upon which we can start charting a path out of this unexpected darkness.

CHAPTER 1

Creating the World We Want to Live In

The world as you know it is experiencing (yet another) seismic shift on all levels of society, and the field of human-computer interaction is no exception. You must broaden your understanding of what interaction truly means in order to adjust to this brave new world. When you do, you'll find that definition is now inextricably linked with some of the forces that drive that transformed society. With great power comes great responsibility. (Thanks, Uncle Ben.)

Until the advent of the smartphone, the shape of a human-computer interaction was fairly well defined. Your computer whirred to life and began the conversation with pictures and visual representations of words on a screen—and occasionally, even sound effects. The human expressed their intent, or response, with the help of a keyboard and a mouse.

Thankfully, the available palette of interaction technologies has become far more sophisticated. The devices of today and tomorrow are capable of supporting far more than a single input and output. And yet so many of our devices continue to party as if it's 1999!

These new technologies allow today's designers to broaden their toolkits and to choose the inputs and outputs best suited to their customers' needs. Some systems already allow customers to choose between parallel input and output modalities on demand—a far more inclusive approach often referred to as *multimodality*.

But as interactive technology became a darling of the consumer market, it also became indispensable to the systems that power human society. Your understanding of your customer's lived experience is more critical than ever, as your experiences affect a majority of their waking lives. Your design decisions aren't just about inputs and outputs anymore. Your decisions are about *impacts* and *outcomes*. Technologists have far more power than anyone anticipated years ago. How can we use our collective skills to create the world we owe to each other?

The Criticality of Context

I was fortunate enough to grow up in a tech enthusiast household (see Figure 1.1). From an early age, I developed an affection for the "blinking black boxes" scattered around the house. I even wrote my college essay about the topic. But I'm clearly no Nostradamus, as I didn't see the blinking black cylinders of my Alexa-powered future looming in the mists of foreshadowing.

Mind you, the devices in my home weren't *always* blinking, particularly after I started reading the manuals. My parents had to contend with a precocious pre-kindergartner who set the VCR's clock and corrected them when recordings weren't set correctly. (As a service for most people reading this book, "VCR" stands for *video cassette recorder*. You didn't miss much.)

FIGURE 1.1
The author, already drawn to the device her father used for computer programming at Amtrak.

For decades, the experience I had as a child was the accepted model for interacting with technology:

1. Purchase expensive hardware (or software).
2. Read the manual.
3. Sit within a few feet of the hardware's input channels (buttons, keyboard, mouse, etc.).
4. Perform a complex ritual of steps you memorized from the manual.

Humans were—and in many ways, still are—expected to adapt their world and their life to their technology. (This is particularly true for those living with disabilities—we'll talk more about this later in the chapter.)

At the risk of rash generalization, surprisingly little consideration was given to contextual design questions like, "Where is the device located?" or even "Can we assume our customers have 20/20 eyesight?" We needed physical peripherals to interact with those devices, so it was safe to assume our customers were within arm's reach of the device. Beyond that, most devices were heavy and needed power, so it was also safe to assume that a device was always in the vicinity of the same power outlet.

Nowadays, everyone theoretically knows that things have changed. But has that "knowledge" changed the way that products are conceived, pitched, and designed? Not as much as you might think. Product teams are still reflexively applying all sorts of shortcuts and assumptions that aged out once laptops, batteries, touchscreens, cell signals, and hands-free devices entered the market.

Context has become a critical component in any designer's work. You can't even assume that customers can *see* the "blinking black box" (or cylinder) anymore. Whether you're designing for devices that travel (laptops, smartphones, fitness trackers, smartwatches, etc.) or designing for dynamic environments (open offices, family kitchens, and public spaces), the context in which interactions occur shapes the perceived utility and success of that experience.

Part of my mission in this book is to encourage you to treat the customer *and* their context as stakeholders in your work. As interactions become more sophisticated, it's risky and in some cases downright dangerous to disregard the tremendous impact a customer's surroundings, relationships, and circumstances will have on the success of your experience.

LEARN MORE

Chapters 2, "Capturing Customer Context," and 3, "Understanding Busy Humans," provide you with tools for exploring and defining your customer's context so that you can keep the human at the center of your human-computer interactions.

Defining Multimodality

What do the terms *modality* and *multimodality* even mean? Those words might be part of your motivation for reading this book. But have designers and technologists ever stopped to consider whether they're all talking about the same thing?

It turns out that this is a tricky question to answer. Merriam-Webster defines *multimodal* as "having or involving several modes, modalities, or maxima." That's fairly general, to say the least. In order for that term to mean anything, a useful definition of the concept of a mode will be required. As it turns out, the terms *mode* and *multimodality* have been interpreted in many ways, even when limited to digital experiences:

- **One input, many interpretations:** The Nielsen/Norman group defines *modes* as "different interpretations of the user input by the system, depending on the state which is active. Same input, different results."[1] The example they provide is the Caps Lock key on a keyboard: when Caps Lock mode is engaged, the way a device interprets an alphabetic keystroke changes. As originally defined, *multimodal* didn't apply to system output.

- **Capability or functionality:** The term *mode* is also more widely used to describe different capabilities or states, like *airplane mode* on a smartphone. Psychologists have defined different sensory modalities for humans: visual, auditory (sound), haptic (touch, movement), and proprioceptive (movement and orientation in space).

- **Type of communication:** Outside of the technology industry, the concept of a *"mode* of communication" is rather widely accepted. Modes of communication can include the written word, pictures, speech, movement, touch, and more.

So where does this leave the industry? In the end, none of these definitions are inherently wrong. The word *mode* has many modes. In his 2019 keynote "Moment Prisons" at Interaction Latin America, Lou Rosenfeld challenged the industry to avoid becoming overattached to specific definitions, saying that it's the context that provides meaning. The relationship between humans and their devices has evolved, and so has the context in which multimodal will be interpreted.

---

1   Page Laubheimer, "Modes in User Interfaces: When They Help and When They Hurt Users," Nielsen Norman Group, April 14, 2019, www.nngroup.com/articles/modes/

In the context of this book, my definition of a multimodal interaction is *"an exchange between a device and a human being where multiple input or output modalities may be used simultaneously or sequentially depending upon context and preference."*

To ease future discussions, it makes sense to establish a common set of modalities that can be applied to both human-initiated input and device-initiated output (see Table 1.1).

TABLE 1.1 COMMUNICATION MODALITIES

Modality	Description
Visual	A projection or rendering of a stimulus that will be interpreted over optical channels—from books and e-readers to GIFs and videos.
Auditory	The use of acoustic waves to communicate meaning: music, sound effects, or language.
Haptic	Communicating meaning with changes to the physical environment: pressure, vibration, force feedback, or direct manipulation like taps or clicks.
Kinetic	Communication based on movement or orientation in space.
Ambient	Inferred meaning driven by environmental or biometric conditions: temperature, heart rate, lighting, etc.

Take note that the input and output modalities at any given moment in an interaction do not have to match. In fact, in some cases a mismatch might be desirable. For decades, our digital interactions have technically been out of sync: humans communicating via haptic input (mouse and keyboard), but receiving system output via visual and auditory modalities. We tapped and typed while computers glowed and beeped. And that's not necessarily bad! It's just not always aligned with the "natural" way that humans have evolved to interact.

LEARN MORE

You'll learn more about the specific input and output manifestations for each of these interaction modalities in Chapter 5, "The Language of Devices" and Chapter 6, "Expressing Intent."

Fluidity over Rigidity

When I first began working with smart speakers, I discovered a peculiar tension. On one hand, smart speakers were receiving rave reviews from customers and media alike as a new, inclusive step forward.

And yet, in the first few weeks of my time as a voice designer on the Alexa voice user interface team at Amazon, I was confronted with evidence that contradicted that perception. In fact, early Echo devices weren't fully accessible to all customers with disabilities. Certain key features (like onboarding) were *only* controllable via the app. These visual-only settings excluded customers with extremely limited vision and members of the Blind community.

That led me to ponder a broader question: If even a smart speaker struggles with accessibility, how on earth are multimodal interfaces desirable? Ethical? Wouldn't we be excluding more customers as we required the use of multiple input technologies, increasing the pool of folks who might encounter an obstacle?

And there's the trick. Requiring multiple inputs *does* exclude more potential customers. Those early Echo devices were implicitly requiring both auditory and haptic interaction to complete some core scenarios.

But multimodality in its strongest form shouldn't be about *requiring* multiple modes of input at all. The most powerful multimodal systems are those that support multiple inputs and outputs and allow fluid transitions between those modes of interaction as a customer's context and needs change.

LEARN MORE

Transitions between modalities are so important that there's a whole chapter devoted to the concept of transitions—see Chapter 9, "Lost in Transition."

Fix the System, Not the Person

Disabled customers have lived in a paradoxical state: they've long been pioneers of multimodality, using voice and haptic controls in unique ways when the "default" way of working wasn't sufficient. But these multimodal experiences were almost always an afterthought; a pervasive "check-the-box" mentality led to subpar and disjointed multimodal interactions.

We can't afford to make that mistake again. We now have a chance to build new systems with disabled customers in mind from the ground up! What an exciting opportunity for a discipline of practitioners who love solving problems and a market powered by discovering new customers. However, this requires a desire to deeply understand the nature of disabilities and the disability culture.

(Re)Defining Disability

The definition of *disability* has evolved considerably in the past few decades. In the 1980s, a disability was largely defined in terms of impairment and missing capabilities. But the definition now acknowledges that a disability is the result of both a person's physical capabilities *and* the systems that person must interact with on a regular basis. From the World Health Organization: "Today, disability is understood to arise from the interaction between a person's health condition or impairment and the multitude of influencing factors in their environment."[2]

This shift restores dignity to those who were made to feel like less of a person. It shifts the focus to fixing systemic exclusion rather than putting the burden on already burdened individuals to "overcome" the system.

> **NOTE** DISABILITY AND DIGNITY WITH LABELS
>
> Different individuals prefer different terminology when discussing a personal disability. Some prefer "disabled person," while others prefer "person with disabilities" or even "person living with disabilities." Some of my sources intentionally vary their language, but when dealing with a specific population, follow their lead. Avoid the use of the word *handicapped* in reference to a person, because it is outdated and not endorsed by the disability community.

---

2   "Disability," World Health Organization, accessed August 8, 2020, www.who.int/topics/disabilities/en/

Accepting Constraint as a Gift

As you explore input and output modalities in the next few chapters, you'll see a number of notes about the potential customers who would be excluded from that mode of interaction due to situational, temporary, or permanent disabilities.

Rather than accept these potential exclusions as limitations, look at them as invitations: invitations to lead with inclusivity. Where you find an exclusion, ask yourself this question: How might a robust multimodal experience use a different interaction to allow those excluded customers to complete a task?

Your designs will be stronger if you begin these considerations at the start of your project when you're prioritizing which modalities and support systems will be supported.

Instead of viewing design for inclusion as a task, reframe the constraints presented by inclusive design as a gift. Don't designers thrive on constraint? Aren't most products considered to be solutions intended to solve a problem? There are many documented instances where inclusive design bore unexpected dividends well past those with disabilities. Here are a few examples:

- **Curb cuts:** The ramps cut into concrete curbs at intersections were designed to allow wheelchairs to access the crosswalk, but were also transformative for strollers, delivery carts, and bicycles.[3]

- **Captioning on streaming media:** Captions created for hearing impaired individuals led to the ability to watch video without headphones on a crowded bus and the ability to watch streams in noisy environments.

- **Text messaging:** Originally designed as a tool for hearing impaired individuals, text messaging fundamentally changed the way that humans interact around the globe.

But don't lose sight of the reason for the accommodations. The "curb cut effect" may benefit all of society, but it does bring *with it* the risk of re-marginalizing the people for whom the original accommodations were made. In a blog post, wheelchair user Scott Crawford wrote: "I've photographed curb ramps that are little more than 'decorative accents' in an otherwise impassable sidewalk that isn't

---

3   Angela Glover Blackwell, "The Curb Cut Effect," *Stanford Social Innovation Review*, Winter 2017, https://ssir.org/articles/entry/the_curb_cut_effect

safe for a mountain goat, much less a disabled person. Wheelchair users use such ramps only to find an obstacle down the sidewalk. We have to backtrack, feeling like a 'rat in a maze.'"[4]

Design Questioning for Systems Design

Along these lines, members of the disability community rightly raise concerns about the way that design for disability has been framed in the past. In her 2019 talk at Interaction Week in Seattle, Liz Jackson shone a light on the hollow motivation behind some of today's design work for people with disabilities.

Liz called out the "pathological altruism" embodied by some of today's design for disabilities and pointed out that the narrative often told is of a savior (the company or designer) and the beneficiary (the disabled person). That narrative diminishes the disabled person and removes their agency, sending a message that they were not competent enough to help themselves. In her words, "We are nothing more than a prop in your stories."

As an alternative, Liz encouraged "design questioning." Rather than focusing on "fixing" the person and restoring a missing capability, you should question the systems that require the use of that capability in the first place.

That's tough medicine to swallow, I know. But this is one of the many reasons multimodal design is so exciting. Multimodal systems allow you to stop treating disabled folks as a prop or a checkbox. By focusing on a flexible multimodal approach that allows people to use different human capabilities to solve a single problem, you're taking important steps toward shifting the narrative from "accessibility for people who lack a capability" to "amplifying everyone's inherent capabilities."

Nothing About Us Without Us

In her eye-opening book *Giving Voice: Mobile Communication, Disability, and Inequality*, Meryl Alper points out that the many projects that lead with technological adaptations for disabled people are missing broader systemic issues.

---

4   Scott Crawford, "Impassible Sidewalks Turn Curb Cuts into Decorative Accents," *Rooted in Rights* (blog), November 16, 2016, https://rootedinrights. org/impassable-sidewalks-turn-curb-cuts-into-decorative-accents/

My Disability Journey

I now self-identify as disabled. After a work-related injury in 2018 (office ergonomics matter—even in temporary workspaces), I was referred to a physiatrist who diagnosed me with a genetic connective tissue disorder in addition to my injury.

Suddenly, so much of my life snapped into place. My history of surprisingly traumatic joint injuries. Migraines, tumors, and other strange symptoms. And most importantly, it provided an explanation for my chronic pain and its resulting impact on my life, interfering with and sometimes preventing my participation in activities like driving and writing.

The process of fully exploring this diagnosis will take a long time. Ironically, I've been living with that disability my whole life and just didn't know that it had a name. There's such a tendency—and even I have been guilty of this—of "othering" folks with disabilities.

But we are all humans with varying spectrums of ability dealing with environmental conditions, known medical conditions, and as-yet unknown constraints. I encourage you to think about how you empower people of any capabilities, rather than trying to "compensate" for the loss of a standard capability.

One popular attempt to honor the disability community's rallying cry "Nothing about us without us" is to arrange accessibility design sprints, where customers who live with a relevant disability are invited for a whirlwind week of participatory design. But to Liz's point earlier, those design sprints generally still frame disability as ancillary to the process, rather than integrating disability as a core consideration.

As an individual who is either actively developing technology or curious about the process, your viewpoint is but one valuable perspective among many at the design table. To better equip your team with the creative perspectives needed to challenge existing systems, consider pursuing more durable representation from disabled voices as consultants, vendors, or full-time team members on your projects.

LEARN MORE

For examples of potential exclusion risks in multimodality, see Chapters 5 and 6. For more about inclusion in the design process, see Chapter 15, "Should You Build It?"

Leading with Anti-neutrality and Anti-racism

We live in a time where brave, radical inclusion is required of all of us in the technology sector. In this liminal state between the injustices of the past and the changes we yearn for—changes which will take years, decades—technology remains disproportionately influential.

Darnella Frazier, the young Black woman who had the presence of mind to capture what became the tragic murder of George Floyd with her smartphone—changed the world. Technology both enabled that brave act *and* enabled the subsequent harassment she endured at the hands of racists and those numb to the intersection of police brutality and racism. It took weeks for Facebook employees to speak

It's Time for Designers to #causeascene

For too long, those with the luxury of power and platform (myself included) have failed to acknowledge that it's not enough to assume neutrality "fixes" forms of discrimination and oppression woven into the fabric of our culture.

Anti-racist economist and tech ethics advocate Dr. Kim Crayton created the #causeascene (Cause a Scene) hashtag on Twitter and the Cause a Scene podcast to deconstruct the harm that tech "neutrality" causes. The #causeascene framework provides four clear but critical guiding principles to help you minimize the harm your own work causes moving forward in these difficult times.

The #CauseAScene Guiding Principles:

- **Technology is not neutral.** A lack of action is the same as inaction, and it reinforces existing systemic bias. On Twitter, heads of state and other people in power are allowed to abuse the platform in direct violation of terms of service that are applied to the rest of the platform's audience. Every product decision you make can help or harm—but true neutrality is an illusion.
- **Intention without strategy is chaos.** How often have you heard "I meant well" after something goes wrong? Positive intent doesn't neutralize actual harm. Strategy can take the form of steps to proactively mitigate potential harm, as well as a plan to listen to your customers, monitor impact, and respond immediately if unexpected harm is identified.

out when the President encouraged violence on their platform without objection from Facebook's CEO. That same indifference led to the environment that empowered Darnella's tormentors.

In Chapter 15, you'll explore a lightweight framework to help you probe your own work for ethical red flags. But this point is important enough to make before you even begin your journey into multimodality: *It is your responsibility as a technologist not just to ensure the systems you envision cause no harm, but that they actively reinforce the society you wish to see.* From not-racist to anti-racist; from accessibility to radical inclusion.

- How might your technology reinforce negative stereotypes and empower abusers?
- How might your technology be used to silence the less powerful?

- **Lack of inclusion is a risk management issue.** This point is best illustrated by the 2020 Oscars, where despite earlier campaigns for greater racial diversity in nominees, both women and minorities were shut out of key categories—leading to the lowest ratings in Oscars' history. Notably, awareness of the racial disparity in Oscar nominations was driven by the #OscarsSoWhite hashtag on Twitter as created by Black media activist and former lawyer April Reign.
- **Prioritize the most vulnerable.** It's not enough to assume good intentions, and it's not enough to stop with "equal" treatment. Today's technologies and societal norms are built on a complex history of colonialism, discrimination, and oppression. Active effort must be taken in order to break these cycles—and it is what we owe each other.

The principles outlined in Dr. Crayton's #causeascene framework provide a useful framing mechanism for those who intend to move the needle on the trickiest, largest-scale problems facing society. Could the lives of trans men and women be saved if social media platforms prioritized their safety as some of the most vulnerable members of society? How would the 2016 U.S. elections have been different if Facebook had acknowledged that technology is not, in fact, neutral? Rather than wait until your idea is fully formed, work these principles into your daily practice.

- Do Black, indigenous, other minorities, and disabled people have equal access to your technology? What happens if they don't? How are they harmed by exclusion?
- Would the introduction of this technology harm or disrupt support systems already in place?

These are hard questions, and I'm no expert. In general, you should be talking to the members of these communities to ascertain the answers to these questions, rather than trying to guess as an outsider. Our record in the first few decades of the millennium proves that we, as a collective, are not great at acting in the best interests of those unlike ourselves. Inclusion means working together, not simply opening the door.

LEARN MORE

For more about potential sources of bias in artificial intelligence—some of the biggest risk areas in technology today—see Chapter 13, "Beyond Devices: Human + AI Collaboration." For a lightweight framework with which to explore the feasibility, desirability, and potential impact of your project, see Chapter 15.

Reconnecting with the Past

Another important part of cultivating an anti-racist mindset is recognizing the relationship between colonialist practices of the past that led many of us to be where we are today—quite literally. Just as with the concept of reparations, the growing desire to confront our past is not an attempt to demonize today's descendants many generations removed, but rather one tiny first step toward making those whose families were harmed by these practices whole again. It's about learning from the past, not reliving it.

Much of this book will talk about centering human context, systems design, and ethical design—practices well-aligned with the oft-challenging reflections about how to reorient our thinking away from outdated colonialist models. There are few corners of the world that are not affected by these models in some way. Designers looking to affect large-scale change or improve equity should include these reflections in their work, and can start by investigating the history of their own hometowns.

This book was written within the traditional territory of Coast Salish peoples, specifically the Duwamish Tribe. Despite hundreds of years of broken treaties and setbacks, the Duwamish people continue to shine a light here in their ancestral lands as the host tribe of Seattle, all while continuing to petition for formal government recognition. I am grateful to the Duwamish tribe, past and present, and honor their land itself.

A Gender Equity Lens

Gender is a difficult topic. Some designers find themselves trapped: you want to do the right thing, but doesn't gender equity mean making gender invisible? Not really—at least, not yet. It's impossible to deny that the gender gap still exists in systems that surround us, from income to legislation. Ignoring gender during the design process risks perpetuating harms represented within those systems.

NOTE WHAT IS GENDER?

The Gates Gender Equality Toolbox defines gender as "The socially and culturally constructed ideas of what it is to be male or female in a specific context."

But it is important to note that gender and gender identity, which includes all forms of nonbinary identities, are very personal topics. For many of you, the products you're designing don't necessarily need to *request* that information. That doesn't mean you don't need to understand the impact these factors may have on your customer's experience. Remember, humans don't put their identities on pause when they interact with digital experiences.

At my current employer—the Bill & Melinda Gates Foundation—we are redoubling our efforts to look at all investments through a gender equity lens. I encourage you to do the same on your products.

- How might your experience be perceived differently based on gender?
- In what ways might your work unintentionally increase or perpetuate existing gender gaps?
- Is there anything your work could do to mitigate or reduce existing gender gaps?

Constraint is a gift—this mindset is not only the right thing to do from an inclusive design perspective, but it also increases the market viability of your work. A rising tide lifts all boats.

Where No Design Has Gone Before

With the advent of smart speakers, some in the industry have rallied behind the cries of "Voice First" or "Voice Only"—implying that all interactions should inherently shift to become voice-dominant experiences. I love the passion represented by those hashtags—and certainly, voice interfaces represent a significant portion of the untapped opportunity in the industry. But in my perspective, focusing on one interaction modality at the exclusion of others is just changing the problem your customers face, not solving that problem.

While voice user interfaces do extend a newly welcoming hand to customers with mobility and vision impairments, they risk leaving others behind. This is why I don't believe the future is truly voice-only or even voice-first. There's no one interaction model that includes everyone equally. When you overemphasize one type of interaction, designs become siloed, and other interactions and customers suffer.

The future is multimodal—support for fluid transitions between various input and output modalities will ensure that everyone is an equal participant in our technological future.

But that shouldn't be disappointing. Actually, this is fantastic news for those energized by interesting, complex design problems. The future is as unwritten as it's ever been. There are so many possibilities, and you're at the helm of a ship pointed toward that seemingly limitless horizon. Which way will you sail? Consider this book as your navigational guide for that great blue horizon.

This book can't serve as a one-stop manual for all of your product design needs. This book exists because the increased complexity of experiences now demands new, bigger-picture, holistic frameworks and systems upon which you can layer the types of design work you've done in the past. You'll still need voice designs. You'll still need graphical user interfaces. But they will co-exist with other modalities, and you'll need systems for connecting those experiences in a coherent, consistent way. *Design Beyond Devices* will shine light onto new techniques you can adopt as your product or service moves boldly into the final frontier of experience design.

Apply It Now

You may say that you're not quite ready for multimodality in your product or experience. But here's the truth: for some of your customers, your experience is already multimodal. No one input modality satisfies all customer needs. But if you're not intentionally supporting these customers, their experience is likely to be fraught with friction as they're driven to third-party tools and workarounds.

Before exploring the rest of this book, take a moment to reflect on your current or most recent product:

- Do you understand the extra tools that customers must use to address modalities not natively supported in your experience?

- What happens as your current customers age and their needs change? Will your experience, as designed, still support them?

- Does your roadmap include more direct support for these excluded customers?

- How does your experience interact with the other people, devices, and systems in your customer's life? Is this interaction positive or harmful?

Odds are that you're *already* working on a multimodal product, but it's much harder to say you're consciously guiding those divergent customer experiences within the full context of your customer's world. In this book, you'll learn the tools and techniques you need to take ownership of that experience, long shrouded in shadow.

CHAPTER 2

Capturing Customer Context

To design for the "real" world, you must first understand it. Now that you can no longer make the assumption that your customer is sitting quietly at a desktop PC, you need to understand the broader context in which your customers live their lives and use your products. You must tell stories. You must tell *human* stories. You must bring the context of use to life—not just for yourself, but for all of your peers and decision-makers.

As you move toward designing experiences that break out beyond the boundaries of any single device, there's no switch you can flip in your brain to reset your assumptions. You'll need to develop a new muscle: contextual curiosity. To begin working this muscle, you can explore frameworks that help you challenge your assumptions. You can adopt processes that force you to ask questions that don't come naturally. And once you've learned about your customer's context, you'll need to learn how to convey that story to your peers through the art of storytelling.

Blending Theatricality with Design

In 1999, Alan Cooper's evocatively named book, *The Inmates Are Running the Asylum*,[1] introduced the concept of personas: fictional characters intended as a useful abstraction of a group of similar customers. In his 2008 blog post, "The Origin of Personas,"[2] Alan described his earliest use of a persona, as manifested during a walk on a golf course waiting for a build to complete:

> As I walked, I would engage myself in a dialogue, play-acting a project manager, loosely based on Kathy, requesting functions and behavior from my program. I often found myself deep in those dialogues, speaking aloud, and gesturing with my arms. Some of the golfers were taken aback by my unexpected presence and unusual behavior, but that didn't bother me because I found that this play-acting technique was remarkably effective for cutting through complex design questions of functionality and interaction, allowing me to clearly see what was necessary and unnecessary...

1 Alan Cooper, *The Inmates Are Running the Asylum: Why High Tech Products Drive Us Crazy and How to Restore the Sanity* (Sams, 1999).
2 Alan Cooper, "The Origin of Personas," *Cooper Professional Education Journal* (blog), May 2008.

As it turns out, Alan's behavior on the golf course as he talked through his first personas wasn't dissimilar to an actor or playwright running lines for a new show. (All the world's a stage, even a golf course.)

However, personas today rarely capture a holistic view of a customer's perspective. Personas tend to be focused on a moment in time, not a passage through time. They may mention the "who" and the "where," but not always the "how" and the "why." Some practitioners certainly go that far. But a few decades after Alan's golf course walkabout, many personas read like a dating profile filled out in a hurry (see Figure 2.1).

 *(Almost like)*
Real customers in your area!

Zoe Chandler (she/her)

AGE:	GenZ ("None of your business!")
JOB:	Self-employed Etsy sticker maker
QUOTE:	"I am not throwing away my shot!"
APPS:	Instagram, TikTok, Spotify, 5 Calls
SAVINGS:	None. Student loans till 2072
LIKES:	British Bake-Off, ACLU, oat milk
DISLIKES:	Capitalism, people sliding into DMs

FIGURE 2.1

Does a persona like this *really* get who your customer is in the moment they're using your product?

How can you develop a greater holistic understanding of your customers and their context without completely boiling the ocean, so to speak? Playwrights and actors—especially improvisational actors—have struggled with this question for years. They need to paint a three-dimensional picture of an experience with limited resources.

For example, how do you convince a room full of stakeholders that your voice-controlled kitchen timer is worth millions of dollars in development costs when a $3 timer can complete the same task?

Perhaps your stakeholders will be inspired by the story of a budding chef who needs to manage three simultaneous timers while their hands are covered in gooey meat juice. Your ability to tell a rich story to your stakeholders might mean the difference between creating a new product line or continuing to build the same old experiences.

But how do you find that story when you're literally inventing new experiences? How do you ensure that you're telling that story in a compelling way?

Improvisational actors face a similar contextual challenge, amplified through the lens of time. They are creating a story on the fly. All decisions that will make their characters and scenarios engaging must occur in real time. In professional improvisation, the added pressure created by a paid audience means that actors are strongly motivated to ensure that their improvised stories are compelling (at least, more often than not).

To become skilled at making compelling theatrical decisions on the fly, improvisors learn about storytelling. They experiment with story structures. And in many cases, they agree upon shared storytelling frameworks to make it easier to evaluate their work and to work at speed with their peers.

If improvisors can learn to create compelling stories in real time, just think what stories you'll be capable of, armed with more than five minutes and an armful of customer research!

NOTE MY IMPROVISATIONAL BACKGROUND

> I've been a professional improvisational performer and instructor for over 15 years, most of which I've proudly spent in the ensemble of Seattle's Unexpected Productions in the historic Pike Place Market. The more you practice improv, the more gratitude you develop for the way that improv teaches you to do the following:
> - Accept any new question or offer as a gift, not an adversary.
> - Explore perspectives different from your own.
> - Tell stories—from documents to presentations—with a clear arc, crisp narrative structure, and confident presence.
>
> Plus, it's often ridiculous fun. I'd strongly recommend it for designers looking to improve their craft in an unexpected way.

Storytelling for Design

Why storytelling? Why now? In 2007, with the arrival of the iPhone, the average human relationship with devices began to change. Suddenly, interactions were occurring more frequently outside the home and office. The specifics of the customer's story in the moment became much more important.

- Where is your customer?
- What is their objective?
- Who is around them?
- How do they respond to the world around them?

The challenge has become more pointed in recent years. Not only are customers not sitting at a PC, but they might not even be in eyeshot of a screen at all! With a wider range of potential customer needs, objectives, and contexts, the storyteller's burden on designers becomes even greater.

Luckily, you don't need to tell brand new stories in real time. And in an ideal world, you even have source material to draw from: your user research. But like actors, you do have an audience: your peers and stakeholders. And that audience is unlikely to be quite as connected to your customers as you are. It's not practical to replay every customer interview for them. You are the storyteller.

And here's the big secret about storytelling in design: *storytelling is design*. The process of selecting what to include and what to exclude in your story is a design decision. You're asking important questions and identifying where you might not have answers, where you might be making assumptions, and where your key insights lie.

The Building Blocks of Storytelling

A large part of improv training and rehearsals revolves around creating mental "muscle" memory around story structure, in pursuit of better storytelling in the moment.

Some improvisors, myself included, use a shorthand for these building blocks of story: CROW, which is an acronym for *character, relationship, objective,* and *where*. The more developed these elements become, the more compelling the resulting scene will be. Not every good short scene or story nails all four of these components, but there's a correlation between CROW and more engaging scenes.

What Is Improvisational Theater, Anyway?

Improvisational theater is often mistaken for stand-up comedy, but they're two very different beasts. In improvisational theater, multiple actors collaborate in real time to simultaneously create and perform brand new scenes or entirely improvised plays, all while witnessed by an audience.

Most (but not all) improv shows get suggestions from the audience prior to or during the show. This serves two purposes: it relieves the actors from the intimidating blank page problem (remember, constraint is a gift), and it *also* demonstrates to the audience that the show is responding in real time as opposed to running from a script. Improv "rehearsals" serve two main purposes: building cast trust and learning a common set of rules, structures, or games upon which the company later constructs their narratives in real time.

By contrast, stand-up comedy is typically scripted: crafted meticulously through countless tryouts and open mic nights and edited to ensure that the timing, word selection, show order, tone, and physicality maximize the emotional rollercoaster that the performer is seeking for their audience.

While any prerecorded media lacks the true immediacy of a live performance or livestream, canonical examples of improvisational theater available for on-demand streaming are the classic TV series *Whose Line Is It Anyway?* and the Netflix improvised play series *Middleditch and Schwartz*.

But improv isn't just about performance—people around the world have found it to be a very useful skill in the workplace. Improv is a framework for active listening, enthusiastic collaboration, and intellectual resiliency.

One of the many beautiful things about improv is the accessibility of the practice to newcomers. Plenty of improvisors start out self-taught, with a group of peers experimenting with exercises learned from a book or website. You don't need to be a trained improvisor to benefit from improv techniques.

Picture a scene where two people are standing and talking about chocolate. Doesn't sound inherently compelling, does it?

- Perhaps one character chooses to display some physical behaviors subconsciously associated with nervousness, like shuffling feet or avoiding eye contact. Things become a little more interesting, thanks to this *character* choice. What's going on? Why is this person nervous about such a mundane subject?

- We may discover the *relationship* between these two characters when they refer to each other by name (Eddie, the nervous boy, and Sarah): perhaps these two people aren't strangers but friends. Why, then, is one of them so nervous?

- By a passing comment about "4th period class," and later interaction with an invisible locker, we discover the *where* of the scene: it takes place in a school hallway.

- And at some point, the audience discovers Eddie's *objective*: to ask Sarah to a school dance for the first time. The conversation about chocolate is their way of building up to the subject.

By establishing CROW as the scene progresses, the scene transforms from a simple conversation to a story with potential.

NOTE THE ORIGIN OF CROW

The storytelling framework explored in this chapter has been used for decades at my improvisational home, Unexpected Productions. It's not well documented, but our founder and artistic director Randy Dixon (along with former cast members Rebecca Stockley and Susan MacPherson) helped me trace CROW to its source—the late Jose Simon, a West Coast improvisor who spread the mnemonic via workshops. Jose's insight continues to influence improvisors and storytellers to this day.

The wonderful thing about a storytelling scaffolding like CROW is that it gives you a process and a framework for asking important questions about your customer as a whole human being, in context. So let's examine CROW in terms of user experience (see Table 2.1). What parts of your story apply to each of these building blocks, and how can you tease CROW out of your scenarios?

TABLE 2.1 THE CROW FRAMEWORK FOR BUILDING
COMPELLING STORIES

Dimension	Description
Character	Define the qualities of an active participant in the story: their attributes, attitudes, and choices.
Relationship	Explore the history, moods, and attitudes *between* two or more participants or objects in the story.
Objective	Understand the desired change in the state of the world that a participant in the story seeks, actively or passively, in the short or long term.
Where	Catalog the qualities of the environment(s) in the story—objects, obstacles, and prevailing conditions.

Character: What Makes You "You"

When storytellers talk about a "character," the term refers to many qualities of an individual (fictional or real). People aren't static beings, but some things about people are more changeable than others over time. To better deconstruct these different levels of fungibility, you can split character into three dimensions:[3]

1. **Attributes:** Fundamental traits, mannerisms, and habits. These tend not to change over time, but may change infrequently throughout a person's life (like preferred gender pronouns). Includes skills, quirks, gender identity, preferred pronouns, disabilities, and the individual's membership in both mainstream and marginalized communities.

2. **Attitudes:** Emotions and reactions to outside stimuli—other people, objects, or situations.

3. **Choices:** The actions you take. But when actions are taken without a clear "why" based on attitude, characterization, or other event, the audience will see that choice as "out of character."

When you look at your customers through these lenses, a few helpful UX-related questions emerge to lead you toward interesting opportunities and key moments (Table 2.2).

---

3   Tom Salinsky and Deborah Frances-White, *The Improv Handbook: The Ultimate Guide to Improvising in Comedy, Theatre, and Beyond* (Continuum, 2008).

TABLE 2.2   EXPERIENCE QUESTIONS INSPIRED BY YOUR
CHARACTER LENSES

Dimension	Questions to Explore Your Customer's Context
Attributes	• Would your customer have any physical mannerisms or limitations that might impact their experience? • How does your customer differ from other customers when communicating? Languages, accents? • How does your customer define their own identity to themselves and others? • Which of your customer's attributes are underrepresented in the greater population, and how might that affect them?
Attitudes	• What cultural influences have shaped your customer's preferences and beliefs? • What is your customer's likely emotional state when starting this experience? • Would this customer have any preconceived opinions or learned behaviors that they would bring to bear on this experience?
Choices	• Why would a customer choose to seek out your experience? Did they have a choice at all? • What choices are you asking your customer to make when engaging with you? • How does your customer express their individuality, and is your experience part of that expression?

Relationship: What Connects You

Relationship is perhaps the most challenging "building block of story" to translate to your work in user experience. But because relationships are also a key to emotional reactions, they are incredibly important for designing context. The closer you are to someone (or something), the more likely you are to get emotional about it. Examine your scenarios and try to define the web of relationships surrounding your product.

- **Human-to-device relationship:** How long has your customer owned the device they're using? Is it shared? Do they own it? Is it expensive and treasured, or cheap and disposable? Does the customer anthropomorphize the device in any way? Did they name it? How much time do they spend together? And how does your customer feel about this device? (See Figure 2.2.)

FIGURE 2.2
Human-to-device relationship, as illustrated by the way a woman holds her personal smartphone.

- **Human-to-business relationship:** Does your customer deal with you directly or through a third party? Did they get to choose to work with you, or are they locked in due to monopoly or limited choice? What are their expectations of you in this situation? (See Figure 2.3.)

FIGURE 2.3
Human-to-business relationship, as illustrated by the way a person interacts with a digital ordering kiosk.

- **Human-to-human relationships:** In some cases, your product may be used by multiple people, perhaps at the same time. What is their relationship to each other? Do they trust each other? (See Figure 2.4.)

FIGURE 2.4

Human-to-human relationship in the context of a product, as illustrated by a family sharing a tablet device to make a video call.

If relationships are key to emotion in storytelling, so too are these relationships key to the elusive emotional state of "delight" in your products. If you simply satisfy the requirements, your customers are satisfied. If you deeply understand the relationships at play and honor those expectations, you are building a stronger foundation for your experiences.

Objective: What Drives You

Product teams already frame customer objectives with concepts like scenarios, top tasks, and jobs to be done. But those frameworks can still fall short. How many times have you seen a user story like this: *"As a user, I want to browse a list of virtual machines."*

Unless you're dealing with recreational content, people don't generally browse just for fun. They browse to achieve an *objective*, whether that's choosing a film on a streaming service or finding an underperforming virtual machine to troubleshoot. When you lose sight of their objective, your "solutions" become self-serving, and you risk totally failing your customers.

For user experience professionals, the O in CROW should serve as a reminder to double-check your assumptions.

- What have you defined as your customer's objective? Is that *truly* their end goal, or simply a sentence written to get the customer to your feature?

- Has your product team assumed that their solution stands alone? Is that true, or are you part of a larger, device-agnostic human objective that might span multiple experiences?

Obstruction of Objective

A conversation that has replayed itself hundreds of times in the 21st century: the dreaded newsletter subscription feature.

MARKETING: *We want to make the Subscribe to Newsletter link more prominent to increase engagement.*

DESIGN: *OK, but what's the customer objective?*

MARKETING: *To subscribe to the newsletter.*

DESIGN: *No, but WHY would they want to subscribe? You haven't explained that here.*

MARKETING: *I don't understand the question.*

If your feature isn't supporting a genuine customer objective, engagement is meaningless. Just increasing the size of elements or their prominence on a page won't create quality engagement. Sure, maybe more folks will click on that link—but if they don't know why they'd want to subscribe or what benefit they'd receive, they probably won't share their email address in the next step.

But a poorly-timed newsletter subscription isn't just at risk of being detached from the customer objective. The "newsletter pop-up upon page load" pattern is actively blocking the customer objective, "I want to learn about this topic." When a customer is confronted with a poorly timed call to action, the effects range from frustration to measurable harm.

Just as you want to make sure that you're aligned with real customer objectives, you also need to make sure that you're not actively blocking

Broadening an Objective with Amazon Echo

In some cases, your initial hypothesis about your customer's objective must expand based on feedback. The Amazon Echo smart speaker shipped with the ability to set verbal kitchen timers. You could set one timer at a time. But once the product shipped, feedback came in from customers asking for multiple timers at once.

As it turns out, a customer's objective is rarely simply "I want to set a timer." Often, it's "I want to cook dinner without burning my house down." (Or, is that just me?) When this objective is examined in context, you start to see that the same cook might need multiple timers at once: one for the potatoes, one for the turkey. The single timer satisfied a single goal, but not the customer's overall objective.

To honor this broader objective, the Alexa platform eventually added support not just for multiple timers, but for named timers. Those features launched at the same time because they were related. Once you have multiple timers, your cook needs to know *which* timer just went off in order to properly satisfy the objective of "I want to cook dinner without burning my house down."

the completion of an objective. If you're not solving a customer problem or helping them achieve an objective, your product or feature will not thrive.

Exploring Objectives

To explore your customer's objective more thoroughly, ask yourself questions like these:

- What is your customer thinking when they engage with your product?
- What does your customer want to achieve when they engage with your product?
- If your customer was going to hire someone to do this task, what would the job description be?
- How would your customer describe their goal to a friend or coworker?
- What might your customer's life goals be for the next month? Year? Five years? Does your product interact with those goals?

Defining technology-agnostic objectives well is the key to true innovation. When you understand what a person wants—and when you're no longer tied to a specific way of achieving the task—you've opened the door to creativity. Even on an existing product where you're assuming a specific tool will be used to achieve an objective, a crisp statement of a customer's objective is a fantastic north star for prioritization purposes.

Where: What Surrounds You

Last but not least, it's time to consider the "where," or your customer's environment. Human factors engineers are well-versed in considering the impact of the physical environment on their interactions, but until fairly recently, user experience designers often took their customer's environment for granted (see Figures 2.5 and 2.6). Phones, tablets, and hands-free UI now open up the world to a dizzying array of possibility.

Limited only by their imaginations, wouldn't it be easy for improvisors to establish an environment for their scenes? In reality, I find this to be by far the hardest skill for my improv students to learn. Even when improvisors do establish an environment, they usually do it verbally. It's very difficult for the adult mind to project an imaginary environment onto a real one.

To begin defining your "where," ask questions you'd normally observe at a contextual inquiry:

- Is it a public or private space?
- Is it usually noisy or quiet?
- Where is the device located? Is it fixed or mobile? Does it need to be near a charger?
- Is a conversation, or a device that makes sound, socially acceptable?
- What is your customer holding? Are they multitasking?
- Where is your customer looking? Do they see the device at all times?

After you understand the answers to these questions, reason through and document the potential pain points. Your job is now to draw attention to those pain points and to help your stakeholders somehow visualize the interesting aspects of your customer's "where" in their own minds.

FIGURE 2.5

When you picture an archetypal context in your head, it often corresponds with sterile media depictions like this editorial photo of a kitchen.

FIGURE 2.6

But there's usually far more richness to be uncovered in your customer's context than what you see on TV. Compared to a TV kitchen, my own kitchen is far more dated, cramped, and lived-in.

Design researcher Bill Buxton coined the term *placeona* as a
mental model for thinking about your approach to documenting
environmental qualities.[4] How would you create a persona for this
environment? What distinguishes it from other environments?

Exploring Your Environment

Do you find yourself creatively stumped when thinking about your
"where"? Table 2.3 provides some techniques you can apply without
ever leaving the office, while Table 2.4 cites some of the most common
techniques used to get real customer context.

TABLE 2.3   GENERATIVE TECHNIQUES FOR EXPLORING
            THE WHERE

Technique	Description
Sketching	Don't worry about Pixar-quality drawings. Use sketching as a design exercise. What elements communicate your environment? What's important? What might vary between locations?
Competitive Wheres	This is a fun little game we often play as a warm-up in Seattle TheatreSports. Two players face off, often with a table to simulate a game show buzzer. Name an environment, and the players take turns quickly naming objects or qualities of that environment. First one to draw a blank loses.
Bodystorming	Mock up the important aspects of the environment at actual size in a space you control. Participate in basic role-play, based on your core scenarios, and see where you encounter unexpected questions or friction.
Stock Photo Hunt	Look at images of fictional environments similar to where you expect your customer to find themselves and note the distinctive elements.

---

4   As described in Bill's keynote "Wild Design for Living in the Wild," February 6, 2019, Interaction 19, Seattle, WA, USA, https://interaction19.ixda.org/
program/keynote--bill-buxton/

TABLE 2.4   RESEARCH TECHNIQUES FOR EXPLORING THE WHERE

Technique	Description
Location Scouting	Act like a cinematographer. Visit typical locations that your experience might use and snap photos focusing on the environment. (This is often done prior to an interview.)
Diary Studies	Ask customers or representative participants to send you snapshots, based on prompts, or as a journaling exercise. Some platforms, like Scout, make this easier from a logistics perspective.
Contextual Inquiry	Seek out permission to interview and observe your customers in the context in which your product might be used. This technique is a staple of ethnographic research.

From Reality to Retelling

As the original designer for the now-retired Echo Look (see the Case Study later in this chapter), I had to rely heavily on storyboards to help my stakeholders visualize the "where" of my stories. It's one thing to say "the phone isn't nearby when customers want to take the outfit photo." It's another thing to depict the sequence of events that shows how the customer must place the phone down when getting changed—so it's not readily at hand when it's time to take the photo (Figure 2.7).

FIGURE 2.7
Selected frames from an early Echo Look storyboard showing important environmental details pulled from contextual inquiry. The human mind is eager to fill in details about an environment. You don't need an art degree to tell an environmental story.

Contextual inquiry is an excellent research tool to help define and understand the "where," and it's often a lost art. You don't know what you don't know about a customer environment until you see it yourself. Even when you believe you understand an environment well—a kitchen or a living room—it's still your job to remind your stakeholders that your customers may have divided attention, and that the decision-making metrics applied to websites don't necessarily apply for apps or hands-free experiences.

Whatever artifacts you generate to depict environmental context, remember that you don't need every detail. You need *salient* details. You have two goals:

- Define just enough detail to suggest the location archetype.
- Shine light on the aspects of the established environment that directly influence the experience.

LEARN MORE

You'll learn more about the application of some of these techniques for exploring environmental context—like storyboarding and bodystorming—in Chapter 11, "Breathe Life into the Unknown." For more about storytelling on the Echo Look project, see the case study later in this chapter.

Story as Shared Understanding

The increased need for storytelling in this age of complex technology means that customer advocates (that's you, even if you don't identify as such) must create an environment where stakeholders can truly empathize with customers, their pain points, and how a proposed solution can improve a customer's daily life meaningfully.

Now that you've explored CROW (character, relationship, objective, and where) in the context of user experience, the next step is accepting that you won't always need or use all four building blocks. Some scenarios are compelling without all four building blocks being well defined.

When pitching new Echo projects at Amazon, any one of my storyboards could be taken out of context. I needed to ensure that each storyboard hit enough CROW to be compelling in its own right. But how do you define those building blocks in the first place?

The CROW storytelling framework can pay dividends for your product in multiple ways:

- CROW functions as a framework of curiosity to reframe your existing understanding of your customers. It helps you ask the right questions early in the process.
- CROW acts as a roadmap that helps you weave more compelling stories from your research insights.

Unless your audience is full of empaths, context and detail usually lead to better, more engaging stories. Why is it that the media responds so empathetically to stories where a few people are harmed or killed, but huge events go by with barely a mention? It's the scale of the context. Human brains weren't built to empathize at broad strokes and large scale. With the right amount of detail, it becomes much easier for others to project themselves into a story, or to picture a story as plausible and relatable.

There's a great tension around detail when it comes to personas. On one hand, personas were ostensibly created to average out details for ease of abstract understanding, at the risk of creating a homogenized "one-size-fits-none" outcome.

But as improv students know, specificity is a magic spell for the mind. Names, emotions, environmental details—specific details are woven together at speed by the human mind to create something almost tangible for the audience.

As you move into a world where your experiences have a broader reach, specificity also allows you to bring life to the edge cases that matter. As technology becomes inextricably woven into the critical moments in human lives, you must find ways to ensure that stakeholders don't forget about addressing edge cases that could cause real physical, emotional, or financial harm to your customers.

By ensuring that your design stories provide CROW, you can avoid making too many assumptions about your stakeholders' understanding of a problem. And a strong design story gives everyone a rich shared context for collaborative decision-making. Rather than designing for the common denominator, it's time for you to design for real people. Tell real stories first. Abstract later.

What story will you tell? The show must go on.

Amazon's Echo Look

To examine CROW as it applies to products, let's deconstruct my team's early exploratory work on Amazon's Echo Look. (The Echo Look was a voice-enabled wardrobe management camera device on the market from 2017–2020.) We wanted to challenge our initial product hypothesis through open-ended user research.

Hypothesis: A hands-free "selfie camera" offers value to our fashion-conscious customers by helping them keep track of their wardrobe.

We partnered with an outside firm to conduct ethnographic research in potential customers' homes, but expanded our study to include some people we suspected might not be customers, too. From what we learned, we could begin to build a series of insights that corresponded to the CROW framework.

- **Character:** Our primary customer was an individual with a large wardrobe. The more fashion conscious they were, the less organized they became: clothes were scattered everywhere, and it was impossible to see all clothes at once. Why? Because they were often trying on two to five outfits while choosing clothes each day.

- **Relationship:** Our customers didn't have much experience with voice interfaces (our study was pre-Alexa). They owned cell phones, but those phones were not always within arm's reach, either due to choice or to circumstance (charging). Selfies were frustrating because their phone camera in a mirror couldn't capture full-length shots.

- **Objective:** Our customers wanted to feel confident about their clothing choices, but sometimes found this challenging. Lack of confidence had a ripple effect into their dating lives, their work lives, and their sense of self. Some customers also had the desire to share outfit photos with trusted friends or family, but phone cameras never captured the full outfit.

- **Where:** Fashion-engaged customers rarely had one single location where all clothes were kept—a major contrast to the assumptions made by some stakeholders who pictured an immaculately organized Beverly Hills style closet. Fashion-conscious customers usually ran out of closet space and made use of secondary closets, drawers, or even piles of clothes. Furthermore, many customers lived in small apartments without an adequate full-length mirror.

By using ethnographic research to explore the CROW of our initial hypothesis, we actually discovered *more* potential value than anticipated—both in the ability to track outfits and as an alternative to impractical full-length mirrors.

Apply It Now

This chapter is called "Capturing Customer Context" to drive home the point that anyone, at any time, can ask important questions about the context of use for your product.

Sometimes, those questions will lead you to research. Sometimes, you're lucky enough to have answers from another source. Sometimes, you might have to build hypotheses before you learn.

If you're at the point where you need to build some hypotheses about the context of your experience, a great place to start applying CROW on your project is a dedicated contextual curiosity workshop. Schedule several hours for you and your stakeholders to brainstorm.

Part 1: Baseline

Begin by ensuring that your team is working from a common shared understanding. (This can be done as pre-work or as a preliminary session if you can't find enough contiguous time together.)

1. Get all known constraints out in the open: budget, timelines, directives.
2. Collect, review, and recap everything you know about the customer. Any previous research should be summarized for the group.
3. As a group, agree upon your goal for the session. Are you looking for a new customer need? Are you preparing to research an existing product idea?

Part 2: Explore

Visiting customer sites can be expensive and impractical for a whole team. Leverage the group's collective creativity and lived experience to explore the basics of your customer's context.

1. Have everyone sketch the customer in context multiple times, using an individual sketching exercise like *Crazy Eights*. This will draw out individual perspectives quickly and raise important questions.
2. Review the sketches, and as you go, start to capture patterns, insights, and questions as they relate to the product or the customer's CROW. This is a good starting point, but you're probably just scratching the surface.

3. Push yourself further into the details. Split into four groups and assign each group one of the elements of CROW. Spend at least 15 minutes identifying as many questions as you can about your assigned dimension. It's OK if you come out with open questions as well as some answers—open questions can inform your future user research and risk analysis.

Part 3: Roadmap

Come back together as a group and synthesize the insights from Parts 1 and 2. Focus on answering these questions with the customer-focused content you've generated:

1. What do we know to be true?
2. What assumptions are we making?
3. What questions do we need to answer?
4. What does success look like for this customer?

The goal of this session isn't to solve the problem. Rather, it's to understand the human context in which the problem occurs. If you're lucky, this process will also create buy-in for further user research and discovery efforts to address your assumptions and unanswered questions.

Exploring Social Context at a Global Scale with Janice Y. Tsai

Janice Y. Tsai, PhD and I first crossed paths at Microsoft, when she was contributing important work on digital privacy for the Windows platform. She's now a research scientist at Mozilla, contributing her considerable expertise to the research and development of multimodal experiences with a particular focus on international usage.

Q: You've done a great deal of research about the use of voice. What's been most surprising for you? How do the attitudes toward voice user interfaces differ in other regions around the world?

Social norms play such an important part in the use of voice. It's important and interesting to understand which norms are malleable, depending on the amount of utility that a new technology can provide. Shouting at a laptop or having something respond to you in a public place is still taboo. People generally seem to have an awareness of their own surroundings and have an ingrained sense that shouting at a robot or computer in a public place doesn't seem right, despite the acceptable nature of having a human conversation either in person or on the phone. We see this constantly evolving, as you have probably seen more and more people having video-based conference calls in coffee shops. It will continue to be important to understand how social norms differ by location and culture when building new products with integrated voice interaction.

Social norms were particularly interesting to study when conducting research on the use of voice assistants in the United States and Europe. In our field study in France and Germany in 2018, we found that there was a much slower adoption of voice assistants. The adoption of new technologies by our European participants was driven more by need or necessity rather than by the convenience and curiosity mindset that we found in our United States–based participants. In Europe, people had a poor impression of voice assistants due to early experiences with failure when speaking accented English. (Most assistants were first launched only in English.) Voice assistants didn't fit into the communication patterns of families: most of our participants' households were multilingual with seamless switching between languages. (Google Assistant is now bilingual.)

The differences in connectivity also helped to drive certain routines, ensuring that people used a minimal amount of data whenever they were on the go. For voice assistants to function, they need to always be connected to the internet and continuously send data back to the provider, even when not being used. On the other hand, social norms may also help drive screen-free interactions. For our French participants, using a screen during meal times was particularly taboo. But for those same French families, the ability to ask a voice assistant to search for information to settle a family debate or to listen to the local news was valuable and fit into people's routines.

Janice Y. Tsai, PhD is a research scientist at Mozilla focusing on voice interaction for an open, accessible web via Firefox Voice. She helped to rate all the privacy products in the "Privacy Not Included" guide so you can pick presents that aren't spying on you. She has a background in user-centered privacy and consumer behavior with a PhD in Engineering and Public Policy from Carnegie Mellon University. As a privacy manager at Microsoft, she helped make the Windows 10 Privacy Settings easier to understand and created a framework for research ethics at Microsoft Research.

CHAPTER 3

Understanding Busy Humans

People deserve devices that take their state of mind and cognitive load into account. Until now, the industry model of "multitasking" has largely been from the device's point of view. But the device-centric model of multitasking no longer holds true when you can't guarantee that any one activity remains tied to a single device. Even listening to music, which has been a fairly device-centric task for decades, can now span multiple devices as you move the song you're listening to from your phone to in-home streaming systems.

Furthermore, in a world where (overly) proactive push notifications often invade daily life, you must also consider what activities your customer might be performing at the moment you interrupt them. That feature announcement your marketing team wants may seem harmless until it interrupts a customer mid-presentation.

Most of humanity's favorite stories revolve around some sort of activity. Humans, like most living creatures, originally evolved as active beings: foragers, always on the move. While the advent of rich media like radio, television, and movies have decreased our level of physical activity, those are still activities of a sort. Even sleeping is a form of activity!

After you define your customer's context and objective, you must model what they want to do. However, what is often overlooked is what else they're already doing. All commerce, all human action is driven by doing. But not all actions are created equal. Some activities are largely passive, while others are incredibly time-sensitive and cognitively taxing.

It's time to turn the concept of multitasking around to keep humans, not devices, at the center of the story.

Turn Contextual Awareness into Activity Models

We've all been there: you attempt to open a document on your laptop, but the loading indicator spins. Rather than stare at the spinner, you move on to email . . . only to be interrupted moments later when the previous app steals your focus and you type a sentence into that document you opened. Why couldn't it wait until the end of your sentence? Or even better yet, what about waiting until the email was sent? What if devices took our current activity into account?

This seems like a good idea, but as you begin to parse human behavior, it feels like it won't scale. The scope of possible human activity seems near-limitless. Rather than being deterred by that dizzying scope, you can reframe your thinking and draw energy from the challenge. There are bound to be patterns in the madness that will make coping with those activities more manageable.

The first step in achieving this what-if world is finding a way to signify what kind of activity a person is engaged in at any particular moment.

When our team first began work on Alexa Notifications, we envisioned the kinds of interruptions we'd need to present to customers—for example, an incoming call. But when we thought about it, the way we'd handle an incoming call might be slightly different based on the customer's current activity, like listening to music or getting driving directions.

A few key questions emerged that helped me categorize the activities in our system:

1. Does the activity have a fixed endpoint?
2. How long is the activity?
3. How time-sensitive is the activity?
4. How much attention is required during the activity?
5. How much effort does it take to restart the activity if our customer is interrupted?

The answers to these questions led us to patterns. We were able to decide which answers mattered and how many patterns were relevant. If you're looking for a starting point, use the taxonomy detailed in Table 3.1. The rest of this chapter will explore each of these common activity types in detail.

By clearly defining an activity taxonomy along these lines and applying it to your products, you give your system greater contextual understanding of human behavior, allowing for more appropriate adaptations in the moment. Once defined, this taxonomy makes it easier for a feature team to work out how their new feature should behave when starting, ending, or interrupting—all based on context.

When communicating these abstractions to others, I landed on the term "activity model." **There is no single "activity model" to rule them all**—the granularity that's appropriate for your own

TABLE 3.1 AN EXAMPLE TAXONOMY OF HUMAN ACTIVITY

Activity Type	Description	Cognitive Load	Length
Passive	Attention is unfocused and not directed at a single device or activity.	(Almost) None	Indefinite
Sustained	A long-running activity usually with a low cognitive burden, that is often without a known endpoint. It can usually be paused, suspended, or even run in parallel with other tasks without loss of detail.	Low	Indefinite
Discrete	An activity that requires directed attention, but may leave some cognitive bandwidth for multitasking or interruption. The activity usually has a known, discrete endpoint.	Moderate	Short
Focused	An activity that consumes most or all cognitive resources: from the creative state of "flow" to operation of a motor vehicle. Recovery from interruptions is costly.	High	Long
Live	A real-time activity, like a phone call. Due to the unpredictable nature of real-time interactions, full attention is required. Any distraction will cause loss of context, if not actual harm.	Full	Long

explorations may vary. But the example activity model above provides a useful scaffolding with which you can better understand why—and how—an activity model makes a difference in multimodal design.

If you're interested in using this activity model as a starting point, you'll need further context about how each activity is defined. The rest of this chapter explores the activity model proposed in Table 3.1 in more detail. Even if your model ends up somewhat different, this should give you a feel for the type of framework you'll need to give your designs a strong and customer-focused foundation.

Passive Activities: Zoning Out

Passive activities are often recreational. Daydreaming. Sitting and thinking. Playing quick casual games or fidgeting. Rewatching a favorite TV show in the background. In many cases, a passive activity might not be a device engagement at all.

In some ways, passive activities are a dream of a time gone by. Today, people live such hectic lives, is there really any passivity at all? And to be very clear, "passive" doesn't mean "ripe for the picking." In some cases, passive time may be the most precious resource that your customers have.

But how do you identify a passive activity? Table 3.2 includes some questions and answers to help you decide what qualifies.

TABLE 3.2 IDENTIFYING A PASSIVE ACTIVITY

Question	It may be a passive activity if your answer is...
How does the activity end?	Passive activities usually continue until interrupted, they rarely have a natural endpoint.
How long is the activity?	The length is usually nonspecific. In some cases, the end of passive activity might be inferred from an alarm, quiet hours, or other signal.
How time-sensitive is the activity?	There is no inherent urgency to a passive activity, except perhaps in a medical scenario like stress management.
How much attention is required during the activity?	A passive activity creates little to no cognitive load.
How much effort does it take to resume the activity if your customer is interrupted?	Depending on the interruption, it may be impossible for customers to return to a passive activity once engaged.

NOTE JUDGMENT CALLS

You'll notice that the tables describing activities use the phrasing "It may be...". In some cases, your classification of activities will feel somewhat subjective or dependent on context. For example, the difference between passive and sustained might vary depending on how expert your customers are at a given task. In the end, your decisions should keep your understanding of your customer centered, not what worked for another unrelated product.

Examples of passive activities:

- Sleeping
- Stretching
- Snacking
- Small talk

Considerations for working with passive activities:

- Is passivity only relevant when no input is received? Or is there an interaction in your system you consider passive?
- Should you allow interruptions of passive activities? Or would you be violating privacy or valuable rest time?
- How can you avoid startling your customer if you're interrupting passive activity—which generally means your system would be "speaking out of turn?"

Sustained Activities: Passing the Time

Sustained activities may take some effort to get started, but once in motion, they tend to stay in motion. In the analog world, running and walking are sustained tasks. It takes a bit of effort to get started in some cases—but once you get going, you can "tune out" a bit and continue on autopilot without much additional interaction. In other cases, sustained activities can continue while completing more discrete tasks, like listening to music while putting on makeup.

Consumption of media has become a critical part of most device experiences; some days it feels like every piece of new home furnishing will become a functional streaming hub by the end of the decade. Media consumption is another example of a sustained activity. Once started, streaming tends to continue until customer intervention occurs. Table 3.3 explains how to classify a sustained activity.

Examples of sustained activities:

- Listening to an audiobook or podcast
- Listening to music
- Watching TV or movies for entertainment (at home)

TABLE 3.3 IDENTIFYING A SUSTAINED ACTIVITY

Question	It may be a passive activity if your answer is...
How does the activity end?	Sustained activities are generally persistent unless ended by customer action, or by end of media being consumed.
How long is the activity?	Passive activities tend to run for many minutes or hours. The end may be dictated by media length or by customer intervention.
How time-sensitive is the activity?	Sustained activities are usually not time-sensitive.
How much attention is required during the activity?	Sustained activities usually continue with little additional interaction, once started.
How much effort does it take to resume the activity if your customer is interrupted?	Sustained activities can usually be resumed if the underlying system is designed thoughtfully.

NOTE SIMULTANEITY AND SUSTAINED ACTIVITY

Amazon Echo devices "attenuate" music playback when a voice request is made, allowing that sustained music activity to continue. The music becomes quieter, and the voice interaction occurs in parallel. But audiobooks aren't attenuated, because the brain can't process two spoken threads at once. You might decide to represent these as two different activity types, or you might decide to apply those rules elsewhere.

Considerations for working with sustained activities:

- Can (and should) another task be completed simultaneously?
- What happens when your sustained activity is suspended?
- How costly is it (in time spent) to resume that activity later as opposed to starting over?

Discrete Activities: Getting Things Done

Discrete activities require a nontrivial amount of your attention while they are in play and are generally directed at accomplishing a single goal. These are activities or tasks where you may be making decisions, looking for feedback, receiving information, or otherwise shaping an outcome based on an input/output loop.

In your workday, you encounter many discrete tasks, like authoring a typical email or scheduling a meeting. Many device interactions are discrete activities, like checking the weather.

Discrete activities are more sensitive to interruption. Distraction might force you to repeat the activity to derive the desired value (for example, hearing the weather report). It's hard to efficiently "multitask" when your tasks are of a discrete nature—in *general*, you're swapping your limited ability to focus between those discrete tasks, not doing them simultaneously. Table 3.4 explores the qualities of a discrete activity.

TABLE 3.4 IDENTIFYING A DISCRETE ACTIVITY

Question	It may be a discrete activity if your answer is...
How does the activity end?	Discrete activities usually have an endpoint when the customer need is satisfied.
How long is the activity?	Discrete activities generally take from a few seconds to a few minutes. The longer the activity, the higher the risk of fatigue or cognitive overload.
How time-sensitive is the activity?	Somewhat time-sensitive. Since attention is required, interruption or delay of a discrete activity may cause loss of context.
How much attention is required during the activity?	Discrete activities generally consume a large portion of our available cognitive resources, as they tend to involve both input and output. In some cases, experts or other attentive individuals may be able to process additional stimuli.
How much effort does it take to resume the activity if your customer is interrupted?	If context is lost, your customer may need to restart the activity. The repetition of work or state established prior to the interruption may cause frustration.

Example discrete activities:

- Checking the weather or the time
- Booking an appointment
- Writing a tweet or an email
- Booking a flight
- Watching a training video

Considerations for working with discrete activities:

- Does the customer start the activity or the system?
- What are the signs that your customer might be getting fatigued?
- Is it appropriate to save the customer's progress if a discrete activity is interrupted? What would you save?
- How long can your customer be interrupted before they "lose their place" in the interaction?

Focused Activities: Going with the Flow

Focused activities usually correspond to creative scenarios like writing or interactive scenarios such as a role-playing game. The brain is generally fully engaged, and the context of engagement may be suppressing your perception outside the boundaries of the activity at hand.

Sometimes focus is enhanced or induced by specific context. People are generally not as focused on a movie at home as they are in a theater. By removing external stimuli and creating pressure not to engage with one's phone, traditional movie theaters transform movie consumption into a focused activity.

It's generally difficult, if not impossible, to multitask while engaged in a focused activity. Even if multitasking is possible, it usually results in decreased quality of experience or output. For example, when I sat down to write this book, I often started with the TV on in the background but ended up pausing it after a few minutes. Too much stimulation interrupts my flow and slows me down significantly. Table 3.5 walks through the unique qualities of a focused activity.

Examples of focused activities:

- Writing an email or a report
- Graphical editing or animation
- Precise handiwork, like art or ornate embroidery
- Watching a movie in the theater

Considerations when working with focused activities:

- How did your customer achieve focus? Time or controlled stimuli?
- Are there natural breaks in the activity?
- Can you tell when attention is failing?
- What would still be important to your customer during a focused activity?

TABLE 3.5 IDENTIFYING A FOCUSED ACTIVITY

Question	It may be a focused activity if your answer is...
How does the activity end?	Focused activities may have an endpoint, but that endpoint is not always apparent.
How long is the activity?	Focused activities tend to run long, as it takes a while just to get into the state of flow. Focused activities may run a few minutes, but can often be measured in hours.
How time-sensitive is the activity?	The added efficiency of a focused state is lost once the focus is gone.
How much attention is required during the activity?	Successful focus essentially replaces awareness of the world with the context of the task at hand, fully utilizing any capacity for attention.
How much effort does it take to resume the activity if your customer is interrupted?	The activity *can* be interrupted, but a state of focused flow is very hard to recapture once it is lost. The likelihood of frustration or lost productivity due to unwanted interruption is significant.

Live Activities: Can't Miss a Thing

Live activities are experienced in real time and are heavily contextual. The immediacy of the activity usually demands your full attention. In most cases, interruption of a live activity will cause significant loss of context—and in some cases, physical or emotional harm.

The most canonical example of a live activity is a phone call. Whether the call is audio-only or full video, circumstances and social norms generally dictate that people devote their full attention to the call, ruling out most multitasking.

Driving rests on the live spectrum as well. Driving is an extremely time-sensitive activity; turns at speed must happen in the span of a few seconds. Distractions and interruptions that cause loss of context can be literally disastrous.

Live-streams are (as advertised) live activities where both the broadcaster and the audience find themselves in a heavily time-sensitive environment. Broadcasters may miss audience comments or lose viewers if distracted. Viewers may lose context if interrupted or distracted while watching a live-stream, and may miss an opportunity to interact meaningfully with others—but one might argue that's less of an issue for viewers than broadcasters. Table 3.6 explores what differentiates this activity from the other less demanding activity patterns.

TABLE 3.6 IDENTIFYING A LIVE ACTIVITY

Question	It may be a live activity if your answer is...
Does the activity have a fixed endpoint?	All live activities will end, but they rarely have a specific predetermined endpoint.
How long is the activity?	Live activities tend to run long, as it takes a while to build up context and rapport.
How time-sensitive is the activity?	Live activities are inherently time-sensitive; they are of the here and now, and are not available at any other time.
How much attention is required during the activity?	Social norms and physics generally dictate that you devote your full attention to live activities like calls.
How much effort does it take to resume the activity if your customer is interrupted?	Interruption of a live activity will cause immediate loss of context. In demanding cases, this may cause physical injury, financial impact, or emotional harm.

Examples of live activities:

- Phone calls (audio and/or video)
- Live-streaming as a broadcaster or viewer
- Participating in team sports
- Performing music or theater
- Driving

NOTE COGNITIVE LOAD VERSUS CULTURAL NORMS

Would watching live theater count as a live activity? That depends on the context of the situation. The performers almost certainly are at high enough cognitive load that they wouldn't be able to complete other activities. The audience, however, might actually be able to text or perform other tasks. The question that follows: Do you want your system to support this? Your activity model will represent both customer engagement and cultural norms.

Considerations for working with live activities:

- What does the live activity mean to your customer?
- Why is your customer willing to focus so intently on this task?

- What is the worst thing that could happen if your customer were distracted or interrupted during a live activity?
- What kind of latency are customers experiencing during a live activity?

Apply It Now

Whether you adopt the taxonomy cited earlier or create your own activity model, your next challenge is to decide what to do with it. On small-scale systems, perhaps it's enough just to codify your activity types and the associated patterns. You can use these definitions to create a more robust, consistent set of interruption behaviors or interactions. But on large-scale or critical-path systems like Amazon's Alexa platform, it pays to do the legwork to represent these activity types as metadata in your system.

An activity model at the platform level requires you to do the following:

- Define concrete activities in your system, like listening to music or checking the weather, with clear start and (sometimes) end points.
- Categorize the type of attention required for each activity.
- Teach the system about appropriate interruptions for differing levels of attention.

If you're working with an existing system, it's likely you don't even have support for endpoint activities, much less classifying them. Adding these capabilities to an existing system is certainly feasible, but often expensive—and it can be hard to justify that expense when an activity model is an invisible construct.

A robust activity model is a step toward better quality assurance, more predictable system performance, and easier future expansion. Early Echo devices didn't represent these concepts, so each individual activity was implemented slightly differently with regard to concepts like interruption.

Once you've successfully extended your platform to allow each activity to be endpointed and classified, you have essentially taught your system a new level of understanding about your customer's state at any given time. And once you understand your customers' activities, you are better prepared to interrupt those activities when need be.

CHAPTER 4

Activity, Interrupted

Once you can represent each activity your customer may be engaged in, you can begin to define the ways in which those same activities might be interrupted. Modern experiences often lean heavily upon interruptions but fail to do so with respect for human time and attention.

Open offices are, justifiably, one of the many banes of modern adulthood. Ethan Bernstein, coauthor of "The Impact of the 'Open' Workspace on Human Collaboration,"[1] said in an interview: "I walk into this space, and I see everyone wearing big headphones staring intently at a screen trying to look busy because everyone can see them... instead of interrupting people, I'll send an email."[2] Interrupting people. It's hard, isn't it? You have to draw on a variety of social and environmental cues to determine what's appropriate in the moment. Headphones typically convey a desire to focus without interruption, so when employees are driven to use headphones to cope with ambient noise, suddenly an entire office seems uninterruptible.

As you learned in Chapter 2, "Capturing Customer Context," context matters. The presence of the headphones changes the context of the interruption at hand. Your behavior when approaching a coworker with headphones is likely to be different than your normal behavior (unless you're some kind of monster).

But when headphones are suddenly the default state, you lose that context. If only you could see past the headphones to understand whether your coworkers are truly focused and uninterruptible, or if they're just seeking solace from ambient distraction.

If it's this hard for human beings, why are we so surprised that our digital systems get it wrong all the time? For example, I am constantly irritated when a system interrupts the sanctity of my home or my work with an apparent lack of respect for my current state.

Your digital systems are operating at a disadvantage, just like an employee in an open workspace confronted with a sea of headphones. How can teaching your systems what customers are doing lead to better outcomes? How can you make your experiences more skilled at interruption?

---

1   Ethan S. Bernstein and Stephen Turban, "The Impact of the 'Open' Workspace on Human Collaboration," *Philosophical Transactions of the Royal Society B* 373, no. 1753 (2018), https://doi.org/10.1098/rstb.2017.0239

2   Jena McGregor, "Open Office Plans Are as Bad as You Thought," *The Washington Post*, July 18, 2018, www.washingtonpost.com/business/2018/07/18/open-office-plans-are-bad-you-thought/

When Interruptions Attack

To start, let's explore the definition of an interruption. What qualifies? What's most common? The range of possibilities is vast, but there are some rather well-defined categories of activity interruptions seen in today's experiences, as summarized in Table 4.1.

TABLE 4.1 SUMMARY OF COMMON INTERRUPTION TYPES

Interruption Type	Initiated by	Example
Activity	User or system	Switching between apps
Proactive Interruption	System	Incoming text message
Wake Word	User	Saying "Alexa" while listening to music
Transition	User	Starting a hotel search on a phone and continuing on a laptop

Activities as Interruptions

Activities replace other activities all the time. Any time you switch tabs on your desktop or tap on a notification, you're replacing one activity with another. Usually, these switches are customer-initiated, but that's not always the case. Either way, when you design your system, you'll want to account for how one activity replaces another.

Proactive Interruptions (aka Notifications, Nudges)

When you first thought of the word "interruption," you probably thought about a notification. Whereas activity switches are generally initiated by the customer, there's another category of interruptions (often referred to as *alerts* or *notifications*) where the system is initiating the interaction. (In Chapter 10, you'll also encounter the term *nudge*.) Proactive engagements are the way that systems present information out of turn to a customer. Not all proactive interruptions are created equal—some call for complete and abrupt interruption (like an Emergency Broadcast System alert in the U.S.), while some are just informational.

LEARN MORE

For more information about coping with notifications as an interruption, see Chapter 10, "Let's Get Proactive."

Wake Words

How do customers indicate their desire to trigger an activity shift or interruption on a device when engaging with their voice? How do smart speakers avoid sending all possible human speech to the cloud?

"Wake words" are special key words or phrases that customers use to indicate their desire to interact with a device verbally. (When idle, many devices have special local hardware systems that only listen for the wake word before sending any other sounds to the cloud—a critical technology layer for any of us with privacy concerns about speech-enabled devices.)

But when customers are already interacting with a voice controlled device and a wake word is detected, that means the customer wants to speak a command and the current activity may need to be interrupted—especially if it's a loud activity that could interfere with speech.

Systems that don't require a wake word often require some kind of hardware control like a microphone button; you'll learn more about this in later chapters.

Transitions

Sometimes, a customer may continue with a single activity, but shift their context of use while doing so. When a customer moves between locations or devices, they're likely to encounter an interruption in their interaction as the experience adapts—or when it fails to adapt. Here are some examples:

- Switching from headphones to your car's Bluetooth when starting the car
- Moving between Wi-Fi and cellular while on rapid transit
- Switching your game console from TV mode to portable mode (see Figure 4.1)
- Focusing on an app that just opened in the foreground
- Switching to airplane mode when a plane is ready for takeoff
- Closing the lid of your laptop when moving between meetings

Transitions are a major factor when you're building an app which co-exists with other apps on a larger system, like a smartphone or a laptop. Office 365 uses the "Welcome back! Continue where you left off" mechanic to restore the thread of engagement when the app loses focus.

FIGURE 4.1

Games on the Nintendo Switch video gaming console are interrupted when the customer pulls the device from its HDMI dock to use it as a portable device—and yet astonishingly, no gameplay state is lost.

Leaving an Activity Behind

In addition to understanding each interruption type and how it behaves, you'll also need to resolve how the interrupted activity behaves.

For short activities where your customer isn't engaged in data entry, you may decide that interruptions mean abandoning the original task.

In other cases—like making a purchase or dictating a note—you may prefer to suspend progress on the current activity until it can be resumed, either automatically or manually, after the interruption is resolved.

For each activity type in your system, explore these questions:

- Does your task still have meaning, or should the original activity be abandoned?
- How long will your system remember the state of a suspended activity?
- If you suspend the activity, how do you help your customer resume their work later?

The possibilities for interruption become daunting for multidevice scenarios, so focus on documenting the high-risk interruptions and what they mean for your customer. The questions you'll need to ask yourself may sound familiar:

- Can a specific activity be handed off between devices or systems at all?
- Is transitioning the activity between the two devices actually desirable?

- How will the customer know the handoff occurred?
- Is there any risk of loss of context? Do you need to warn the customer?

LEARN MORE

For more information about coping with different types of transition, see Chapter 9, "Lost in Transition."

Interruptions and Inclusion

Interruptions may seem like a minor annoyance if you're not living with cognitive impairments, but many of your customers are constantly and invisibly managing conditions like Attention Deficit Disorder and autism. A single interruption may have vastly different impacts on your customers in terms of frustration and even harm, depending on a person's environmental and mental circumstances.

Microsoft's guide, "Respecting Focus" (part of their broader Inclusive Design Toolkit), proposes a spectrum of potential needs for interruption control, as depicted in Table 4.2.

TABLE 4.2   WORKING STYLES AND INTERRUPTIONS

Style	Description
Isolated	The need for an isolated environment in which to work effectively. That could mean working in a quiet, private space, or having a computer desktop that's free of clutter.
Informed but in Control	Comfortable with alerts, but wants control over their form and timing.
Neutral	No preference for alert timing, style, or mode.

These preferences may sound familiar to you. It's entirely possible that you're fluidly moving between these engagement styles based on mood or environmental conditions. But for others, the lack of control or isolation can be a deal-breaker leading to loss of productivity, pain, or other distress.

If your product relies heavily on interruptions in any way, look for ways to include customers in the design process whom you don't identify as neurotypical. Their insights will lead to stronger design choices that can benefit those with more rigid constraints, as well as those who have the luxury of adapting.

Build an Interruption Matrix in Three Easy Steps

As you learned in Chapter 3, "Understanding Busy Humans," an activity model tells you what types of things a customer may be doing in the moment. Once your system "understands" this, the system can also potentially adapt an interruption based on the currently specified (or detected) activity. "Focus assist" on Windows is one such example (see Figure 4.2). Use of certain app modes, like projection in PowerPoint, is interpreted as a "focused" activity. The system takes this into account and suppresses interruptions until that focused activity is deemed complete.

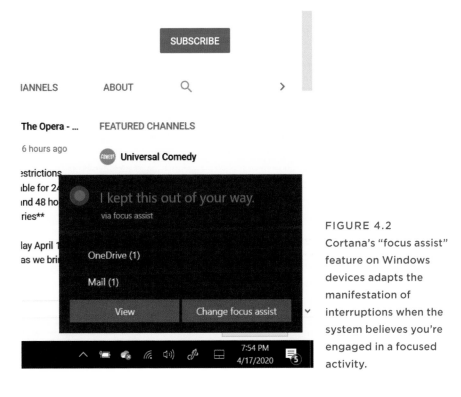

FIGURE 4.2
Cortana's "focus assist" feature on Windows devices adapts the manifestation of interruptions when the system believes you're engaged in a focused activity.

Your systems are likely to support multiple potential activities and multiple potential interruptions. Single-tasking systems may handle interruption in a much different way than a multitasking system, but both must cope with interruption.

To define concrete patterns of interaction during each of these interruptions, I've deployed an interruption matrix as both a design and communication artifact. Through the remainder of this chapter, you'll learn how to build your own interruption matrix with a step-by-step guided example. (Buckle up for lists and tables galore!)

After you've identified all of the major categories of activity and interruption that your system will support, use these steps to build your own interruption matrix:

1. List all of your activity types along one axis of a table or spreadsheet.

2. List all potential interruptions along the other axis of a table or spreadsheet.

3. Fill in all the blanks.

4. (Optional) Profit

Interruption		Short-running activity (e.g. Weather TTS)	
Urgent Notification (e.g. Incoming Call)	VUI	STOP Weather TTS *RING* "Incoming Call from Prof. Plum"	
	GUI	Full Screen App (Active Call) ("Professor Plum is calling.")	
Scheduled Notification (e.g. Timer)	VUI	CONTINUE Weather TTS *Short Timer Alert Tone*	
	GUI	[LAUNCH] Full Screen App (Timer) Full text: "Turkey timer is complete"	
Standard Notification (e.g. Message)	VUI		
	GUI	Notifications with preview (e.g. Message): Notifications w/o preview (third party skills):	
Customer Speaks to Device (Wake Word)	VUI	STOP TTS Only (Retain context of last prompt)	
	GUI	Display voice chrome and retain context	
Wake Word + Error		REPEAT Weather TTS	
User Requested Live Activity (e.g. Pick up an Incoming Call)	VUI	STOP Weather TTS	
	GUI	SWITCH to Full Screen App (Active Call)	
User Requested Short Activity (e.g. "WW, what time is it?")	VUI	STOP Weather TTS	
	GUI	SWITCH to Full Screen App (Clock)	
User Requested Long Activity (e.g."WW, play Spotify")	VUI	STOP Weather TTS	
	GUI	SWITCH to Full Screen App (Spotify)	

Fine, maybe they're not actually easy steps. And no one has ever profited from an interruption matrix on its own, least of all myself. But this is an incredibly valuable road map. Within these cells lie some of your most challenging moments and difficult design problems. It's like a treasure map, except the treasure is tough problems.

Filling in the Blanks

But *how* do you fill in the blanks? Within those blanks, you want to represent the sequence of events that occurs when a given activity is interrupted by a potential interruption. For a reconstructed example of how I've approached this problem in the past, see Figure 4.3.

- What happens to the existing activity?
- How is the interruption manifested via output channels?
- How is any potential action indicated to customers?
- Can the previous activity resume after the interruption is complete?

Current Foreground Activity	
Live Activity (e.g. **Active Phone Call**)	Long-Runing Activity (e.g. **Music Service**)
CONTINUE Phone Call *RING* *(No Announcement)*	SUSPEND **Music** *RING* "Incoming Call from Prof. Plum" RESUME **Music**
Full Screen App (Active Call) ("**Professor Plum is calling.**")	Full Screen App (Active Call) ("**Professor Plum is calling.**")
CONTINUE Phone Call *Short Timer Alert Tone*	SUSPEND **Music** *Long Timer Alert Tone* RESUME **Music**
Full Screen App (Timer) Full text: "Turkey timer is complete"	Full Screen App (Timer) Full text: "Turkey timer is complete"
CONTINUE Activity *Notification Earcon*	
Banner Notification with the Message preview	
Persistent card on the home screen after screen times out to Home.	
CONTINUE **Phone Call**	SUSPEND **immediately**
(if user's to-do list was on the screen before the user spoke, it remains)	
CONTINUE Phone Call	RESUME Music
STOP original Phone Call	PAUSE Music
SWITCH to Full Screen App (Active Call) (for the new call)	**SWITCH** to Full Screen App (Active Call)
CONTINUE Phone Call START Short Activity	SUSPEND Music
SWITCH to Full Screen App (Clock)	**SWITCH** to Full Screen App (Clock)
CONTINUE Phone Call START Spotify	STOP Prime Music
Chrome Transport Controls	**SWITCH** to Full Screen App (Spotify)

FIGURE 4.3

A reconstruction of an interruption matrix I built out when working on a smart speaker notification framework. Note that the table format in complex scenarios doesn't leave much room for flowery text, so you'll likely need to supplement with additional documentation.

In many cases, some of these steps can be represented by a reference to one amongst a robust set of notification patterns. But the notification itself isn't usually sufficient on its own. You'll probably still need to address the existing activity in some way, which isn't a job for a notification.

> **NOTE** DEVICE CAPABILITIES
>
> If you're designing across multiple devices with significantly different capabilities with regard to input and output, you might need separate interruption matrices. Start with a single matrix with a well-formed series of callouts for exceptions on certain devices, but if you have more exceptions than not, it's time to split your matrices.

The Light at the End of the Matrix

Your interruption matrix will pay off in a few critical ways:

1. It forces you to explore complex edge cases early in the development process.
2. It shines a light on inconsistencies in design decisions and motivates the team to streamline those decisions in favor of patterns.
3. It gives new features a fast and easy way to determine how they should behave in any interruption scenario.
4. It can be built at the platform level to automate these transitions and reduce the cost of development and quality assurance for new features.

To get the most out of the interruption matrix, it should be supported by system architecture and platform functionality. But that's an invisible framework-level investment that won't sell well in a commercial. You'll probably have to make a strong case to stakeholders that the investment will pay off.

Putting It All Together

To understand why it's more cost effective and reliable to build an interruption matrix, let's run a thought experiment. Let's say you're designing a voice-enabled smartwatch with a small screen. You start out with three features: weather, music, and phone calls. Since you only have three features, perhaps a full activity and interruption model at the start feels redundant. You can just map the features against each other with a simple matrix: active feature on the vertical axis and interrupting feature on the horizontal axis.

For every one of the cells in your matrix (Table 4.3), you have to decide how the system behaves under those conditions. It's harder than it sounds. In this example, you face gnarly questions like these:

- If someone asks for the weather during a call:
  - Should the system deliver an audio response at full volume?
  - Would the system just show the data with no audio if you have a screen?
- What happens if the customer asks for weather before the previous weather response is done?
  - Do you keep delivering the first one?
  - Do you abandon it in favor of the second one?
- If someone asks for weather while they're listening to music:
  - Should the system pause the music?
  - Should it stop the music entirely?
  - Would it deliver both at the same time?

Every one of those conversations can turn into a meeting. Or two. (Or ten, depending on how many stakeholders are involved!)

TABLE 4.3 ACTIVE FEATURES VERSUS INTERRUPTING FEATURES

Active/Interrupting	Weather	Music	Phone Call
Weather	Cancel previous response	Keep speaking weather over music	Stop speaking
Music	Turn volume down during weather	Switch songs	Pause music
Phone Call	Deliver response at full volume	Play music during call	Call waiting prompt

You didn't apply any activity types here—you just mapped features to all other possible feature interruptions. Not too unwieldy. Nine cells, nine interactions. But what if you decide to add support for sports score requests? You'll have to add a new row and a new column to the matrix.

Table 4.4 sees your matrix growing from nine possible interruptions to sixteen—that's seven more interruptions that you need to define.

With a single new feature addition, you've almost doubled the number of possible interruption patterns... and by association, the design work required.

TABLE 4.4 ADDING A NEW FEATURE TO THE INTERRUPTION MATRIX

Active/Interrupting	Weather	Music	Phone Call	Sports Score
Weather	Cancel previous response	Keep speaking weather over music	Stop speaking	Cancel weather response
Music	Turn volume down during weather	Switch songs	Pause music	Turn volume down during score
Phone Call	Deliver response at full volume	Play music during call	Call waiting prompt	Deliver response at full volume
Sports Score	Cancel sports response	Keep speaking sports over music	Cancel sports response	Cancel previous response

The growth doesn't stop if you keep adding features; the matrix spirals out of control pretty quickly. And needless to say, devices like the Amazon Echo and Google Home have *many* more features than we're showing here. Each new feature introduces dozens of potential interruptions, and the more you define, the less likely you are to be consistent. Think of the QA nightmare: do you want to walk through Alexa's seemingly endless features to ensure that each new interruption behaves properly?

All is not lost, however. Tables 4.3 and 4.4 are mapping features to features. It's time to apply an activity model and an interruption model to reduce the complexity of your potential interactions.

Even if you're not sure where to begin, a draft matrix like this can shed some light. A pattern is already emerging. It turns out that asking for sports scores and asking for weather are pretty similar activities. Both are a short, defined response to a clearly scoped request. Let's look back at our definition of a discrete activity from Chapter 3:

> An activity that requires directed attention, but may leave some cognitive bandwidth for multitasking or interruption. The activity usually has a known, discrete endpoint.

If you categorize both Weather and Sports Score activities into the "discrete" activity type, you can simplify your table again. Table 4.5 shows how the interruption matrix looks when you replace those two activities with the broader "Discrete" activity type.

TABLE 4.5 APPLYING AN ACTIVITY TYPE TO AN INTERRUPTION MATRIX

Active/Interrupting	Discrete	Music	Phone Call
Discrete	Cancel previous response	Keep responding over music	Stop speaking
Music	Turn volume down during response	Switch songs	Pause music
Phone Call	Deliver response at full volume	Play music during call	Call waiting prompt

This kind of design and taxonomy rigor is the gift that keeps on giving. If you later decide to add support for a simple date or time request, that, too, falls into the Discrete activity type. No additional interruptions are needed. The team working on that feature doesn't need to worry about design arguments or the QA associated with new interruption patterns.

Start Early

As your interruption matrix takes shape, it's important to involve your development partners sooner rather than later. In a perfect world, where you're designing from scratch, these models can be baked in at the system architecture level from the beginning.

But there are countless experiences that shipped without an activity model, interruption model, or interruption matrix. And while those taxonomies aren't *required* to get a product off the ground, layering them into an existing system when you need them can be far more complicated and costly than doing it from the start.

Defining a strong activity model gives you an excellent foundation that will help you scale your experience over time in a more reliable, less costly fashion. Sure, it's overkill for small systems. But know where you're going. If there's any chance you may want to scale up over time, build a strong conceptual foundation and work with your development partners to represent these concepts in your system architecture from the start.

Apply It Now

The activity and interruption taxonomies explored in this chapter might initially seem trivial since they're largely words on paper. In reality, your interruption matrix and the work supporting it are a manifestation of your team's shared understanding of the human behavior and system responses core to your customer experience.

Your interruption matrix can be *so much more* than a design pattern. Ensure that you're pursuing critical conversations at many points along the way to give that vision its best chance of becoming reality.

- Review your activity model with the product owner and user research to make sure that you're aligned.

- Build a shared understanding with stakeholders around your proposed interruption model to ensure that key use cases are represented.

- Test your hypotheses about interruption types with potential customers in context. Include customers who do not self-identify as neurotypical to avoid causing unintentional harm.

- Get involved in system architecture discussions. You may feel like a fish out of water, but this is platform-level design work, and you'll need to be in those discussions.

- Seek out developers early and find allies on the platform side who will include support for this work in their product backlogs.

- Ensure that feature owners understand the implications of your interruption matrix and have adequate technical documentation to leverage the implementation.

My work designing and socializing the interruption matrix for the Echo and Echo Show was some of the most challenging fun I had as a systems-minded designer on those projects. It's a long road, but I hope you'll find the process just as fulfilling.

CHAPTER 5

The Language of Devices

E ven the most human-centered of designers will find themselves adapting their mental model to cope with the baggage of a device-centric world when speaking with engineering partners. When engineers talk about *input* and *output*, those terms are defined from the device's perspective.

- A person's expression of intent via the keyboard is "input" via the keyboard as an "input device."
- The system's response to the typed request in this example over video and audio channels is the "output."

While I'm always a fan of keeping things human-centric, in this case, trying to change this framing would be wasted energy. As the Borg would say, "Resistance is futile." Let's instead focus on working within this frame.

Because devices exist in the service of human beings, it also makes sense to align one's understanding of these inputs and outputs with the human context: the senses and human context to which these interactions apply. In Chapter 1, "Creating the World We Want to Live In," you learned about five core communication modalities: visual, auditory, haptic, kinetic, and ambient. All of these communication modalities are tied to at least one human sense (and in the case of kinetic and ambient communications, potentially multiple senses). Every device will have a specific set of input and output capabilities tied to some or all of these modalities.

But why focus on device capabilities at all? (Isn't this book called *Design Beyond Devices*?) We're inherently looking *beyond the boundaries of a single device* when we discuss inputs and outputs at a more granular level. Rather than thinking about a device first and its capabilities second, this chapter and Chapter 6, "Expressing Intent," are focusing on the more universal range of possible interactions *across* devices.

This broader perspective has become more critical as devices become more capable. For example, thinking about speech interaction as a *capability* independent of a smart speaker enables you to get creative, supporting similar speech interactions on additional platforms where speech interaction is supported (like smartphones).

To fully embrace this device-agnostic design perspective, you should be starting with your customer *and their context* at the center of your designs.

- Given your customer's current environment, what communication choice is most appropriate?
- In what ways does your customer want to interact?
- How is your choice of communication modalities going to affect your customer's perception of the interaction?

These questions transcend device boundaries. By looking at inputs and outputs holistically, you might discover more appropriate device specs or even change what platform you're targeting based on the context. Maybe your customer is closer to their PC than their smart speaker, and as a result, you consider implementing your feature on a different platform.

Admittedly, not every project has the luxury of controlling its inputs, outputs, or platforms. That doesn't mean there's not ample opportunity to bring truly multimodal and cross-device experiences to your customers. As devices become more capable, you'll want to evaluate what devices and capabilities are *already available* to your customer. Those are opportunities to make the most out of untapped potential instead of sticking to old, device-bound ways of thinking.

Visual Output: Displays and Indicators

Half of the typical human brain is dedicated to processing visual stimuli. Since human brains are so optimized for processing visual stimuli, it's no surprise that a majority of output innovations have been rooted in visual mediums, both analog and digital. Table 5.1 explores a few broad categories for visual displays and their capabilities.

The Amazon Echo and Rich Indicators

Amazon's original Echo device featured a "light ring" indicator (Figure 5.1), a circular arrangement of LED lights that used color and animation to differentiate between states. Despite that increased sophistication, the light ring was still an indicator tied to a narrow set of system states like setup, connection failure, processing, and active listening.

TABLE 5.1 THE WIDE WORLD OF VISUAL OUTPUT

Display class	Description	Examples
Static Displays	Solid objects that do not change form once created.	Books Paper, posters
Indicators	An affordance tied to specific, variable aspect(s) of a system's status. Status may be conveyed by indicator color, indicator shape, illumination, symbols (including numbers and text), physical position, or animation.	Fuel gauge Speedometer Amazon Echo light ring
Dynamic Displays	Arrays of dynamic pixels used to convey rich visual information. Constrained displays require stronger information architecture to help customers navigate the increased cognitive load when information is hidden off-screen.	Kindle e-readers Apple Watches Smartphones Monitors Televisions
Immersive Displays	Immersive displays output visuals designed to overlay or replace most of our field of view. They are rarely traditional "screens."	Large format (IMAX) Augmented reality Virtual reality

FIGURE 5.1

Amazon's Echo device uses a dark blue ring when listening, and light blue to indicate the direction of the speaker.

The "dynamic display" class covers a wide range of possibilities, both mainstream and irregular. Dynamic displays may be limited in one or more ways that require particular design attention (see Table 5.2).

TABLE 5.2 DYNAMIC DISPLAY CONSTRAINTS

Constraint	Considerations
Output Type	Constrained displays may focus on a single type of output, like text and numbers.
Pixel Density and Screen Size	Constrained displays are often incapable of displaying full HD output, and may have a limited ability to render readable text.
Screen Shape or Size	When a display uses a nonstandard aspect ratio or irregular borders, special interface considerations begin to apply. Irregular shaped screens include the Google Nest or the Echo Spot.
Refresh Rate	Screens with lower refresh rates won't support rapid-fire interactions or animations.
Screen Size	It's impossible to specify a hard limit to screen size. In fact, this is a relative measurement that may change as technology evolves.

From Exclusion to Inclusion

According to the World Health Organization, "At least 2.2 billion people have a vision impairment or blindness," based on a study of global population data from 2015. While your mind may leap first to the concept of total blindness, the American Foundation for the Blind reports that only 15% of people with vision impairments are totally blind. The remaining 85% have some form of sight.[1]

Color Blindness

Color blindness is incredibly common, affecting hundreds of millions of people worldwide.[2] While the severity and type of color blindness varies from person to person, *no interface should depend solely on color to convey meaning or status.*

---

1   "Low Vision and Legal Blindness Terms and Conditions," AFB.org, American Foundation for the Blind, www.afb.org/blindness-and-low-vision/eye-conditions/low-vision-and-legal-blindness-terms-and-descriptions

2   "Colour Blindness," Colour Blind Awareness, www.colourblindawareness.org/colour-blindness/

Immersive displays, as used in extended reality experiences (augmented, mixed, or virtual reality), are quite impressive, but they are not without drawbacks. The more immersive the display, the more likely viewers are to experience motion sickness.

When a display replaces a person's visual field, their body generally interprets that input as "real" and reacts as such, expecting physical stimuli that match the perceived motion. Disconnects between these two simultaneous outputs can confuse their minds and cause nausea or headaches. Furthermore, immersive displays render the viewer unable to respond to stimuli in the "real" world, which may make them vulnerable or at risk of physical harm.

You should weigh the potential exclusion caused by this "simulator sickness" carefully when deciding whether to utilize an immersive display. Some appropriate examples where immersion is genuinely useful:

- Emulating real-life conditions to safely measure human response

  Example: Driving simulators to test automotive interfaces

- Integrating seamlessly with existing environments

  Example: Microsoft's HoloLens

- Building a rich sensory memory that can be recalled later

  Example: Immersive emergency responder training

For more about the wide world of extended reality—including augmented reality, mixed reality, and virtual reality—see Chapter 14, "Beyond Reality: XR, VR, AR, and MR."

Low Vision

Uncorrectable reduction of some but not all vision may take many forms, including central or peripheral vision loss, blurring, or the inability to see in low lighting conditions.[3]

To help your customers with low vision:

- Support *high contrast mode* and utilize platform settings when available. If possible, *emphasize contrast in your default styles* as well; even fully sighted folks benefit from high contrast.

---

3 "Eye Conditions and Diseases: Low Vision," National Eye Institute, last edited May 5, 2020, www.nei.nih.gov/learn-about-eye-health/eye-conditions-and -diseases/low-vision

- Any text-based output should support *customizable text sizing* for those who struggle with small type. If your chosen platform (OS, web browser, etc.) supports resizing content via system commands, make sure that your experience responds to those interactions.

The Blind Community

Customers in the Blind community will be completely unable to use a visual interface and must rely on alternative forms of input instead. To support the use of these devices correctly, your developers will likely need to add metadata to aid in describing or replacing on-screen elements.

- Refreshable Braille displays replace the visual stimuli of text with a haptic stimulus (see Figure 5.2).

- Screen readers turn visual stimuli into an auditory signal, describing the content and controls on the screen, often at high speed.

©ZLIKOVEC–STOCK.ADOBE.COM

FIGURE 5.2
Refreshable Braille displays provide a steady stream of characters so that unsighted customers can take in language-based content.

The good news: accessibility for visually dominant displays is a very well-explored problem, and numerous best practices have been defined and even referenced in legislation. If you're just beginning your visual accessibility journey, the Web Content Accessibility

Guidelines (WCAG),[4] as defined by the Web Accessibility Initiative (W3C), is a comprehensive checklist of best practices.

> **NOTE** ACCESSIBILITY AND COMPLIANCE
>
> The U.S. government requires adherence to many of these guidelines for any software it uses, so that most large companies like Microsoft and Google have baked enforcement of WCAG guidelines into their software engineering process. If you're not yet familiar with these guidelines, make that learning a priority for you and your team.

Auditory Output: Sound Effects, Speech, and Music

Humans are capable of understanding quite a bit over audio channels, and often this understanding is reflexive. Even if your customers can turn down the volume, don't turn down your opportunity to consider audio as a primary or secondary output modality. You can start with lightweight earcons or go all the way to a high-fidelity approach that incorporates music, sound effects, and spoken language, and there are many stops in between the extremes.

Sound Effects and Earcons

The broad term "sound effect" refers to any (generally nonverbal) audio signal intended to convey some kind of meaning. If you've not worked with audio output before, your understanding of sound effects may be tightly associated with more narrative media like video games and films: footsteps, a crash of thunder, the creak of a door hinge, etc.

In the world of device interaction, there's a subset of sound effects designed to mark a specific event or condition. Designers often refer to these interaction-bound sound effects as *earcons*—icons for the ear. Avoid the temptation to dismiss these as simple stock sound effects.

---

4 "Web Content Accessibility Guidelines (WCAG) Overview," W3C Web Accessibility Initiative, last edited June 22, 2018, by Shawn Layton Henry, www.w3.org/WAI/standards-guidelines/wcag/

As Bill Buxton said, "There's as much care and art in the design of good earcons as there is in good icons."[5]

Earcons aren't just a flourish added to a voice interaction: they communicate without words. Well-designed earcons can communicate source, direction, frequency, magnitude, and urgency. Earcons are often fairly short, abstract, and designed for repetitive use—but there are exceptions to each of these generalities.

The power of earcons lies partly in their ability to transmit meaning faster than speech, and partly in their ability to create a sense of place without requiring narrative descriptions. Cathy Pearl describes one such example in *Designing Voice User Interfaces*: "In the 511 IVR system (which provides traffic and transit information), when the user returns to the main menu, a specific, short audio clip plays. When the user goes to the traffic menu, a short car horn beep is played. This is called *landmarking*, and it helps users to quickly understand they have been taken to the right place."[6]

The art of designing earcons is far more complex than you'd think. Shorter abstract sounds are harder to differentiate and harder to integrate into an overall sound strategy.

- Do you ease into the sound, or do you need to jolt people into awareness?
- How long is too long?
- How will it sound after hearing it 100 times?
- Will it sound the same on a phone speaker and a surround sound system?

NOTE QUALITIES OF SOUND

Volume, dynamics, tone, and more all combine to create vastly different impact for your customers. Choose carefully. Bryce Johnson, Inclusive Lead from Microsoft Devices, shared a playful mental image, "I like to say try for the ice cream truck over the fire truck."

---

5 Tom Warren, "Microsoft Had to Blindfold Me So I Could Hear the Future," *The Verge*, November 6, 2014, www.theverge.com/2014/11/6/7164623/microsoft-3d-sound-headset-guide-dogs

6 Cathy Pearl, *Designing Voice User Interfaces: Principles of Conversational Experiences* (San Francisco: O'Reilly, 2016).

Communicating Nonverbal Information

If you've worked primarily on the Web during your career, sound effects may seem like a gimmick (at best). But there's plenty of room for sound effects and earcons to enrich your experience in the event that volume is audible. The world around you is full of both subtle and prominent audio cues from which you're deriving both passive and active information. Does that pipe banging mean you need a plumber? Did the lock click into place as expected? Why is your computer fan still running on the weekend?

Safety

You're probably familiar with the sound of trucks beeping to indicate operation in reverse. But newer consumer electric and hybrid engines run effectively silent, posing a safety hazard in close quarters. In their article, "The Danger of Too-Quiet Cars," Edmunds.com points out a 2009 study that found "hybrids and electrics were twice as likely as nonhybrids to be involved in a pedestrian crash" at low speeds. The solution: the U.S. government's Pedestrian Safety Enhancement Act of 2010, which mandates the use of sound effects to alert pedestrians of nearby slow-moving vehicles.

Status

Even short sounds can impart information. It's less common now that elevators can make spoken announcements, but a former best practice for accessible elevator design included a standard for sound effects. The cheapest way to impart elevator status to the Blind? One ding for going up, two dings for going down. Admittedly, it requires training—but once you know, you know.

Position

In stereo or immersive audio systems, audio can be "placed" relative to the listener's head, implying a position in space. Microsoft's Soundscape app is a carefully engineered example of this phenomenon. As described by Tom Warren in The Verge in 2014: "One feature on the headset allows you to push a button and hear a list of nearby places of interest. They're processed through the headset dependent on the direction you're facing so that when a store is read aloud you'll be able to hear the direction of where it's located. That might be in the rear left or out in front, but the audio gives you a clear sense of where that store is along a route through just sound alone."[7]

Music

Music is distinguished from sound effects by its relative length, its rhythmic component, and the tendency for music to involve multiple audio sources (like instruments, percussion, and sometimes the spoken word). Music can create an emotional response, improve focus, evoke memories, and even inspire a state of flow—but when it doesn't align well with the current task, it can cause cognitive dissonance, distraction, or even frustration.

Language

The ability to understand spoken language is one of the first skills we acquire—and if we're lucky enough to live a long life, one of the last abilities we lose. Human brains have adapted unique specializations for language processing, like the "cocktail party effect"—the ability of the human brain to pick out one voice over a cacophony of voices.

> **NOTE** SPEECH AT SPEED
>
> Those who use spoken UI regularly often develop an astonishing ability to recognize speech at speed. If you've never had the opportunity to observe a customer's use of a screen reader, seek out that experience—and note how fast they are able to consume the speech generated by the system.

Language is effective, even in critical situations. Voice evacuation systems have become more popular in newer buildings to announce fires and other urgent situations. Not only is the sound of the spoken voice arguably less traumatic than a klaxon, but the words also make the alarm more versatile by imparting important information that humans can't help but process, even in a crisis, because the human brain is so optimized for speech.

Even as spoken interfaces become more mainstream, there are problems:

- Humans are rarely alone. Spoken UI does not offer good privacy, and can be embarrassing in the wrong context.
- Like conversation, spoken UI is prone to interruption—and in many cases, interruptions mean starting over completely.

---

7 Warren, "Microsoft Had to Blindfold Me."

Spoken output requires generation of the audio prompts the customer will hear. Today's smart speakers use sophisticated text-to-speech systems in the cloud in real time, enabling them to generate arbitrary strings. Older systems and systems without cloud access may instead rely on prerecorded prompts.

Output Hardware

Not all speakers are created equal. Odds are that as technology improves we'll all need sounds that hold up across a wide range of speaker fidelities. Cell phone speakers, smart speakers, headsets, and immersive or surround sound systems all satisfy different needs and have different acoustic properties. Figure 5.3 depicts just a few of the widely varied physical builds in Amazon's Echo family of devices.

- Does your speaker support full music playback at a reasonable quality?

- Is the sound rich or tinny?

- Do you need a stereo system to convey positional information? If so, how will you calibrate it?

PHOTO CREDIT: AMAZON

FIGURE 5.3
Sound design for device families like Amazon's Echo family of devices is surprisingly complex, as each device's form factor and speaker combine to create unique acoustic properties.

Sound design is a parallel discipline and far more complex than it seems. Many sound designers work on a freelance or contract basis. You should reach out to a professional, even if you think your needs are fairly minimal. A good sound design professional can help you narrow down what sound cues you have, develop a common acoustic aesthetic for your sounds, and make sure that your sounds perform well on many different devices.

From Exclusion to Inclusion

In the heady early days of the smart speaker craze, podcasters and bloggers around the world speculated that voice-only interfaces might be the wave of the future. But moving completely from the visually dominant output of the 1990s and 2000s to an acoustically dominant output model doesn't solve an inclusion problem—it just shifts the problem to a different set of customers. Furthermore, the world is a noisy place, and it's risky to place all of your interaction eggs into that audio basket. Audio output excludes customers who cannot rely fully on their sense of hearing, whether that sense is impaired, unavailable, or temporarily diminished.

Hearing Loss

Some people lose some of the sensory cells in their ear that help them perceive audio signals (known as *sensorineural hearing loss*). In other cases, the vibrations associated with sound aren't making their way all the way through the ear (known as *conductive hearing loss*).

In both cases, customers may experience a muffling of sounds, loss of clarity, and complete inability to hear quiet sounds.

In some cases, your customers might use hearing aids or bone-conduction headsets to augment their hearing. Some of these assistive devices can pair up with your device or app, which could lead to a much more seamless experience for these customers.

The Deaf Community

Your system will need a nonaudible way of interacting with customers in the Deaf community. To include these customers, you need to provide an *alternate output*, like digital Braille systems or visual output of comparable fidelity. Earcons can be replaced with haptic feedback, and, in fact, phones do this today with "silent mode."

This challenge remains generally unsolved for smart speakers, but the rise of devices like the Amazon Echo Show help bridge this gap. Consider that many customers will have a smartphone. Could you use a nearby visually dominant device to transmit any spoken or acoustic signals in an alternative fashion?

Environmental Interference

As the Microsoft Inclusive Design Toolkit[8] points out, situational disabilities are also a consideration. Customers in an already noisy environment are effectively operating with a hearing impairment in relation to whatever information you may convey over the audio channel. And on the flip side, not all environments are conducive or safe for audio output. Be sure to consider your customer's environment before including prominent audio feedback in your product and also to provide alternatives.

Haptic Output: Touch and Force

The *Oxford English Dictionary* defines the term *haptic* as "the perception of objects by touch and proprioception, especially as involved in nonverbal communication." In layman's terms: haptic feedback engages your sense of touch.

> **NOTE PROPRIOCEPTION**
>
> *Proprioception* is a term used in cognitive psychology to refer to a person's sense of the position and relative movement of their body through space. Ballroom dancers develop a very acute sense of proprioception.

The world is constantly providing us with haptic feedback. Digital haptic technologies are simply trying to mimic that feedback. Table 5.3 provides an overview of four types of haptic feedback, along with examples from both the physical world and digital interactions.

---

8 Albert Shum et al., *Toolkit: Inclusive 101* (Microsoft, 2016), www.microsoft.com/design/inclusive/

TABLE 5.3 SOME EXAMPLES OF PHYSICAL AND DIGITAL HAPTICS

Feedback	Physical World	Digital
Vibrotactile (Vibration)	Rumble strips: heavily textured road markings that cause the steering wheel to vibrate when a car is drifting dangerously	Modern smartphones that vibrate briefly to alert us to an incoming notification
Force Feedback	Vehicles without power steering, where certain maneuvers encounter significant steering wheel resistance	Video game joysticks that push back when you're attempting difficult actions
Electrotactile	The feel of your clothing against your skin	A haptic suit that can convey a sense of texture
Atmospheric	The feel of wind on your face when you're biking at speed	Disney's Soarin' IMAX ride, where air is used to create a sense of speed on a stationary ride vehicle

Vibrotactile Feedback

The most common form of haptic output today, *vibrotactile feedback* engages human skin receptors, which are finely tuned to detect vibration around them.[9] Vibrotactile devices typically use motors and vary the oscillation, pulses, and shudders of those motors to provide information. Magnitude, scale, or frequency can be communicated by changes to the vibration sequence, strength, and duration. For example, your smartphone likely supports a "silent" mode where vibrotactile feedback is generated via a motor when a call or notification comes in.

Force Feedback

When you hold an object in the real world and try to squeeze it, you'll encounter some level of resistance, depending on the rigidity of the object. To provide this kind of tactile feedback for virtual objects, *force-feedback output devices* react to your actions to simulate the force you would encounter in a physical interaction.

---

9   Dimitri Mikhalchuk, "What Is Haptic Feedback (Haptics)?" *TESLASUIT* (blog), VR Electronics Ltd., March 28, 2017, https://teslasuit.io/blog/haptic_feedback/

Most force-feedback output is active force feedback—the device actively exerts resistance against human movement using motors or other interventions. Passive force feedback uses proxy objects: a technique seen in some VR environments where, for example, a digital chair might correspond to a chair in physical space.

Electrotactile Feedback

A form of haptic input that requires no moving parts, *electrotactile feedback* devices use electrical signals not unlike medical-grade electrical muscle simulation systems. Electrotactile feedback can be received by more than just the skin's receptors, making it more versatile than the previously mentioned vibrotactile feedback. The use of electrical signals enables these signal data to go deeper, to the nerve endings in the skin, unlocking a much broader range of possibilities.

Figure 5.4 depicts a next-generation device that combines several of the aforementioned technologies. Haptic suits and partial body peripherals like the upcoming TESLASUIT GLOVE attempt to track human motion in space at a granular level while stimulating our sense of touch with both vibration and electrical signals.[10]

FIGURE 5.4
The TESLASUIT GLOVE employs technologies like force feedback and biometric sensors to enable a rich set of physical interactions.

---

10 Dimitri Mikhalchuk, "TESLASUIT Introduces Its Brand-New VR Gloves," *TESLASUIT* (blog), VR Electronics Ltd., December 27, 2019, https://teslasuit.io/blog/teslasuit-introduces-its-brand-new-vr-gloves/

Atmospheric Haptics

There are a few types of haptic output that *don't require* any direct interaction to transmit information.

- **Air:** The use of pressurized air provides resistance or a sense of movement.

- **Ultrasound:** Ultrasonic fields, generated by an array of transmitters, can disturb a region of air so that the skin detects affordances that are invisible to the human eye.

- **Thermal:** The manipulation of ambient temperature provides information about a space or object. (Haptic suits can also provide direct thermal feedback, but it's very power-inefficient.)

Applications of Haptic Feedback

The most common use of haptic feedback in today's world is *vibrotactile feedback*, primarily deployed simplistically in smartphones and wearable technology like fitness trackers to provide invisible "nudges" in lieu of an audible notification.

From the more sophisticated rumble motors inside next-generation video-game controllers to the use of atmospheric feedback in immersive VR experiences, haptics offer a unique escalation to customer immersion when applied to entertainment scenarios.

But there's much more potential as the actuators used for physical feedback become more lightweight and efficient. Could a wearable fitness tracker provide meaningful haptic feedback on technique when weightlifting? Could a pair of gloves provide directional guidance?

It's still early days for the exploration of haptic output patterns. User researchers are exploring exactly how deep that rabbit hole goes. In their book exploring the cognitive psychology implications of multimodal design, Christine Park and John Alderman describe one relatively new concept in this space: "Differentiation and recall, tests that can be used to measure the usability of icons, are also being used for haptic vibrations, sometimes called *hapticons*; these gauge how well a person can remember a vibration pattern or tell two different patterns apart."[11]

---

11 Christine Park and John Alderman, *Designing Across Senses: A Multimodal Approach to Product Design* (O'Reilly Media, 2018), Kindle Edition: Locations 444–445.

Regardless of your customer's situation, haptic output is rarely sufficient to convey meaning *on its own*. In general, it's too coarsely grained. Haptic output is most useful when replacing physical sensation you'd expect while interacting with a purely digital system, but haptics can also be useful when you want to tap into human reflex reactions.

> **NOTE** GAME HAPTICS AND REFLEXES
>
> Some video games use haptic feedback to trigger nearly automatic physical responses. For example, Nintendo's *Animal Crossing* games use vibrotactile feedback to jerk the controller and hopefully entice you to reel in a curious virtual fish by smashing a button on that controller.

From Exclusion to Inclusion

Vibration and force feedback will be of limited use to anyone already suffering from mobility impairments of some kind. Paralysis also impacts the sense of touch, and thus physical feedback on an impaired body part would not have an impact.

Even if your customer is able to perceive haptic output, they might prefer not to experience it. Haptic feedback can feel invasive or even painful, especially to those sensitive to overstimulation. Consider how you might provide the ability to opt out of haptics and ensure that the experience is still coherent without that feedback.

Atmospheric haptic experiences are difficult to categorize. Specific to the use of air, customers with contact lenses, respiratory conditions, or sensitive skin may find aggressive use of air problematic.

> **NOTE** A COMMON ASK
>
> According to Bryce Johnson, Inclusive Lead at Microsoft, the #1 requested feature ask in the accessibility feedback forums after the launch of the Xbox One was the ability to disable controller vibrations. (That feature has since been added to the Xbox OS.)

Scientists at the University of Pennsylvania found a measurable improvement in the efficacy of teaching physical movements when haptic feedback was added to existing verbal and visual instruction for test participants.[12]

> The conducted study showed that augmenting visual feedback with vibrotactile feedback through our low-cost (~$216 total cost for parts), wearable motion guidance system helped users reduce their motion errors as they learned and practiced 1DOF (one degree of freedom) arm motions.

More complex movements with multiple degrees of freedom didn't see the same benefits, but the authors of the study hypothesized that participants found the design of the feedback difficult to interpret, opening the door for improved designs and greater results. These findings bear particular interest for fields like physical therapy, where the customer's motivation and the goal-oriented engagement might lead to even better results.

---

12 Karlin Bark et al., "Effects of Vibrotactile Feedback on Human Learning of Arm Motions," *IEEE Transactions on Neural Systems and Rehabilitation Engineering* 23, no. 1 (January 2015): 51–63, doi:10.1109/TNSRE.2014.2327229.

Kinetic Output: Movement and Motion

Kinetic output relies upon motion to convey meaning. This is different than communications where motion is used to move between distinct states. For example, a ballroom dance is kinetic communication, but the traditional dance to the Village People's classic song "YMCA" is interpreted more as purely visual communication as participants mime those four letters.

With kinetic output, the movement itself is the data, not the destination:

- The pendulum in an antique clock tells us the clock is working and gives us a measure of time (see Figure 5.5).
- Your dog's tail provides kinetic output corresponding to their current mood.
- Audio-animatronic figures use both audio output and kinetic output to create the illusion of life.

FIGURE 5.5

The pendulums of antique clocks are an enduring example of meaningful kinetic output—although one can't quite say they're timeless.

The digital systems of today don't frequently rely upon kinetic output, but there are circumstances where it might be appropriate. Kinetic output tends to look and feel very analog, so in situations where we want to blend in with our surroundings as much as possible, kinetic output could be compelling. And kinetic output will become more relevant as robotics become more mainstream.

Certain animations on a digital screen are also kinetic output, since they are based on motion. If the meaning changes if the motion is disabled, then you're creating kinetic output.

From Exclusion to Inclusion

Motion can be very evocative and exciting, but there are a wide range of individuals who find motion difficult to contend with. For example, look at the following examples:

- Accessibility advocate Val Head describes the struggle of those with visually triggered vestibular disorders: "As animated interfaces increasingly become the norm, more people have begun to notice that large-scale motion on screen can cause them dizziness, nausea, headaches, or worse."[13]

- Cognitive impairments can render people more sensitive to animation. Those with ADD and ADHD, for example, can be particularly distracted by animation.

- The scientific community continues to investigate whether people with autism may face higher thresholds for perception of coherent motion.[14]

Adaptive affordances to cope with motion have lagged, but standards are finally evolving so that the major operating systems—and many websites—allow customers to express their desire to minimize or suppress interface animation. To include as many people as possible with your experience, do the following:

- Don't use animation as the only way any information is communicated in your interface.

- Honor any customer preferences in the OS or browser to dynamically minimize animation in your UI.

Ambient Output: The World Around You

Digital output has up until recently been limited to audio, video, and limited haptic output. But there's more in the environment than just devices. The term *ambient* is defined by the *Oxford English Dictionary* as "relating to the immediate surroundings of something." What *surrounds* your customer? General environmental conditions like light, scent, or background sounds—and changes in conditions—can also contribute to your customer's perception of an experience.

You may have noticed that a few human senses have as of yet been ignored in this assessment of potential outputs. Taste will remain outside the scope of this book (although you'll forgive me for hoping you find its contents tasteful). As of yet, no reasonable technology exists for dynamically outputting taste.

---

13 Val Head, "Designing Safer Web Animation for Motion Sensitivity," *A List Apart*, September 8, 2015, https://alistapart.com/article/designing-safer-web-animation-for-motion-sensitivity/

14 Martha D. Kaiser and Maggie Shiffrar, "The Visual Perception of Motion by Observers with Autism Spectrum Disorders: A Review and Synthesis," *Psychonomic Bulletin & Review* 16, no. 5 (2009): 761–777, doi:10.3758/PBR.16.5.761.

However, there *are* some (currently fairly limited) ways of outputting olfactory—or scent-based—signals. But beyond any outputs you control, additional incidental output events may occur in the vicinity of your device that influence the way your customer will perceive the end-to-end experience.

Olfactory

While your design or development education likely didn't include anything around the human sense of smell, there are some good examples of olfactory output being used to significant effect already in use today:

- The use of scent generators in public spaces to create a brand experience (Vegas hotels).
- The introduction of scent to indicate danger (sulfur in odorless gas).
- The use of scent in immersive experiences (Disney rides).

Our sense of smell is more likely to trigger emotional responses, or instinctive responses, like disgust. Smell is highly subjective, and some people (for example, pregnant women) are highly sensitive to smells to the point of distraction or discomfort.

Furthermore, human brains haven't developed sophisticated heuristics for separating scents, as opposed to the ability to separate voices from background noise. If there are competing scents in the area, it will be difficult to differentiate between them.

For these reasons, olfactory output should be used extremely sparingly, and with a strong eye toward unintended side effects and environmental context.

Incidental

Some feedback is obtained through changes in the world independent of the device you're controlling. For example, when you ask your smart speaker to turn off the lights, you know your request was successful if the lights proceed to turn off. This is a visual form of output, but it's not system output—it's system-adjacent. Incidental feedback doesn't just have to be visual: think of the vibration of a garage door closing, or the sound of a door locking behind you.

Incidental output or feedback is generally only useful if it's in close proximity and very closely timed to the initial triggering action. The less tight the pairing, the harder it is for customers to infer the two events—the request and the change—are related.

In most cases, incidental feedback shouldn't be your primary output or feedback mechanism, as the passive nature means it's perhaps easy to miss. To return to the smart home example previously, what if a customer asks the device to turn off a light in another room? Incidental feedback won't be enough, because your customer can't see the light going off (see Figure 5.6).

FIGURE 5.6
Smart homes are full of opportunities for incidental feedback, but the bigger the house, the less likely that feedback is reliable.

Apply It Now

It's always exciting to work with new technologies, but work at the cutting edge assumes that your customers have the ability to pay for hardware capable of depicting your vision. The reality is that most advanced output technologies remain out of reach for many customers.

The more you can accomplish with more modest output technologies, the greater your impact will be because your experience will be accessible to more customers, regardless of socioeconomic status. As you begin your design journey, ask yourself these questions:

- What output modalities are available on this platform?
- What output modalities are neglected or overlooked?
- How might you be even more inclusive by allowing customers to choose their preferred form of system output, either up front or in the moment?

CHAPTER 6

Expressing
Intent

While the late 20th century saw great leaps in *output* technology, the early years of the 21st century brought forth a renaissance of *input* innovations: capacitive touchscreens, sensors, natural language understanding, computer vision and gesture control, and beyond.

Humans are capable of so much more when communicating intent than the last few decades of devices have afforded us. Think about the simple act of greeting someone. You might speak the word "hello." You might wave and make eye contact. You might shake hands or hug someone. Different combinations of expressions for a single intent: to greet another human being. And the recipient interprets that expression as input.

Thanks to significant improvements in sensor technology, a single human intent can now be expressed to our technology via multiple input modalities. Each input modality has its strengths and weaknesses that may vary significantly based on the context of use.

As long as humans have lived, they've relied upon *multiple* modalities to communicate. Sometimes, you use multiple modalities at the same time, and sometimes you switch fluidly between them. The human desire to adapt in the moment is unlikely to change any time soon. It's time for designers to stop and reassess the many input technologies now available for mainstream use. How might you combine multiple input modalities to provide greater value?

NOTE ARTIFICIAL INTELLIGENCE AND INPUT

Many of the input technologies you'll read about in this chapter are partially powered by specialized artificial intelligence systems. The use of any AI requires additional ethical scrutiny to avoid unintentional bias or harm. For more information about AI, see Chapter 13, "Beyond Devices: Human + AI Collaboration."

Auditory Input

Auditory interfaces allow you to express your desires with sound. While many people perceive voice user interfaces to be a product of the new millennium, the history of voice interfaces goes back much further. (In fact, the first functional demos of a voice control system took place a decade before *Star Trek* ever aired!)

Signal with Sound

Sound-activated systems generally interpret a specific volume or type of sound as a binary switch. The classic Clapper home appliance from 1985 listens for sound within a specific range of frequencies. The same theory can be applied to listening for other sounds—whistles, alarms, or simply the absence of silence.

While simplistic compared to the smart speakers of today, sound-activated devices have long been a very useful adaptation for those with mobility issues, and they remain on the market today—a testament to the fundamental value of the hands-free control scenario.

Voice User Interfaces

Voice user interfaces (aka *speech interfaces*) provide customers with the ability to speak their intent to a device without any manual intervention. Contrary to popular belief, most voice user interfaces are *not* a monolithic artificial intelligence. Today's voice user interfaces are each powered by a network of separate services, each powered by systems trained by machine learning to specialize in a different part of the recognition process, working together to turn the sound of speech into digital understanding.

All voice interactions start with a spoken request, which is generally referred to as an *utterance*. Before the system can apply meaning to spoken words, the system must discern *what* words were spoken. *Automatic speech recognition (ASR)* chops up the recording of the utterance into tiny pieces and attempts to match those pieces with a known phoneme of the selected language. As the speech recognition system goes along, it chooses the most likely word or words based on the sequential arrangement of phonemes.

> **NOTE** WHAT'S A PHONEME?
>
> Voice user interfaces (ironically) come with a lot of jargon for a technology that makes interaction as simple as speaking. *Phonemes* are the building blocks of language: the shortest distinct language-related sounds we can perceive.

Matching Speech with Intent

After the ASR settles upon its best guess at the words spoken, it's time to derive the customer's intent. There are generally two models used to match language with intent:

- **Grammar-based:** Grammars are essentially dictionaries for speech recognition. Grammars are subsets of a language that pair words and phrases with intents that the system can recognize. Grammars are relatively easy to set up, but somewhat rigid and fragile. For example, if all of the words in your grammar sound similar, you're unlikely to get good performance.

- **Natural language understanding (NLU):** NLU systems are a specialized form of artificial intelligence trained to extract syntax, sentence structure, and meaning from arbitrary text. NLU systems are "trained" with hundreds or thousands of utterances paired with both the transcription of those utterances *and* the desired intent. The resulting systems take the output of automatic speech recognition systems and return a list of the most likely intents based on what's been learned from the training data. For an illustration of how these systems work, see Figure 6.1.

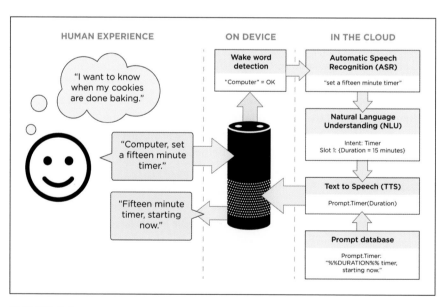

FIGURE 6.1

A simplified look at the various systems that drive your favorite smart speaker or other voice-controlled device.

Choosing the Right Language Model

While most of the devices you now use in your everyday life are powered by natural language understanding, grammar-based systems can still be useful in some situations. Table 6.1 explores the key strengths and weaknesses of the two approaches. Some systems go so far as to support a grammar-based system as a "fallback" system when internet is not available to power NLU processing, but beware that the inconsistent behavior in no-connection scenarios will be jarring.

TABLE 6.1 GRAMMARS VERSUS NATURAL LANGUAGE UNDERSTANDING

	Strengths	Weaknesses
Grammar-based System	Works well for sets of unique words and short phrases No NLU system required No internet connection required Easier to localize	Requires careful tuning to avoid acoustic similarities Often requires training on the "right" phrasing
Natural Language Understanding	More forgiving of missing words Supports longer and more complex utterances Can extrapolate unexpected phrasings	Requires reliable internet connection or advanced onboard processing Requires training of NLU with recorded utterances and human coding Very hard to localize

Microphone Technology

Whether you have control over your device's microphones or not, the type of microphone used has a significant impact on performance. The assumptions you can make about the customer's context also vary significantly based on the type of microphones used.

Near-Field Microphones

Near-field microphones generally only work at close range, and are designed for use in situations where the microphone is directed at a single person—a bit like a singer's microphone. Odds are, your phone, smartwatch, and television remote are also using near-field microphones. Figure 6.2 illustrates what the microphone affordance looks like on the Amazon Fire TV remote control.

Because the speaker must be so close to the microphone, designers working with near-field microphones can generally make a few useful assumptions:

- The customer is within line of sight of the device.
- The customer is within arm's reach of the device.
- The customer *may* be holding the device.
- The customer is unlikely to be drowned out by ambient noise or other speakers.

PHOTO: AMAZON

FIGURE 6.2
The small opening on the top of this Amazon Fire TV voice remote is a near-field microphone, which only works at close range.

Far-Field Microphones

When it's unreasonable to expect your customer to stand or sit immediately adjacent to your device, it's time to turn to far-field microphone technology. Far-field microphones (often in the form of an array of multiple microphones) can "hear" at greater distances, and can often pinpoint approximately where the voice is coming from.

Far-field microphone technology allows smart speakers to detect voices anywhere in a room, but this comes with its own drawbacks.

The more the system can hear, the more likely it is to be derailed by interference. How many times have your requests to an Alexa or Google Home device failed because someone around you interrupted your request? Eventually, far-field microphone technology may enable devices to participate in group conversations, but for now, that feature is generally out of reach at consumer scale.

The broader active listening zone also means you can no longer make the assumption that your customer is within arm's reach of the device. In some cases, your customers can't even see the device that's listening to them!

From Exclusion to Inclusion

Voice technology has been hailed as a new bastion of inclusivity—and indeed, voice interfaces include many customers for whom traditional systems were difficult to use. For customers with mobility or vision impairments, voice user interfaces transform lives by solving old problems—like turning off the lights or turning up the thermostat—in new ways.

In a 2017 article for *Consumer Reports*, Allen St. John described an interview with quadriplegic Nate Higgins about his life with Amazon's Echo:

> "People with spinal cord injuries like myself, we can't regulate our body temperatures like most people can. I can't really sweat like everybody else does," he explains. The Echo-Nest interface allows him to manage an important aspect of his daily life without help from a caregiver. "It's really awesome. I can turn the heat up and down in the middle of the night without hollering at my mother."[1]

This example isn't about a brand-new activity. Simply transforming the input modality Mr. Higgins uses to control the thermostat brings an unprecedented level of agency to his daily life.

Still, customers with speech disorders are unable to interact with voice-only interfaces. At smart speaker companies like Amazon and Google, the effort to re-include these customers is slow but steady.

---

1   Allen St. John, "Amazon Echo Voice Commands Offer Big Benefits to Users with Disabilities," *Consumer Reports,* January 20, 2017, www.consumerreports.org/amazon/amazon-echo-voice-commands-offer-big-benefits-to-users-with-disabilities/

The phrase "augmentative and alternative communication" (AAC) encompasses the communication methods used to supplement or replace speech or writing for those with impairments in the production or comprehension of spoken or written language.

One of the most common technological tools in use today for AAC is a specialty iPad app called *ProloquoToGo*. This tool allows those facing verbal communication obstacles to express their intent to others using visual and haptic interactions.

AAC doesn't have to be high-tech. Laminated glyph cards for pictoral communication and American Sign Language (ASL) also qualify as AAC.[2]

When considering how a person with a speech disability might interact with a system that is primarily voice, look at the alternate ways in which these customers are communicating. Computer vision could provide your customers with a means to accept ASL as visual input. An integration with an app like ProloquoToGo could also open new doors for other customers.

---

2   Meryl Alper, *Giving Voice: Mobile Communication, Disability, and Inequality* (The John D. and Catherine T. MacArthur Foundation Series on Digital Media and Learning) (The MIT Press, 2017).

In 2019, Amazon's "Alexa for Everyone" team released their first accessibility features, allowing customers to interact with Alexa through touch or text input and bringing captions to display-enabled devices.[3]

Because voice recognition requires the use of multiple artificial intelligence-based systems, there is a significant risk of bias and exclusion based solely on the selection of the training data for these systems. Countless stories highlight how accents, dialects, and even gender can decrease the accuracy of these systems if not accounted for in the initial training data, excluding many.

---

3   Robin Christopherson, "Hear, Hear! Here's to the Woman Behind Making Alexa Inclusive," Abilitynet.org.uk, April 23, 2019, www.abilitynet.org.uk/news-blogs/hear-hear-heres-woman-behind-making-alexa-inclusive

Visual Input

The amount of data in a single digital image can be quite astonishing. Early computer vision (CV) algorithms dodged this complexity by focusing on detecting a single feature in an image. Here are some examples:

- The Nintendo Entertainment System's NES Zapper gun could be interpreted as an early form of computer vision. The gun's sensor detected a hit by looking for a special square feature within the frame displayed onscreen immediately after the trigger was pressed.[4]

- Sony's Aibo robotic dog had a computer vision algorithm dedicated to its favorite pink ball. When it "saw" the pink ball, it chased the pink ball. Hilarious antics ensued (see Figure 6.3).

©ALEXEI SYSOEV–STOCK.ADOBE.COM

FIGURE 6.3
Sony's Aibo robotic dogs were "taught" to recognize their favorite balls by shape and distinctive color, which allowed the robot to chase the ball whenever it was detected.

---

4 "NES Zapper," Wikipedia, Wikimedia Foundation, last edited July 12, 2020, https://en.wikipedia.org/wiki/NES_Zapper

In recent years, the advent of more sophisticated consumer-grade infrared (IR) sensors has unlocked exciting new computer vision scenarios. Just a few years ago, these scenarios were the stuff of movies and science fiction.

- Videoconferencing apps like Zoom and Microsoft Teams can use the infrared signal from newer laptops to separate background pixels and replace them with arbitrary backgrounds.

- Windows PCs and Apple's Face ID technology combine infrared signals with camera signals as a replacement for passcodes or fingerprints.

Visual Signals

At their most basic, computer vision (CV) algorithms tend to look for one or more simple visual features. The most common examples are the following:

- **Depth:** In general, depth sensing is useful because it can separate foreground from background pixels. This may not sound interesting, but it is. Depth sensing has unlocked experiences like live background removal (in conferencing apps and the Echo Look) and Face ID.

- **Light and heat:** Some light sensors are extremely simplistic, like that inside the NES Zapper. In recent years, infrared technology is used for depth sensing, biometric identification, skeletal detection, motion capture, and even health care.

- **Color and shape:** In digital terms, the detection of color and shape requires identification of regions of pixels that fall within a specific RGB or contrast range.

- **Gaze detection:** If your visual sensors are at a particularly close range, you *may* be able to ascertain what your customer is looking at. It's hard to use gaze *directly* at a controlling input because human eye movements can be rapid and erratic—but gaze *can* provide needed context to make other inputs (like gesture) more effective.

- **Facial detection:** Once a device is capable of recognizing contours and shapes, the logical next step for developers is detecting the *presence* of a face. Facial detection doesn't provide ID—it merely identifies the pixels most likely to be a human face or faces. This technology is perhaps best known as the tech behind Snapchat lenses.

- **Facial recognition:** Facial recognition, on the other hand, requires a large database of known faces. When provided with a new image or video, facial recognition systems deconstruct the size and placement of unique features of the face and compare those properties against the set of known faces—or, in the case of Apple's Face ID, scrutinize the face observed against the owner's facial features. (See the sidebar for the risks associated with facial recognition.)

Under the Hood: Artificial Intelligence

The sensors that feed into computer vision technology don't "know" much about the things they're recording. Most of the previous features are actually nontrivial to interpret: implementation of those features requires training artificial intelligence via machine learning techniques.

For example, at their most basic, vision sensors don't see "color." They see numbers. It's the development team that teaches the system which numeric RGB ranges correspond to a specific relative "color."

NOTE SUBJECTIVITY AND THE HUMAN EYE

If you think about it, color isn't absolute for humans, either. My husband and I have argued several times about whether the paint in our living room is blue or green. (It's blue.)

As the objects and patterns a CV system recognizes become more complicated, it typically requires the application of machine learning techniques to "teach" an algorithm to look for those patterns. In general, this requires the following information:

- A set of training data. For CV projects, this usually means a set of photos or videos paired with data describing each of the photos or videos.

- Machine learning tools that take the training set and "learn" from them, returning an algorithm that takes new input and reports back on what metadata most likely applies to that input.

For example, you might use a set of photos, with data about which photos contain a hot dog, to train an algorithm that answers the question "Is this a hot dog?" for any given photo. (Fans of the TV show *Silicon Valley* will recognize this scenario.)

Recognition and Abuse

Facial recognition is one of the most dangerous technologies in use today, and its use is now common in law enforcement. (In January 2020, the *New York Times* explored the usage of facial recognition systems in the state of Florida, and in doing so, documented many common issues.[5]) The use of facial recognition technology to initiate any sort of law enforcement proceeding is placing a great deal of faith in a system that is known to be flawed.

As the Electronic Freedom Foundation points out, facial recognition systems have been shown to misidentify Blacks, women, and youth at higher rates than white male adults.[6] If facial recognition systems misidentify a person in a law enforcement database, racial profiling and systemic discrimination place innocent individuals at higher risk of criminal investigation or prosecution than white men. Meanwhile, Black people in the U.S. are three times more likely to be killed by police than white people.[7] Under these circumstances, a misidentification of Black people by a facial recognition system could be deadly.

As tensions increased between government forces, citizens, and immigrants in the United States in mid-2020, this metaphorical pot began to boil over. On June 30, 2020, the Association for Computing Machinery's U.S. Technology Policy Committee issued an open letter including this strongly-worded statement: "USTPC urges an immediate suspension of the current and future private and governmental use of FR technologies in all circumstances known or reasonably foreseeable to be prejudicial to established human and legal rights."

Any use of facial recognition technology—military, law enforcement, government, or commercial use—should be thoroughly reviewed by neutral third parties and independent review boards. Even consumer facial recognition systems should be subject to this scrutiny, as they can be just as dangerous in the wrong hands.

---

5   Jennifer Valentino-DeVries, "How the Police Use Facial Recognition, and Where It Falls Short," *New York Times*, January 12, 2020.

6   Brendan F. Klare et al., "Face Recognition Performance: Role of Demographic Information," *IEEE Transactions on Information Forensics and Security* 7, no. 6 (2012): 1789–1801.

7   "Mapping Police Violence," MappingPoliceViolence.org, last updated June 30, 2020.

This might be straightforward if all of your photos were taken against the same background, at the same angle, and in the same lighting. But real-world variability brings complexity. The more varied your potential inputs, the more training data you'll need to prepare your algorithm. The data collection and training period for computer vision can take weeks, months, or even years. (It took us years to train the Echo Look to reliably tell the difference between various people and their backdrops.) In some cases, you may get lucky and find that an off-the-shelf solution can give you a head start.

From Exclusion to Inclusion

On August 16, 2017, Nigerian technologist Chukwuemeka Afigbo (now Head of Developer Programs at Facebook) tweeted: "If you have ever had a problem grasping the importance of diversity in tech and its impact on society, watch this video." (See Figure 6.4.)

FIGURE 6.4
Chukwuemeka Afigbo's viral video, as depicted in this screenshot from his original tweet, rightly calls out this soap dispenser for failing to detect Black hands.

The video in question depicts a Black man's hand as he attempts to obtain soap from a hands-free dispenser. Unfortunately, the dispenser does not respond. Rather than give up, the video then shows the same individual taking a piece of folded white tissue into his hand and trying again. The soap dispenses immediately. The computer vision system in the dispenser was trained to look for white skin.

The tweet and the story of the racist soap dispenser went viral, but they aren't an isolated example of bias in computer vision systems. Computer vision systems can be misused in many ways—either to exclude by lack of identification, or to harm by (mis)identifying or profiling people for harmful ends.

As with all machine-learning powered artificial intelligence projects, diversity in the team and your testing participants is key to avoid unintended exclusion, bias, and potential downstream harm. Even when you turn to publicly available datasets to reduce training time, you must consider the possibility that the underlying data is biased. Take the time to examine where and how the data was collected, how it was labeled, and the nature of the consent any human participants provided.

Haptic Input

In the beginning, there were haptic interfaces. When humans first created fire, they used their hands to directly manipulate tools like flint and kindling to act upon their intent to create fire. Haptic inputs are tools that humans manipulate physically to express an intent or concept.

Getting a Grip

Physical tools continue to be our most prevalent form of digital communication, although the tides are turning. Most of the tangible interface peripherals you're familiar with qualify as haptic interfaces, for example:

- Our ubiquitous keyboards, mice, and most other pointing devices
- Discrete controls like buttons, knobs, dials, pedals, and switches
- Complex controls like joysticks, throttles, and controllers

Human intents can be infinite, but our hands have finite capabilities. To cope with this imbalance, specialized haptic controllers emerged. Most physical controllers are modal in some way: they are specifically optimized for a narrow category of intents.

- Keyboards are scoped to express human language in symbolic form.
- Joysticks and controllers are usually scoped to convey direction and action.
- Mice are optimized for selection of pixel(s) from a visual display.
- Buttons, switches, and toggles are optimized for binary selections.
- Dials and knobs are optimized for expressing magnitude or selection from a fixed set of values.

Even when touchscreens, voice, or keyboards are available, highly optimized physical controls still have a place. Physical controls provide direct access to frequently used features. They also offer the added benefit of leveraging muscle memory for eyes-free operation when designed well.

For more sophisticated scenarios, like telepresence operating rooms, these finely scoped controls are not enough. Instead, haptic input technologies like sensor gloves are paired with haptic output to provide a sense of realistic real-time feedback when attempting to manipulate *virtual* objects.

A Touch of Magic

Touchscreens are a unique form of haptic input. While we do engage our sense of touch when interacting with touchscreens, today's touchscreens don't give us the same kind of feedback (haptic output) that we expect from physical controls.

Not all touchscreens are created equal, either. At present, there are two competing technologies, although one is fading as time progresses:

- **Resistive touchscreens** detect physical pressure from the finger or a stylus. Soft touch may not register; this is why older airplane seat-back systems are a nightmare for the migraine sufferer in front of you.
- **Capacitive touchscreens** detect an electrical signal from your finger on the screen, making them much easier to use. These more sophisticated touchscreens can support soft touch, multitouch (multiple points of contact at once), and gesture input (swipes, etc.) since they don't rely on a mechanical action.

Resistive touchscreens are far cheaper but also less versatile, and they are falling out of favor. Ironically, you'll still find them in surprisingly expensive venues like automobiles and airplanes, since the replacement cycle tends to be slower and more price-sensitive.

LEARN MORE

> For more on the gestural interactions made possible by capacitive touchscreens, see the section titled "Kinetic Input" later in this chapter.

Choosing the Right Haptic Model

Countless concept cars and sci-fi movies over the ages have envisioned "glass cockpits" that lack the old-fashioned arrays of buttons and dials in favor of a clean, touchscreen-only (or gesture-only) interface. Now that touchscreens are available, why keep old-fashioned physical controls at all? This now-classic debate continues in the world of dashboard and cockpit design.

Muscle memory and haptic feedback are especially important in the operation of motor vehicles, where taking one's eyes off the horizon for more than a split second can have disastrous consequences. In the United States, the NHTSA (National Highway Transportation Safety Administration) guidelines for automakers dictate the maximum allowable dashboard-driven driver distraction: any single glance away from the road should be no more than two seconds.[8]

Physical controls allow operation of key functions without taking one's eyes away from the real world. Touchscreens can't leverage this benefit since controls don't have edges and contours that can be detected by tactile feedback alone. Physical controls often convey not just location via tactile signals, but in some cases, status as well. Still, automakers like Tesla continue to push the envelope toward a touchscreen-only "glass cockpit" for motor vehicles.

LEARN MORE

> For a tragic example of a dashboard replacement gone wrong, see the Case Study: "The USS *John S. McCain*" later in this chapter.

---

8   *Visual-Manual NHTSA Driver Distraction Guidelines for In-Vehicle Electronic Devices* (National Highway Traffic Safety Administration, April 26, 2013), www.federalregister.gov/documents/2013/04/26/2013-09883/visual-manual -nhtsa-driver-distraction-guidelines-for-in-vehicle-electronic-devices

From Exclusion to Inclusion

As humans age, many people must adapt to life with decreased dexterity due to conditions like arthritis. Even without a physical impairment, haptic interfaces might prove problematic—for example, folks with limited vision may have difficulty interacting with haptic interfaces optimized for selection of visual stimuli (like a mouse). Customers with limited mobility are likely to be excluded by many traditional haptic controls. There are alternative inputs that don't require the use of hands and arms, including the following:

- Sip-and-puff controllers interpret binary intent from a customer's breath via a tube.
- Tongue joysticks and eye-controlled mouse input allow directional control without manual control.
- Voice input can also be used to replace physical input.

Seek out and engage with customers who will not be using their hands to engage with your product. To avoid excluding customers with limited mobility, consider adding support for voice control to your systems. If possible, consider how your experience might be adapted for use with nontraditional haptic controllers. The Xbox Adaptive Controller (see Figure 6.5) is an excellent example of such a consideration transformed into a useful product.

PHOTO: MICROSOFT

FIGURE 6.5

The Xbox Adaptive Controller allows its owner to choose additional peripherals that suit their specific needs for each of the specific inputs, like X, Y, Start, and the directional pad.

The USS *John S. McCain*

Tragically, the glass cockpit trend turned fatal for the U.S. Navy in 2017. The destroyer USS *John S. McCain* featured a hybrid helm featuring a combination of both traditional haptic controls and a series of touchscreen panels that allowed for more complex and dynamic control sets.

On the morning of August 21, 2017, the crew detected what they believed to be a loss of steering, and their efforts to correct the situation caused the destroyer to collide with a nearby tanker. Ten lives were lost and forty-eight people were injured, in addition to damages in the hundreds of millions of dollars across both vessels.

The final NTSB report published in 2019[9] states that "The design of the *John S. McCain*'s touchscreen steering and thrust control system increased the likelihood of the operator errors that led to the collision."

A March 2020 paper[10] examining the user interface implications of the NTSB report confirmed that the loss of haptic feedback was cited in the report. "It was concluded that the transfer of thrust control was unnecessarily complex and that the touch-screen throttle controls removed tactile feedback for helmsmen, making it more difficult to identify unganged or mismatched throttles . . . The NTSB report found that the perceived loss of steering by the crew of the destroyer was due to the helmsman unintentionally transferring control of steering from the helmstation to the lee helmstation. The unintentional transfer misled the destroyer's bridge team, placing their focus on a perceived malfunction of the steering system (even though it was working properly)."

While it's impossible to say definitively whether a physical set of controls would have prevented this tragedy, the touchscreen allowed accidental transfer of control in a harmful way. A physical control could potentially have provided haptic feedback to make dangerous changes more difficult to execute accidentally.

In high-stress situations, the extra guidance provided by tactile feedback can be critical. When using touchscreens in lieu of more tactile controls, consider your customer's context and cognitive load carefully. In some cases, this design decision is a matter of life or death.

---

9 "Collision Between US Navy Destroyer *John S McCain* and Tanker *Alnic MC* Singapore Strait, 5 Miles Northeast of Horsburgh Lighthouse August 21, 2017," *NTSB Marine Accident Report*, June 19, 2019, NTSB/MAR-19/01 PB2019-100970.

10 Steven Mallam et al., "The Digitalization of Navigation: Examining the Accident and Aftermath of US Navy Destroyer *John S. McCain*," *The Royal Institution of Naval Architects Damaged Ship V*, March 11, 2020, London, UK.

Kinetic Input

Kinetic input allows customers to express their desires by treating motion as an input medium. Essentially, kinetic inputs, like gesture, add the dimension of *time* to a visual, haptic, or kinetic input system. Table 6.2 provides an overview of the different models of kinetic input in use today.

Gesture on touchscreens is usually discrete, as in gestures repurposed for commanding purposes. The simple pairing of a swipe gesture with the next/previous intents was transformative for touchscreens, because it allowed some visual simplification, but was never a high-granularity interaction.

By contrast, pen input is about the journey. You can still point with it, but the pen is specifically optimized to turn motion into meaning. Think about cursive writing. It's not about the beginning and the end—it's about the path you take *between* those two points. Where haptic systems are generally about discrete inputs, kinetic systems are about the aggregate of an input over time.

TABLE 6.2 COMMON FORMS OF KINETIC INTERACTION

Interaction	Example	Pros	Cons
Touchscreen	Modern smartphones	Direct interaction or identification of objects.	Gestures (swipe, triple touch) are generally invented and must be taught.
Pen input	Wacom tablets, Windows ink, Apple Pencil	High granularity of input.	Requires additional hardware.
Hand Gestures	Control of video playback on Google Home Hub	Limited physical impact. No tools required.	Limited granularity. High cultural variability.
Skeletal Gestures	Xbox Kinect	Physically and emotionally engaging. Expressive. Immersive.	Hard to train on all body types. Requires large field of vision and open space. Not fully accessible.

Is a mouse a kinetic input system? Only partially. The *movement* of the mouse pointer *is* kinetic input. However, apps often ignore mouse movement and treat button clicks—a haptic input—as the primary source of interaction.

Using Gestural Input

Gesture-based systems are difficult to design and tune because they are highly relativistic. What qualifies as a "swipe" may vary widely between a 10-year-old girl and a 30-year-old woman—and that sort of challenge is just the tip of the iceberg.

Most fundamentally, gestural input is a coarsely-grained input; it's very hard to be specific with gestures on their own. Gestures don't shine until very specific context is applied: a swipe of the arm might mean anything, but within the context of menu navigation that swipe becomes specific and meaningful.

David Rose, former futurist-in-residence at IDEO Labs, described their experimentation with gestural interactions: "In messing around with these exercises, we discovered that gestures need to be either sequential, like a sentence—noun then verb, object plus operation. For example, for "speaker, on," one hand designates the noun, and the other the verb: You point to speaker with left hand and turn the volume up by raising (your) right hand."[11] IDEO also observed generational gaps in gesture: volume for older generations was turning a knob, but for younger generations it manifested in more linear gestures.

Just as with natural language systems, gesture-based systems must be trained on a *wide* variety of inputs to account for this spread, and they are subject to the same bias problems that you see in other AI-based systems.

NOTE DO NO HARM

I stopped playing Wii *Tennis* due to shoulder pain, and Wii's *Cooking Mama* was so intense that I returned the game after 48 hours! Just because a system can interpret arbitrary motion doesn't mean that motion is comfortable or safe for humans.

---

11 David Rose, "Why Gesture Is the Next Big Thing in Design," *IDEO* (blog), January 25, 2018, www.ideo.com/blog/why-gesture-is-the-next-big-thing-in-design

Companies like IDEO and Google have identified a few conditions bounding the successful use of gesture interactions. The most commonly cited strengths and weaknesses are included in Tables 6.3 and 6.4.

TABLE 6.3 STRENGTHS OF GESTURE INTERACTION

Strength	Context
Speed	Gestures are faster than speaking sentences, navigating nested menus, or walking to a device.
Distance	If your customer is far away from the device, gestures provide an alternative to shouting across the room.
Scoped interactions	Gesture works well for very limited sets of interactions. For example: • Media playback control • Navigation (pinch, zoom, etc.) • Manipulation (rotate, scale, move)
Expressiveness	Like the conductor of a symphony, elements like speed, direction, and sharpness can communicate emotions and moods in addition to intent.

TABLE 6.4 WEAKNESSES OF GESTURE INTERACTION

Weakness	Context
Physical Strain and Fatigue	Gestures are not suitable for extended use, especially when full limb engagement is required for a minute or more at a time. What seems natural for a designer might subject a different body type to potential injury, especially with repeated use.
Discoverability	Not only are most gestures invisible, but they are also difficult to explain in text or the spoken word. Explicit tutorials are usually required.
Accuracy	Fatigue, distraction, and normal human movement can introduce enough noise that even known gestures are not interpreted correctly.
Cultural Variance	For example, a "thumbs up" gesture is widely accepted in the United States as being a positive sign of support, but in the Middle East and parts of Africa the same gesture will be interpreted as offensive.

While gesture is still a nascent specialty, it bears particular promise in scenarios like the following:

- **Creative production:** The act of creating new content is often highly input-intensive, and the ability to add gestures to a toolset can unlock new possibilities.
- **Entertainment:** Gestural input can create a more immersive, optional experience when layered on top of traditional control schemes.
- **Augmented, virtual, and mixed reality:** AR, VR, and MR systems overlay or replace your customer's senses and often allow them to manipulate virtual objects and views as if manifested physically.

From Exclusion to Inclusion

For those with limited vision, gesture can *hypothetically* be a way of expressing general intent without requiring manipulation of physical controls. In practice, it's difficult for these customers to position themselves correctly in front of the camera or sensors.

Furthermore, mobility is an issue for millions upon millions of your customers. From arthritis sufferers to quadriplegics, there are many for whom gesture will *never* be the most desirable option. Make sure that your gesture-based system is backed up by an alternative form of input, and take special care to ensure that the gestures you're requiring are not putting your customers at risk of injury.

Consider consulting with physical therapists, physiatrists, or kinesthesiologists if your gesture-driven product will see heavy use. In just a few sessions at my hand therapist, I overheard multiple people describe injuries caused by repetitive actions like cutting and pasting across windows. The same will be true of gestures in years to come.

Ambient Input

Ambient input allows devices to *infer* your intent from the world around you, without any conscious effort from you in that moment. Ambient input often requires customers to first express their *future* intent through traditional UI, allowing that intent to come to bear later when conditions are right. Table 6.5 describes three of the most common ambient input scenarios.

TABLE 6.5 COMMON AMBIENT INPUT SCENARIOS

Scenario	Description
Presence-based	Detect a living being's presence in a space (using RFID, Bluetooth, door sensors, etc.), in order to take action based on that knowledge.
Environmental	Detect changes in the surrounding environment and take action based on those changes: like smart thermostats and light sensors.
Biometric	Detect changes in the functioning of a person's body and take action based on that information, usually driven by activity or thresholds (emotion and mood detection, fitness and health monitoring, etc.).

From Exclusion to Inclusion

Ambient input could potentially be incredibly inclusive from a disability perspective. Your family members or medical aides could program your device once to allow your devices to take action on your behalf dozens of times down the line. Even if you don't need formal aid, ambient input can help reduce cognitive load, letting you focus on what's important in the moment.

Biometric scenarios bear particularly interesting potential with regard to more humanistic experiences. If your devices can detect your moods reliably, can they take actions that are more appropriate in the moment? Can they get out of your way and take automatic action when needed?

But, at this time, ambient input systems are still a relative luxury— from smart homes to fitness trackers. In many ways, the broader utility (and in some cases, ethical implications) of these experiences is not fully explored. What does it mean to share your biometric data with third parties? Be sure to remember your responsibility to your customers as human beings and treat ambient inferences with extreme care.

It's also important to note that the invisible nature of ambient input does open the door to abuse, particularly when power imbalances are present. In 2018, the *New York Times* documented the use of automatic smart home actions in domestic abuse scenarios.[12] As a design team, consider how your ambient input might cause unintended harm if the person receiving the output doesn't control the input settings.

Apply It Now

In reality, it's rare to have any control over the input technologies available to your customers. You can sometimes direct a product team to choose one platform or another based on available input, but more often than not, you're simply dealing with what's available.

That said, there is much room for innovation on mainstream systems, like mobile phones and laptops. Some of the areas ripest for exploration and further innovation are the following:

- **Built-in voice recognition** is revolutionizing search on phones, but is barely used on laptops.
- **Capacitive touchscreens** are standard on nearly all mainstream personal devices (except Mac laptops), but little attention has been given to the way this changes the customer's relationship with the keyboard. What makes people lift their hands from the keyboard? When is that a good thing?
- **Infrared depth sensors paired with device cameras** unlock a whole new world of no-contact gesture interactions, but only a small handful of those interactions exist. For example, the Google Nest Hub Max allows customers to hold up their hand to the device to stop video playback.

Your next step is to take full stock of the input technologies available to you on your platform. Evaluate the possibilities against what you're actually using.

- What input technologies exist on your platform, but remain unused in your product?
- What does mainstream usage for those inputs look like on your chosen platform?
- What types of problems might these unused input technologies help you solve?

---

12 Nellie Bowles, "Thermostats, Locks and Lights: Digital Tools of Domestic Abuse," *New York Times,* June 23, 2018, www.nytimes.com/2018/06/23/technology/smart-home-devices-domestic-abuse.html

- Who might be excluded by your current inputs that could be included if you added support for a new input technology?

Will input technologies continue to evolve? Absolutely. Technology's sophistication and resilience in changing conditions will only improve with time.

Will humans ever get to a direct neural interface that doesn't necessarily require additional interpretation? Anything is possible.

No matter what, the need for thoughtful, holistic designs that effortlessly blend multiple modalities (as humans do every day) will only continue to grow.

Beyond a Single Spoken Language with
Syed Sameer Arshad

*Linguists have a critical role to play in the design of truly conversational and multimodal experiences. **Syed Sameer Arshad** is a powerhouse, bringing not just experience in linguistics but also in computer engineering, speech science, and human insight. I had the good fortune of welcoming Sameer into my improv class years ago, and now I've asked him to share his perspectives on speech interfaces beyond single-language command and control.*

Q: When designing hybrid experiences that combine voice user interfaces and visual user interfaces, what common traps or issues are most likely to come up?

One of the most common issues that comes up here is the confusion of referents. What I mean by this is situations where the voice interface is referring to something in the user interface, that may not be visible yet or may be placed in a difficult-to-spot location, or even the wrong location. When a voice interface says something like, "Please press the START button" and for some latency-related reason, this start button isn't visible yet on the screen, it creates a moment of frustration that can compound further and further as the latency issue persists across the session. People take voice commands very seriously and may avoid the correct visual element if it isn't in the location they have been instructed to look for it. That level of end-to-end testing sometimes is missing when a patch comes in to change a visual design without a corresponding voice-interface update. This can also happen in the other direction, such as a change in a vocal cue happening without a corresponding change to a visual design.

Another issue that comes up is not accounting for the multiple ways that a user can express something vocally. For example, a user might utter the word "begin" when the voice interface is expecting to hear the word "start." A synonym like that should be accepted as an alternative. But if it isn't, the user might quit the interaction in frustration.

There are many ways to say something, but probably only one way to click on or tap on something. Funneling the multitude of possible voice-based alternative commands is something that often doesn't happen in multimodal interfaces, because an assumption is made that a failing voice interaction can be appeased by a successful visual interaction via a touchscreen or pointing device. The result is often a mediocre voice interaction but an acceptable visual interaction.

Q: With your extensive background in linguistics and a variety of languages, have you observed any gaps in the industry's approach to voice interfaces for a global market?

I have noticed that people keep assuming that a human's performance at processing language can always be accomplished by a sufficiently well-trained AI. I don't think this is true. Language is alive, growing, evolving, and splitting into new forms. When a human hears a novel utterance, containing words they have never heard before, there is a level of conjecture that can happen on inferring the meaning of those new words. This is how children learn language, without having to ask for the meaning of every single word. We know that the typical American teenager knows 15,000 to 20,000 plain words in the English language. They picked up on the meaning of these words through observation of their usage, not by asking someone "What does _____ mean?" 15,000 times. This is the kind of instinct that allows humans to follow the evolution of new colloquialisms, neologisms, and jargon, without having to look things up explicitly. This happens in all languages, not just English. An AI cannot be expected to keep up with this kind of evolution on its own, without humans who are connected to every relevant speaker community providing training data and ontological information about new word forms.

Q: What should designers keep in mind about localizing these experiences?

Regarding localization and internationalization, the one problem I see occurring often is assuming that there is a "standard" version of every single language. For example, when many software businesses plan for the Spanish or Arabic version of their product, I always ask them "Which Spanish? Which Arabic?" and I am often responded to with a confused pause and blinking eyes, and the phrase, "What? There's more than one?" When we approach problems like these, we need to identify the dialectology of a language, figuring out what speaker groups exist and what kind of clustering has happened in that speaker community. There may not be a standard dialect they have all aligned to.

Many times, a standard dialect is arbitrarily chosen, in-line with whatever the government of a country has decided to embrace, leading to state-run media to align to that dialect. From a business perspective, one needs to think about what population groups for that language are being excluded from accessing the product just because their dialect was not targeted.

Another problem I see is the grouping of many dialects into one large cluster and arbitrarily calling that the standard. This happens for American English as well, where we see African-American English, Chicano English, Southern American English, and other various region-specific and city-specific dialects all getting labelled as "Standard American English." This approach really only works when every identifiable speaker-group's representative data is included in an AI's training set. That still involves some level of machine learning generalization criteria that can lead to poor results for people interacting with the AI in their specific dialect.

Sometimes, language elements are common across national boundaries. Sometimes, language elements split into multitudes even within national boundaries. We can't assume that all the people in one country speak the same dialect of a language. We can't assume that all the people in one country even speak the same language. With the advent of mass media distributed via the internet, we are seeing some clustering of large populations around specific ways of speaking and writing, leading to some dialects becoming understandable and producible by far-flung populations, for example, African-American English being culturally appropriated by East Asian and South Asian populations living outside America.

Language is dazzlingly complex and the right trade-offs need to be made when designing for diverse speakers. Hire a linguist! They can really help!

Syed Sameer Arshad is a computer engineer, speech scientist, and computational linguist, who focuses on problems in natural language processing, user-interface design, and internationalization in text, speech, and visual modalities. Feel free to reach out to him on LinkedIn: www.linkedin.com/in/sarshad/

CHAPTER 7

The Spectrum of Multimodality

You've now explored the full spectrum of options (currently) available to you when breaking beyond the old-fashioned paradigm of a screen, mouse, and keyboard. But pulling those things together requires a broader perspective. A galactic perspective, perhaps?

In *Star Trek: The Next Generation,* the officers of the Starship Enterprise use technology to navigate through space, scan and catalog planets, communicate in short range and across solar systems, and even to entertain themselves. The crew may have ready access to a variety of touch panels and physical throttles, but they can also ask nearly any question in spoken language. The system can reply with language in kind, but when the answer isn't well-suited for a spoken reply, they may move seamlessly back to a screen (or even the Holodeck). They might ask for a damage report and hear a spoken summary, while seeing a map of the damage. By tapping on a part of the ship, they can ask the computer to seal off that specific section; or they can ask the computer verbally to take action.

NOTE STARFLEET DREAMS

> Yes, like many technologists I'm obsessed with *Star Trek*. I've immersed myself in that world for years as a member of an improvised parody of the original series called "Where No Man Has Gone Before." The more I explore the world of *Star Trek*, the deeper my admiration becomes for its optimistic, (usually) inclusive futurism.

The bridge of the Starship Enterprise (Figure 7.1) is a shining example of what today's designers often refer to as a *multimodal interface.* The Enterprise supports multiple input modalities, like touch and voice, and it supports multiple output modalities, like screens, VR, and speech. What's most remarkable is how effortless it is for the crew to change the way they interact with the ship's computer and its various modes of input at a moment's notice.

Now that next-generation technologies like conversational user interfaces and computer vision have arrived, the most immediate challenge that today's multimodal experiences face is the tension between visual interface elements and audio interface elements. No matter how much hype surrounds voice user interfaces, voice is not necessarily best suited to all interactions.

Early voice-enabled interfaces like the Xbox Kinect relied on a "see it, say it" model where customers could speak the written name of an interface element to interact with it, as depicted in Figure 7.2. In contrast, early automotive systems treated voice and touch as separate ways of performing the same task with no synchronization or support for transitions. Mercifully, those experiences are fading away in favor of more integrated approaches to multimodality.

FIGURE 7.1

The bridge of the Starship Enterprise in the TV series *Star Trek: The Next Generation* is the ultimate multimodal interface. Officers interact meaningfully with the system in different ways, depending upon their proximity to physical affordances.

FIGURE 7.2

Some early voice-enabled multimodal interfaces like Microsoft's Xbox Kinect relied heavily on direct reference of UI elements.

Years later, the experience of designing for Amazon's voice-enabled countertop tablet device, the Echo Show, put us in uncharted territory. As we worked on one of the first devices to attempt a tight pairing between interactive visuals and natural language speech, we faced a number of new interaction design questions. Could we use the same responses as the Echo itself? What level of display was appropriate? How did an interaction with the Echo Show differ from the Fire TV? How would we help customers switch between physical interactions and spoken interactions?

As we waded more deeply into the product design process for the Echo Show, it became evident that the introduction of the screen to what had *previously* been a voice-only interaction was far from cosmetic. This particular combination of screen and natural language interface was yet another new paradigm. It seemed silly to read a full forecast when the screen could display it so much more efficiently. Some requests, like "show me stock prices," might not even warrant a spoken response due to the context.

Coping with this added complexity required us to make intentional choices about the relationship between our primary input and output modalities. Over time, those choices became patterns, and my first multimodal interaction model was born. But much of my thinking has evolved since those early days when I, like the industry, was still quite device-focused.

Before you begin designing specific interactions for your experience, you must first make a conscious choice about what multimodal interaction models your product will support.

Dimensions of Multimodal Experiences

Early attempts to chart these new voice-enabled experiences placed a heavy focus on the voice aspect of the interaction. At Google I/O 2018, a "Multimodality Spectrum" with a single axis was presented: the support for voice interactions, from voice only to no voice (see Figure 7.3).

While voice is undeniably a critical element of many multimodal interactions, simple support of voice features isn't necessarily the defining feature of multimodal interactions. Furthermore, the terms *voice forward* and *screen forward* are inherently device-centric.

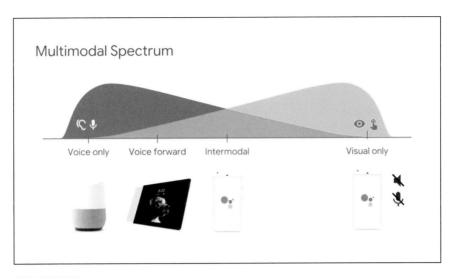

FIGURE 7.3

A single-axis "multimodality spectrum" depicted in "Design actions for the Google Assistant: beyond smart speakers" from Google I/O 2018.

In order to create a more robust interaction model that will stand the test of time, take a step back and consider the human impacts of multimodal systems. While you've explored many input and output modalities thus far, there are two dimensions that have the greatest impact upon your customer experience:

- **Proximity:** The typical or average distance between your customer and the device(s) involved in the interaction.

- **Information density:** The amount of information presented to your customer in a typical interaction. In this case, information includes length and complexity of spoken prompts; any visual information like images, lights, or written text; and any tertiary information provided over channels like haptic feedback.

To understand what multimodal interaction model applies to your experience, begin by asking yourself these two questions about those critical dimensions of the experience:

- Where will your customer be in relation to the device? (See Table 7.1.)

- How much information is presented to your customer during a typical interaction? (See Table 7.2.)

TABLE 7.1 WHERE WILL YOUR CUSTOMER BE IN RELATION TO THE DEVICE?

Distance	Description	Examples
Close Proximity	The customer must be within arm's reach or closer in order to interact with the input sensor(s) in question.	Remote controls, smartphones, and controllers
Mixed Distance	The device supports both close-range interactions and long-range interactions (several feet or more).	Echo Show Google Hub
Long Range	The customer is typically 2–10 feet (or more) from the device or interface when interacting.	Amazon Echo Xbox Kinect

As discussed in Chapter 6, "Expressing Intent," the nature of the input sensors you've selected will directly impact the assumptions you can make about the distance between your customer and the device they're interacting with. Note that close proximity is determined by the location of the input sensor, which is not always on the primary device, as seen in streaming devices with microphone-enabled remote controls.

TABLE 7.2 HOW MUCH INFORMATION IS PRESENTED TO YOUR CUSTOMER DURING A TYPICAL INTERACTION?

Density	Description	Examples
Low Density	Extremely constrained output that usually relies upon external context for meaning.	Fitbit trackers Thermostats
Standard	The information provided to the customer is sufficient to perform specific tasks, but little additional context is provided.	Amazon Echo Apple CarPlay
High Density	The system provides much more than the minimum amount of context required to complete tasks.	Amazon Fire TV Google Hub

High-density information is often provided on high-resolution screens. Multimodal rich output also typically includes robust voice and sound interactions. Low-information density interactions usually include very constrained visuals: either a small screen, an LCD readout, or an LED display of some sort. Figures 7.4 and 7.5 illustrate two ends of the information density spectrum.

FIGURE 7.4
Low information density:
a Fitbit wristband.

FIGURE 7.5
High information density: Netflix on Amazon's Fire TV.

Observant readers may have already noted that these dimensions aren't necessarily fixed, even for a single device. A person can be near or far from their Amazon Echo. Some devices are more constrained—customers are unlikely to use streaming video devices out of eyeshot. But, in other cases, a single device might support multiple "stops" on both of these spectrums, depending upon customer context.

While the examples here tend to be device-based, in reality you could say that an adaptive device is technically switching between intangible and anchored experiences. A single device could support multiple interaction types. The difference is that an adaptive experience has affordances that allow customers to choose how to interact in the moment.

Mapping the Multimodal Quadrants

Once we've answered these two questions, we can begin to understand where our product fits in what was once a dizzying spectrum of experiences. What have our customers learned to expect from experiences like this one, and where have those experiences fallen short?

By placing relative customer proximity on the X axis and information density on the Y axis, you can place most multimodal scenarios firmly into one of four quadrants, as shown in Figure 7.6. Note that there is no superior quadrant: each has its own strengths and weaknesses.

To apply this multimodal interaction model to your designs:

- For your experience, answer the two questions specified earlier.
  - Where will your customer be in relation to the sensors you're using during the scenario?
  - How much information is presented to your customer during a typical interaction?
- Use the answers to these questions to place your experience in one of the four multimodal interaction quadrants.

> **NOTE** CROSS-CHANNEL EXPERIENCES
>
> If you have multiple devices or apps in your broader experience, you might end up working within multiple quadrants for a single project.

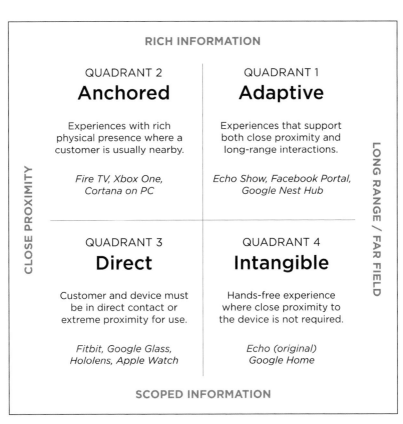

RICH INFORMATION

QUADRANT 2
Anchored

Experiences with rich physical presence where a customer is usually nearby.

Fire TV, Xbox One, Cortana on PC

QUADRANT 1
Adaptive

Experiences that support both close proximity and long-range interactions.

Echo Show, Facebook Portal, Google Nest Hub

QUADRANT 3
Direct

Customer and device must be in direct contact or extreme proximity for use.

Fitbit, Google Glass, Hololens, Apple Watch

QUADRANT 4
Intangible

Hands-free experience where close proximity to the device is not required.

Echo (original) Google Home

CLOSE PROXIMITY

LONG RANGE / FAR FIELD

SCOPED INFORMATION

FIGURE 7.6
Multimodal interaction model spectrum.

Understanding what quadrant you're designing for helps you understand what assumptions, constraints, and possibilities should inform your team's work, and will help you make more consistent decisions.

Adaptive Interactions (Quadrant 1)

Rich output, long-range interactions

In the Adaptive quadrant, your experience is capable of both close-range and long-range interactions. You can leverage this potential in a few different ways, as explained in Table 7.3.

Deciding to inhabit this quadrant is a conscious choice and requires both robust hardware capabilities *and* a willingness to implement an adaptive methodology to allow customers flexibility of input in the moment. Once your customer makes a choice of input modality, your designs may feel a bit like designs from other quadrants—the differentiating factor here is the ability to choose.

NOTE CHOICE AND CONSEQUENCE

If you decide you will *only* support hands-free interactions, you're actually designing for the Intangible quadrant. If you decide you will *only* support close-range interactions like touch, you're designing for the Anchored quadrant.

TABLE 7.3 EXAMPLES OF ADAPTIVE METHODOLOGIES

Methodology	Description	Notes
Switched	Design each scenario to use the inputs best matched to the need.	Not inherently accessible. Requires clear delineation of anchored interactions vs. intangible interactions.
Amplified	All tasks support hands-free completion. Screen and physical input are alternatives and extensions where appropriate.	Any task that is only hands-free may still require additional accessibility work.
Fluid	Customers can complete most or all tasks with close-range or long-range interactions. Switching is supported, not just at the scenario level, but at the task level.	Most expensive option. While switching between modalities is supported mid-scenario, the number of steps may vary.

NOTE WHO'S ON (VOICE) FIRST?

The #VoiceFirst hashtag on Twitter has long been a rallying ground for passionate voice designers who were eager to see voice overtake haptic input as the dominant interaction model. However, there are so many other input modalities out there—not just for voice, but also for hands-free technology like gesture. Calling the Adaptive category "voice first" would ignore future potential, but it certainly *includes* experiences perceived as "voice first."

Anchored Interactions (Quadrant 2)

Rich output, close-proximity interactions

Anchored experiences include a rich physical presence, and the customer typically remains close to the device involved in the interaction.

> **NOTE** SCREEN FORWARD
>
> We initially used "screen forward" to refer to experiences in the Anchored quadrant during my time on the Alexa team at Amazon. However, this was in the context of the Echo Show and Fire TV, without considering the broader range of opportunities beyond the confines of a specific screen.

The assumption that your customer must be close to the device opens up many interaction opportunities:

- Use of smaller fonts and higher density of written text.
- Use of high-resolution photos, videos, or UI elements.
- Reliance upon physical input devices like touchscreens, keyboards, or remote controls.
- Use of voice as a shortcut for tasks that are time-consuming using physical input.

Anchored experiences that support voice often include near-field microphones, in which case you can assume that your customer is near the device and the screen when they are speaking. This enables you to use voice as a shortcut for your visual interface, as the Xbox did with Bing search.

However, this doesn't necessarily mean you must support all tasks with voice. Navigational tasks like forward and back are particularly ill-suited to voice, and a remote control or touch control will yield a much better experience if available.

An emerging category of anchored experiences is virtual reality headsets like the Oculus Quest. Because these devices must be worn on the customer's head, you can always assume proximity to the device, and the output tends to be richly immersive. Most of these headsets support both voice input and some form of controller-based haptic input, and in some cases, gesture interactions.

Direct Interactions (Quadrant 3)

Limited output, close-proximity interactions

Direct experiences are usually associated with small, self-contained form factors, like a Fitbit or Nest—or head-mounted mixed reality or augmented reality displays like Google Glass and Microsoft HoloLens.

The technical limitations associated with the form factors of these devices often lead to limited displays of information and associated context. It's likely that these experiences require some form of training during the out-of-box experience.

The smaller these devices get, the more constrained their interactions become. Some in this category might only support voice via grammar-based voice interactions, due to processing power or internet access considerations. Others might support haptic input only, via one or two dynamic functional buttons.

Intangible Interactions (Quadrant 4)

Limited output, long-range interactions

The wave of voice-only smart speakers launched a thousand multimodal ships. These devices proved once and for all to the mainstream market that voice interactions could work on their own merit, without the crutch of a screen.

> **NOTE** INTANGIBLE VS. VOICE-ONLY
>
> While the dominant intangible interfaces at this time are certainly the ubiquitous voice-controlled smart speakers, calling this category "voice only" ignores the other hands-free input technologies on the market, like gesture and computer vision.

Most intangible experiences today are voice-only experiences, designed so that the entirety of their feature set is accessed via audio output (usually earcons and speech) and audio input (usually voice). These devices do not require (and sometimes do not support) visual or physical interaction with the device to complete any key task. Note that this category of experiences can provide accessibility challenges for consumers with auditory disabilities.

Despite relying mostly on invisible interactions, these devices often provide alternative visual information, like limited LED status indicators. Intangible devices also often have a few physical controls for intents like volume adjustment and "cancel," which could be hard to express during high-volume situations.

Choosing Your Interaction Models

If you're so early in the product process that you haven't locked on input or output hardware, then the fun begins with research. You'll want to evaluate the context in which your customer desires to use each of your different devices, apps, or features.

- What tasks will your customer want to complete?
- Where will your customer's hands be? Will they be full or empty?
- Is it likely that your customer will be dealing with significant ambient noise?
- Will the interaction take place around many people?
- Will the tasks be sensitive or involve security checks?

Anchored experiences are a good compromise for situations where voice will frequently fall short, especially loud rooms full of people. And if your customer's request ends in a rich response—like playback of a movie—all the more reason to enhance the rich output rather than replace it.

Adaptive and intangible experiences are most useful in situations where your customer is moving or their hands are busy. However, the current state of far-field natural language experiences makes them fairly unforgiving in situations where multiple people are talking.

If your end-to-end experience includes multiple device types, you might end up supporting different quadrants for different devices. Perhaps a bedside table experience is anchored (or even direct) due to the assumed proximity, but the experience for the kitchen scenarios support full adaptivity—and a third bathroom scenario optimizes for an intangible experience, since bathrooms and touch don't mix well at all.

Orchestrating Multimodal Transitions

One last question you will likely need to answer very early in your design process: How will your customer switch between the various input modes implied by the "multi" in "multimodality?" Table 7.4 describes the three common methods of multimodal orchestration.

TABLE 7.4 MULTIMODAL ORCHESTRATION METHODS

Model	Description	Examples
Parallel Multimodality	The system supports multiple input modalities, but there is no easy switching between them after a session is initiated.	Early automotive interfaces
Sequential Multimodality	Customers may switch between input modalities, as desired, based on the task. In some cases, a switch may become "locked in" for certain subtasks.	Cortana on Windows
Simultaneous Multimodality	Multiple inputs can be accepted at the same time, and are processed together to determine a single intent.	Voice-directed navigation to a point on a map

In general, supporting simultaneous multimodality helps customers further streamline their interactions using indirect reference. Our "holy grail" on the Windows Automotive project was a scenario where a customer could touch a point on the map and provide instructions via indirect reference, like "Add this to my trip" or "Help me get there."

Most multimodal systems in this generation only support sequential multimodality, and that seems unlikely to change at scale. That's not necessarily a bad thing, although it sometimes represents a missed opportunity.

The amount of added complexity introduced by simultaneous multimodality is costly in both implementation and testing time. In many situations, sequential multimodality is enough.

> **NOTE** NOT ALL OR NOTHING
>
> Simultaneous multimodality can also be applied in concert with another orchestration method, applied to only the scenarios that most benefit from the added complexity. However, any temporary extension in your interaction model like this will likely require customer training.

So which orchestration method is appropriate for your scenario?

- If your tasks are generally **short, single-turn interactions**, parallel multimodality may suffice.
- If you have **multiturn interactions** that typically take a nontrivial amount of time, consider supporting sequential multimodality.
- The complexity of simultaneous multimodality becomes worth it when your system involves **large-scale rich visuals** like maps, or when you're dealing with a **large set of tasks** that are bound to a large set of specific objects.

Regardless of the orchestration method you choose, some challenges in multimodal design transcend orchestration techniques or interaction models. You'll learn more about the biggest challenges in Chapter 8, "It's a (Multimodal) Trap!"

Example: Sequential Multimodality

When interacting with a sequentially multimodal system, customers transition between different input modalities as desired or required.

1. Begin an interaction by saying "Cortana, remind me at 8 a.m. tomorrow." (See Figure 7.7.)

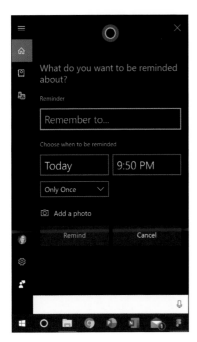

FIGURE 7.7
The result of asking Cortana on a desktop to schedule a reminder.

2. Cortana replies with "Sure thing. What do you want to be reminded about?" The device turns on the microphone. Speak the reminder.

3. You've changed your mind on the time, or perhaps it's wrong. To correct the time, tap on the value displayed on the screen in Figure 7.8.

FIGURE 7.8
When a customer touches the reminder time to correct what was heard via voice, the interface pivots to allow touch interaction.

4. However, once you've switched to a touch interaction, you can't go back to voice. The microphone icon is disabled, and you must tap the screen to complete the task.

In this way, Cortana is leveraging an assumption that since you touched the screen once, you'll remain close enough to touch it again. It's sequential multimodality—you can switch between modalities in the middle of a scenario, but in this case not all switches are reversible.

Apply It Now

The "holy grail" experience is the Starship Enterprise from *Star Trek: The Next Generation.* All requests are richly supported in voice, but can just as easily be sent to a screen whenever appropriate. Multiple speakers are processed seamlessly and gracefully, and there are no microphones to track. State is tracked seamlessly all over the ship, and identity is verified via communicator.

There are many gaps yet to be filled before we can bridge our current technology with that utopian future. (Bridge? See what I did there?) If you believe your customer needs a system that straddles multiple quadrants, by all means, do so. But quality matters even more with voice-enabled interfaces. They hit humans at an emotional level not seen with traditional graphical user interfaces.

Ask yourself the following questions:

- In what quadrant are your competitors focused?
- Does your product or scenario work in multiple quadrants?
- Do you have experiences that support devices in multiple quadrants?
- Do you have experiences that move between quadrants during a single scenario?

In the near term, it's better to execute well in one quadrant than to stretch yourself too thin and fall short. As momentum in the industry builds, we will all collectively move toward a more robust multimodal future.

The Voice-Forward Path Forward with Cathy Pearl

Cathy Pearl, author of the O'Reilly book Designing Voice User Interfaces, *is a veteran voice user interface designer who brings considerable multimodal design experience to the table. She's also one of the still-too-few designers who have worked at executive levels, so her insight is infused with strategic wisdom. I asked Cathy to reflect on this point in the evolution of multisensory experiences.*

Q: Has the explosion of hybrid experiences where both rich visuals and voice are key elements of the experience changed your approach to design?

I think so. For example, smart displays. That, to me, is a big change. Because it's what we call a voice-forward device. It's not a tablet; it's not a phone. With my phone, I might sometimes type, I might sometimes tap, I might sometimes speak. With a smart display, the primary mode of interaction is speaking, but there's this visual support component that's really important. Like, if I want to say, "Watch cute cat videos on YouTube," I want to obviously watch the videos on the screen. The screen is really important.

So that has been a really interesting thing to wrap our heads around. How do you design for something like a smart display? And so one of the things we believe is the best approach is—if you're designing across multiple surfaces, we recommend starting with the voice-only experience first. Because it's often surprising to people, but it's also the most challenging or most constrained case. And so, we say, "Look, if you work it out first on voice first, you're gonna work through a lot of these problems and issues you're gonna have." And then you move to a visual device and think, "Okay, where do visuals enhance the conversation?"

I think one of the issues we have now is that there are a lot more visual designers in the world than there are conversational designers. And if you're a visual designer, what is your go-to? Visuals, right? That's how you're trained, and how you think. So it's important to try not to go too much in that direction. To say, "Okay, hold on, let's do voice-only first."

And then I like to give this analogy: when we were planning our wedding, we went to a florist. She sat down with us and asked us a bunch of questions. That was the voice-only part. And then when she got a bunch of information, she pulled out a bunch of magazines. She's like, "Okay, well what do you think about this? Now, what do you think about this?"

And to me, that's the point at which visuals came on board. That was really, really important. But she didn't just rely on visuals. It was different modes for different contexts.

So, again, with voice-forward devices, sometimes we're hands busy. Sometimes, we're three feet away. It has made me think, because I was in the voice-only world for so long: what about TTS? Should we show the same TTS on the screen that they're saying out loud?

Having had a smart display in my home for a while now, I have some opinions about this. Here's another screen in the house. I have an 11-year-old kid. Here's another distraction for him. So we're eating dinner, and someone asks a question like, "Where is Mesopotamia?" And it starts speaking, but it also starts scrolling the answer across the screen. What he does, he gets out of his chair, he goes across, and he goes and starts looking at the screen. And I'm like, "Argh!" You know?

One of the concerns I have is that we're like, "Oh! A new screen! Let's make it beautiful, let's make it visually appealing, let's . . . when you ask for the weather, let's make some beautiful animations!" And I'm like, "No! No! No!" We don't need yet another screen to have to manage. So I want to emphasize to folks, like, tread wisely with these things and these screens. Yes, they can be really useful and great. But don't just say, "We have a screen, therefore we must use it." Think . . . think about it.

 *Cathy Pearl* is the author of the O'Reilly book, Designing Voice User Interfaces, *and a conversation designer at Google. She's been designing and creating voice user Interfaces (VUIs) for 20 years and is passionate about helping everyone make the best conversational experiences possible. Previously, Cathy was VP of User Experience at Sensely, whose virtual nurse avatar helps people stay healthy. She has worked on everything from programming NASA helicopter pilot simulators to designing a conversational iPad app in which* Esquire *magazine's style columnist tells users what they should wear on a first date.*

It's a (Multimodal) Trap!

As designers begin to tackle the wide world of multimodal user experiences, it's easy to get tied up in the execution of direct customer interaction. After all, there's so much unexplored territory in conversational design or gestural control. After two decades of exclusively mouse-and-keyboard mainstream devices, product teams and designers tend to leap at new opportunities to innovate.

Yet, things are rarely as simple as they seem. There's far more driving a multimodal interaction than what meets your customer's senses. The foundations of your multimodal experience must be laid long before you get to "traditional" design. It's critical to consider the relationship between the experiences you want and the systems that will be required to enable those experiences. Unfortunately for many teams, this realization comes far too late to execute correctly.

But why is there so much complexity lurking beneath the surface? This added complexity is a consequence of the vast possibilities unlocked when you allow your customers to move between devices or modalities at will. Suddenly, customers need to be able to pause or pick up a task at any time. They need their products to recognize them and to share state across sessions. These sorts of features require considerable implementation effort.

For those less experienced with systems or service design, this foundational level of work seems intimidating and possibly infinite. Where do you begin? Many multimodal projects run up against a few core challenges, as depicted in Table 8.1. Exploring these common challenges early in your product design process will contribute greatly to the potential success of your designs.

TABLE 8.1 TOP CHALLENGES FOR MULTIMODAL USER INTERFACES

Challenge	Question
Synchronization	Are your inputs and outputs drawing from a shared understanding of your customer's current state?
Context	How does your system model your customer's behavior and device state for use over time?
Discoverability	How will your customers discover functionality they can't see?
Ergonomics	Can extended use of your interactions cause physical harm to your customers?
Identity and Privacy	How will your experience adapt to use by multiple people or in shared environments?

Synchronization: Do You Have a Shared State?

A multimodal user experience has extremely limited potential when its various input choices are not synchronized. In an unsynchronized system, the various input modalities do not share the same understanding of the customer's state.

To better understand this particular challenge, the automotive industry is an excellent case study. Automotive infotainment systems began to combine both haptic input and speech input in the early 21st century.

Despite the great promise of these early systems, they frequently treated voice and physical input as mutually exclusive. A common practice was to block out any visual interaction affordances with a list of potential voice commands when the push-to-talk button was activated, as illustrated in Figures 8.1, 8.2, and 8.3.[1] While the screen was technically used for output during the interaction, you couldn't interact with anything except an "exit" button while the system was engaged. Eventually, some automotive systems made limited use of the screen during voice interactions, particularly during disambiguation.

FIGURE 8.1
The home screen for Ford's SYNC® 3 when voice interaction is not engaged.

FIGURE 8.2
In Ford's SYNC® 3, once voice interaction is engaged, the home screen disappears and is replaced by a voice capture screen. Any state from Figure 8.1 is lost and obscured.

FIGURE 8.3
The contact disambiguation screen for Ford's SYNC® 3. This experience relies heavily on touch, so it's jarring that the experience in Figure 8.2 is so incompatible with touch.

1   "SYNC® 3 Voice Commands," Ford Motor Company, https://owner.ford.com/support/how-tos/sync/sync-3/voice-controls/sync-3-voice-commands.html

Why have automotive systems taken so long to reach fluid multimodality? The complexity lies "under the hood," so to speak. Transitions between modalities require all input *and* output systems—voice, touch, etc.—to *draw from a single shared understanding of the customer state*. But many legacy systems save the customer state *based on the modality chosen*. It's complicated work to untangle that state from the interactions driving the state.

This problem isn't unique to automotive infotainment systems. Many product teams are composed of smaller teams working in isolated silos. Any project that separates its voice user interface (VUI) team and its graphical user interface (GUI) team runs the risk of developing two separate models of customer state unless the proper work is done up front to define a single, common way to represent and share that state across modalities.

Your ultimate system design should allow customers to fluidly move back and forth between input modalities and devices without concern for loss of context or work. That outcome requires tight partnership between you and your development partners, along with up-front clarity about what customer state is actually relevant across input modalities.

Be Prepared to Plan the Platform

Synchronization is usually driven by the platform or operating system, so the most critical step is to get design representation at business requirements and platform definition discussions early in the project. It is costly to reverse-engineer solutions to desynchronized interactions later on in the process, but often very little extra cost to do things the "right way" the first time.

But to contribute meaningfully to those discussions, you'll need to be well prepared. Ideally, you'll use customer research or competitive analysis to identify the core elements that define a customer experience on your platform prior to these requirements discussions. Ask yourself these questions:

- What are the potential customer scenarios or intents?
- How likely are people to transition between inputs?
- When would customers be likely to transition between inputs?
- What information would be needed to hand those scenarios off to a different handler?

What does it mean to say "customer state is stored locally?"

Consider a standard website accessed through a desktop browser. If you're using Javascript embedded in HTML to track your customer's state, that means the state is probably stored in your customer's web browser and not in the cloud.

How would you then make that local state available to a voice assistant on another device?

- If you're working on a legacy system, you and your development partners must track down where that state is stored locally and adapt it for cross-device use.

- If you're working on a new system, get involved in early system architecture discussions to ensure that your customer's need for a cross-device state is being considered when making decisions regarding cloud storage or network communications.

Either way, these conversations can be tricky. It's hard to assign a dollar value to a persistent state across devices, and any persistent session data has the potential to be a security risk. Be prepared to make an efficient case by assembling a crisp list of the parameters you'll need to share across devices to meet customer expectations.

When considering the information needed to successfully transition, it may help to reframe the problem as a transition between human assistants. If one assistant were handing off your customer's task to another human assistant, what information would be transferred in that conversation?

Armed with this insight, you can then advocate for a system design that allows critical information to be represented centrally, as opposed to being tracked by the current modality (your natural language understanding engine, for example).

Context: What Just Happened?

You've already read about the challenges inherent in synchronization. When customers switch between devices or modalities in the midst of a scenario, there must be a shared understanding about what they are doing.

But it's also critical to think about a customer's context across interactions. In this case, *"context" refers to attributes of the interaction that should be tracked over time to enable smarter responses in subsequent interactions.* Context is yet another system design need that's incredibly expensive and risky to "fix" if missed in the early stages of design.

What Did I Just Say?

Human beings don't reset their conversational context at the start of every new sentence. There's a social expectation that a conversational partner will pay attention and store away salient pieces of the conversation to influence later conversational turns.

The first generation of smart speakers applied this concept, but on an extremely limited basis. For example:

CUSTOMER: "Computer, what's the weather in Orlando?"

DEVICE: "In Orlando, Florida, it's 53 degrees and sunny."

CUSTOMER: "What about New York?"

DEVICE: "In New York City, it's 32 degrees and snowing."

The second customer utterance—"What about New York?"—doesn't actually include a specific intent! It only includes a new value for the "city" slot in the intent (New York). And yet the system is able to continue the conversation because it's "remembered" that the context of the conversation is weather in American cities.

Just because this conversation is possible today doesn't mean that the conversational context problem is solved. Most systems only store context for a few seconds or minutes. And there's generally only one context tracked. Human conversations can be more nuanced— for example, two or three contexts threaded through a single conversation.

Rich contextual understanding is an exciting, complex problem. What should be stored? For how long? Should context be maintained through multiple conversations? How might you access extended context, like "What was the phone number of the restaurant I asked about last week?"

Situational Awareness

Conversational context isn't the only way to enrich and enhance your customer interactions. The more input modalities and output modalities you support—and the more devices in your ecosystem—the more nuanced the opportunities become to do the right thing at the right place and the right time.

For example, the ubiquitous "Play" intent. It's particularly challenging for speech interactions, as folks tend to ask to play a title without context about the medium or device. Does "Play Pirates of the Caribbean" mean play the movie, the game, or the soundtrack?

One solution in this scenario is to give your experiences awareness of a device's inherent capabilities. It doesn't make sense for your customer to play a movie on an audio-only device, so rule out the movie on a smart speaker (unless the smart speaker is paired with a video device). Table 8.2 goes into greater detail about some of the elements of situational awareness you might want to add to your experience.

TABLE 8.2 COMMON DIMENSIONS OF CONTEXT

Context	Examples
Device Capabilities	Video, audio, games, touch, voice, etc.
Customer Location	Closest device, time in room, etc.
Customer Mood	Sentiment detection, rate of speech, etc.
Time of Day	Cross-reference with customer habits
Device Location	Bedroom, public space, private space, etc.
Conversational Context	Last intent, last three intents, identity, etc.
Interaction Context	Most recent input method, available output methods, customer habits
Customer Data	Preferences, habits, calendar, contacts, etc.

Don't treat this list like a checklist—that's a recipe for feature bloat. Instead, review it thoughtfully.

- Which elements of your customer context are most impactful?
- What is the relative cost and feasibility for that context?
- What are the ethical and legal implications of tracking that context?
- Do you have explicit consent to track or infer this context?

Context can be complicated and costly, but it's also a fast track to "magical" experiences when applied correctly. As with synchronization, it's important to pursue context early in the product planning process.

Discoverability: How Will People Learn?

Traditional PC-oriented interfaces have long basked in their ability to cheaply add microcopy text and tutorial overlays to forms and pages with abandon. Discoverability—the rapid ability for a novice customer to discover a new feature quickly—was the driving force behind countless "Design vs. Product" intellectual cage matches.

NOTE MICROCOPY

> *Microcopy* refers to short phrases or sentences, typically placed inline within a graphical interface, intended to provide context in the moment without additional documentation.

Now that audio and even gesture interfaces are consuming a progressively larger portion of the market, discoverability is becoming a much harder problem. You can no longer assume that people can "see" new features. You can't even assume that customers can browse your experience. Voice and gesture interfaces have always suffered from a discoverability problem.

If your experience lacks written words or icons in some form—for example, smart speakers, many virtual reality experiences, and gestural interfaces—you will no longer have the option of including microcopy or teaching toast "just in case." And while documentation is always an option, documentation is increasingly not included with products, forcing customers to dig for your information against all of your product's reviews, critiques, and competitors.

Dynamic Instruction

The first step to tackling the discoverability challenge for multimodal systems is, as with many problems, research. You will ascertain what information is essential and find some way to impart that information to your customers within the experience itself. Whether you gain this knowledge via ethnographic research, usability studies on existing experiences, or competitive research is up to you.

Once you know what information your customers are missing, you must find a way to impart that information when you cannot rely on the written word. Table 8.3 provides a variety of alternative methods to consider when attempting to draw attention or clarity to a feature.

TABLE 8.3 ALTERNATIVES TO WRITTEN DISCOVERY

Method	Definition	Possible Uses
Imply	A concept or feature is referred to but not explained.	Demonstrating specific word choice that can be used to initiate other features Inviting interaction with kinetic or audible clues
Teach	Proactive, explicit instructions or a tutorial about how to use a feature. Explanations come at the cost of customer time. Typically, a spoken interaction if the written word is not available.	At first use of a system or feature, also known as *out-of-the-box experience* Provide help after lengthy periods of inactivity Explain a feature by request
Model	Customers learn about functionality by seeing others use it. This works best for public experiences.	Demo stations at stores Modeling common behaviors in advertisements Providing livestreams, videos, or podcasts that mimic desired scenarios
Reframe	Direct existing customer behavior to a new modality.	Suggest an alternative method of completing the task a customer just completed
Converse	Model and respond to common customer questions, like "What can I do?"	Narrow down a customer's area of curiosity to provide exactly the assistance needed
Interject	Add "advertisements" for features around or after other interactions.	Introduce new features once a customer's initial goal has been completed

No matter what methods you choose—and you'll likely need many of them—consider some guidelines for success:

- **Never get in the way of a customer and their current goal.** If trying to expose a new feature, wait until the customer's current task is completed. As a bonus, waiting until a task is completed means that you may get the benefit of the doubt from your customers if they were satisfied with the previous task.

- **Look for invitations to interact.** Whether it's a wandering gaze, a statement like "I'm bored," a question, or a long idle period, it's likely your customer may give passive or active signals that a discovery moment is appropriate. Learning is most effective when your customer is in a receptive mindset.

Alexa Interjections

During my time on the Alexa platform, we struggled with the challenge of discoverability for pure voice experiences like the Echo. The Echo Show, a later entrant into the Alexa ecosystem, relies on the written word as manifested in a graphical interface for discovery of new features, as seen in Figure 8.4.

FIGURE 8.4

Amazon's Echo Show uses a few visual affordances to expose potentially undiscovered features to the customer.

- **Stay relevant and contextual.** If you're teaching a customer a feature they've already discovered, your system comes off as inattentive or unintelligent. That change in perception can have lasting impacts on your customer's relationship with your product. Where ethical and possible, consider tracking first use of features and only teaching features yet to be used.

- **Idle time isn't yours—respect the customer's space.** Introducing too much information can overwhelm customers, cause mental fatigue, and possibly even abandonment of your experience.

- **Don't focus on a single channel.** Be mindful that people learn in different ways, that multimodal systems are used in a variety

Unlike the Echo Show, smart speakers can't assume any graphical interface is present. Certainly, there is the Alexa app—but it's not fully synchronized in real time with any one speaker's status. Back in 2015, while tackling the Notifications feature, I worked with my peers to propose an interjection system for Alexa.

Specifically, we could flag certain interactions as "interjection enabled." These intents ended neatly, without a frequent need for follow-up questions. During that moment of success, our hypothesis was that customers might not mind a suggestion about another feature on the device. It wouldn't be as invasive as a notification, because we were already speaking to the customer.

In 2019, Alexa began to launch this feature. Most commonly, Alexa interjects after the completion of an intent if there are new notifications, suggesting that the customer follow up. But other interjections are possible, too—suggestions of additional information, for example.

CUSTOMER: "Computer, what's the temperature for tomorrow?"

ALEXA: "On Friday you can expect sun, with a high of 72 degrees and a low of 52 degrees. **Do you want to hear the weather for the weekend?**"

The feature isn't perfect—it's hard to figure out when this is welcome versus an annoyance, and as of this writing they haven't yet managed to scale interjections back enough with time. But it's an exciting new tool to broaden interactions beyond the single-turn transactional model, and I can't wait to see how future designers further adapt this model.

of contexts, and that many systems are used by multiple people. If you focus entirely on out-of-the-box experiences, how will the next person learn to use your system?

NOTE BETTER TOGETHER

Rather than consider these discovery methods individually, consider developing an overall discovery journey that takes into account the customer, context, and time spent with the product. The larger your experience is, the more likely you are to need a comprehensive plan for the discovery challenges your customers will face.

Ergonomics: Are You Hurting People?

For decades, ergonomic considerations were generally limited to vehicle operators and a handful of extreme computer use cases—for example, computer animators whose jobs were incredibly mouse-intensive or 911 operators who had to optimize for speed.

Any gestural or physical interface has the potential to cause real and lasting physical harm. As a user experience designer who sustained a work injury when ergonomic conditions were compromised, I can speak to this risk firsthand. As the era of multimodality arrives, ergonomic considerations must take greater focus.

However, your usability participants may never complain about ergonomic issues between modalities, because most usability tests are fixed-length. These tests do not adequately explore extreme or complete usage. Acknowledge this as a blind spot and ask deeper questions:

- What does extreme usage look like?
- Do our customers have full control over switches between input modalities?
- How can our testing explore the impacts of extended use?
- What is the worst impact we might have on the human body?

In particular, keep an eye out for these two categories of common ergonomic risk: repeated use and impact caused by input transitions.

Repeated Use

Seemingly innocuous motions, like a click, drag, or switch between keyboard and mouse can cause significant injury if repeated over time. This risk can be heightened for voice interfaces (where the customer is already making an effort to speak slowly and loudly) and gestural interfaces (that may be using unfamiliar muscles).

Repeated use is a particularly salient concern for the designers of immersive experiences, like video games and virtual reality. These systems are most likely to push customers to physical limits through motion or repetition.

For any experience you're building, ask yourself these questions:

- Does your experience require any gesture or movement to be repeated frequently?

- Have you considered the muscular strain of that repetition?
- What impact will the customer's environment have on this action?
- What control does your customer have over breaks, variety, and rest?
- What can you do to limit the risk of injury to your customer?

Even if there is no traditional physical motion involved in your task, consider that even the voice manifests in the physical world. Long or repetitive voice asks may push your customer, though, in general, the risk is lower than motion-based input.

Transitions Between Input

For designers of more traditional experiences, it is the "cliffs" between input modalities that hold the greatest danger.

Every switch between physical inputs—whether between haptic inputs like a keyboard and a mouse, or between haptic and gestural interfaces like a touch panel and an infrared sensor—can potentially cause physical harm.

Any time you ask your customer to switch between physical motions—whether that's typing and mouse, typing and touch, touch and gesture, or typing and gesture—you're asking for significant muscle engagement. Movement of the right hand to the mouse can require rotation, movement, and even extension of the wrist, forearm, and arm (Figure 8.5). Twisting in particular has a tendency to cause injury. Combine that with repeated use, and you have a recipe for significant injury.

NOTE LITTLE MOVEMENTS, BIG PAIN

My own case of tendinitis was brought on by the repetition of two simple acts: mouse movement (arm extension) and the transition between keyboard and mouse. I wasn't alone. My hand therapist's office was constantly full with folks with similar repetitive stress injuries. Many of them cited a repeated need to copy and paste across apps—a task that requires both the mouse and keyboard—as a factor in their injury.

PHOTO © LIGHTFIELD STUDIOS—STOCK.ADOBE.COM

FIGURE 8.5
Your customer is physically rotating and moving their hand each time you ask them to switch between keyboard and mouse input. Repeated over time, such motions can cause real injury.

Ergonomic Considerations

Always remember that your customers are human beings with joints and bones and muscles. They have inherent limits, and those limits may vary from day to day, hour to hour, or even minute to minute, based on personal and environmental considerations. Two common ways to combat this risk are the following:

- **Allow your customers to switch between input modalities freely as they desire.** Let voice compensate for haptic and kinesthetic movement in periods of strain, and vice versa.

- **Minimize the required involuntary switches between input devices.** Most software development apps place a particular emphasis on keyboard shortcuts, precisely for this reason: the majority of programming is keyboard-driven, so optimizing all interactions for the keyboard reduces physical strain on customers in general.

Identity and Privacy: Whose Turn Is It, Anyway?

While smartphones have been transformative, they've also made many designers lazier when it comes to considering questions of identity. In the era of desktop computers, a common scenario was family usage of a single machine. Whether it was in-app identity or OS-level identity, software had to adapt to the needs, skill levels, and preferences of different people.

By contrast, smartphones are intensely personal devices. Aside from some "kid-friendly" sandbox modes, most phones are designed to pair with one user. How would you react if someone asked to use your phone for five minutes? Few people today would readily hand their phone over.

But at the same time that humans are developing an almost codependent relationship with their phones (not throwing stones here—I live in this glass house, too), smart speakers and the Internet of Things are redefining the nature of human relationships with devices.

Have you done the work to explore the environments in which your customer will use your experience? Do you understand your customer's relationship with your device and your device's relationship to a whole household or office space? The complexities of identity in your system are easy to overlook if you don't properly explore the context of use.

Table 8.4 details some of the most common identity and privacy considerations for multimodal experiences, which apply not only to smart speakers and smart displays, but also to laptops, desktops, streaming media devices, and other Internet of Things devices.

The subtleties regarding identity and privacy vary by environment. Your metaphorical mileage may vary, but here are a few common scenarios: home usage, office usage, and public spaces.

TABLE 8.4 GENERAL IDENTITY CONSIDERATIONS FOR MULTIMODAL EXPERIENCES

Consideration	Details
Varied Preferences	People may have different configuration preferences, like: • Streaming media defaults • Quiet hours • System voice or visual theme
Different Tastes	Taste in consumable media like movies, music, and books can be polarizing—and "polluting" one person's queue or favorites can cause actual arguments.
Information Security	Large screens and audio user interfaces are inherently less private than a laptop or smartphone screen. Care must be given to the type of information that is displayed and how it is displayed.
Interruptions and Concurrency	When "natural" user interfaces like gesture and voice are used in a shared space, it is difficult to get a "clean" signal, because many people may be detected by your sensors.
Physical Variations	For any visual or physical input, different heights and body types may require frequent readjustment or recalibration of those sensors and related preferences.
Age Restrictions	In a space with underage children, natural user interfaces that do not require regular authentication can be a big risk.

Home Usage

Many smart speakers, smart displays, and streaming media devices reside in bustling households where multiple customers may live and where group gatherings with outsiders are not necessarily uncommon.

- **Groups:** How will your experience be used during gatherings? Do you need to know the identities of the people in the room?

- **Personalization:** When different people interact with your experience, do they expect different things?

- **Adaptivity:** Does your experience change when a group interacts with it, or is it the same 1:1 experience delivered to the group?

- **Privacy:** Could your experience accidentally result in an embarrassing oversharing of information or behavioral insight?

Office Usage

Offices are still largely dominated by 1:1 pairings between devices and employees, and that's likely due to privacy and identity challenges.

- **Workspace:** Is your experience being used in a conference room or an open office? (Private offices are possible, but rare.)

- **Company hardware:** What peripherals is your customer using? Are they shared or individually assigned? Close range or long range?

- **Privacy:** Is the interaction you're expecting something that could potentially cause embarrassment, either due to experience failure or the nature of the input?

Exquisite Embarrassment

Perhaps the risk of embarrassment seems abstract—you're not a shy person, or your colleagues are super easygoing people. Take this example of one of the many ways in which public interactions can go awry.

During my time working on the now-defunct Cortana in the Car project, a group of colleagues on the Connected Car project were discussing the relative capabilities of Cortana on Windows Phone with respect to address book functionality. At the time, we all had Windows Phones, and the Cortana experience on those devices was surprisingly robust.

Name has been changed to protect the innocent.

CHERYL: "Cortana actually supports nicknames and indirect references when accessing your address book now. I think that'll really help here."

KERMIT: "Really? I've never seen that."

ROWLF: "Oh, sure, let me show you! (Picks up his Windows Phone.) Cortana, call my wife."

CORTANA: "Okay! Which wife?"

Laughter pretty much ended the meeting, as Rowlf turned bright red. To the original product team, this might not have even crossed their mind! "Wife" was just a nickname that could be given to a contact. Maybe his wife had multiple entries in his address book, and Cortana was asking an innocuous clarification. But to a room full of people, there was a flash of a question in the air . . . how many wives did Cortana know about, anyway?

Words have meaning, and your experiences aren't used in a vacuum. Consider how your interface might give the wrong impression in a group scenario.

Public Spaces

Designing multimodal experiences for public spaces is so hard that even theme park giants like Disney and Universal have trouble making these experiences work at scale in their controlled environments. Be sure to consult experts on the ethical and legal ramifications of experiences that involve recording or data capture in any way.

- **Consent:** Have your customers explicitly consented to the use of sensors to process their interactions? How can people opt out from interacting with your systems?

- **Awareness:** Do people know when they are being recorded, when the recording stops, and where the sensors are located? If data is stored, how will customers know how to retrieve or delete it?

Apply It Now

When beginning the product design process for a new multimodal experience, start by evaluating your proposed experience against these five challenges. Which will be the biggest issues? Where must you focus your efforts in the early days of product development?

1. **Synchronization**
   - Advocate for your customer's needs during the platform and system design experience.
   - Ensure that your back end includes a shared representation of critical aspects of your customer's state during common activities, accessible across any input modality.

2. **Context**
   - What customer insight will you need over time to make better assumptions and default decisions about how to respond?
   - What context is already tracked by the platform or tools you're using?
   - What can you track and model ethically, and how can you model transparency about the use of these insights?

3. **Discoverability**
   - How will your customer discover your invisible functionality, particularly when driven by nonvisual inputs like gesture or voice?
   - Can you develop a cohesive plan that unifies your customer's learning journey over time?

4. **Ergonomics**

   - The human body has limits: what impact will repeated use of your product have on the human body?

   - How can you optimize for voluntary transitions and minimize involuntary transitions?

5. **Identity and Privacy**

   - In what circumstances will your experience be used by multiple customers at once?

   - Are your customers being observed when they interact with your system?

   - Does your system threaten your customer's identity through embarrassing circumstances?

   - How will your system distinguish between multiple customer identities or accounts?

   - If you're using sensor-based input modalities, be extra mindful of leading with consent and transparency about what you're collecting and how to back out.

CHAPTER 9

Lost in Transition

One constant in truly multimodal systems is change. When you could assume a customer would remain in the same context for the duration of an interaction, the only change that designers had to consider was the change in the customer state enabled by the UI. Don't want a change? Then don't build an affordance for that change. Simple.

Multimodal systems are defined by their flexibility. Without the ability to transition between inputs and outputs, all a multimodal system provides is a single choice up front about an engagement. It's essentially several mutually exclusive single-mode interactions.

In reality, multimodal design is about so much more than the customer state. Within an individual state or moment, the interaction is constrained and can be designed via fairly traditional means. The highest risk and greatest challenge in multimodal design lie in the transition states. Transition can take many forms in advanced experiences:

- Changing input or output modalities
- Switching devices during a single, end-to-end task
- Multiple customers sharing a single device

Design of a truly multimodal system requires you to look *between* moments. Channel your inner child and look back to the classic connect-the-dots puzzles. While the dots are the foundation of those pictures, you experience the image by exploring what's in between.

Between Modalities

Some designers refer to a transition between different modalities as an *interaction cliff*. When your customer transitions from one input or output method to another, they are at risk of losing context, time, and even safety to the transition. Table 9.1 details several cliff archetypes that can threaten the cohesion of your customer's experience.

Input Transitions and Fluid Multimodality

Increasingly, it's possible to move fluidly between input modalities.

In some cases, this transition is *voluntary*: a customer is changing their preferred mode of interaction because they believe the new input modality will be easier or more appropriate for use.

In other cases, the transition is *involuntary*: the current input is deemed insufficient by the system, and the customer must switch inputs to continue their desired activity.

It's important to look out for both voluntary and involuntary input transitions. Either way, these transitions are critical moments in the successful completion of an end-to-end scenario. Table 9.2 includes several example transitions from past and present consumer experiences.

TABLE 9.1 COMMON MULTIMODAL "CLIFFS"

Cliff Type	Description
Input Transition	A customer transitions between two or more input modalities during a single activity.
Output Transition	The system changes the way it communicates with a customer in the middle of an activity.
Input/Output Mismatch	A system responds to a customer request using an output modality that does not match the input modality the customer used to make the request.

TABLE 9.2 EXAMPLE INPUT TRANSITIONS

Initial Input	New Input	System	Example
Voice	Haptic	Cortana (Desktop)	A customer uses voice to set up an appointment, and the system recognizes an incorrect time. Rather than speaking the correction, the customer uses a mouse and keyboard to make the change.
Gesture	Haptic	Google Home Hub	A customer moves their hand in front of the camera to pause a video, and then decides to use touch to scrub backward for something they missed.
Haptic	Voice	Amazon Fire TV	A customer uses a remote control to browse featured movies and doesn't see anything good. Instead, the customer launches another streaming app using their voice.
Haptic	Gesture	iOS	A customer is interacting using touch, but decides abruptly to switch apps and does so by using a system gesture.
Gesture	Voice	Xbox Kinect	A customer is using their hands to interact with a game, but must say "Xbox, open that" to get the contents of a notification.

Voluntary Transitions

Observe your customers interacting with your system.

- What input do they typically start with?
- What input do they prefer, if shown all options?
- Are they naturally driven to switch modalities partway through?
- Are there common points in the process where the switch occurs?

Patterns in voluntary input transitions are both educational opportunities (attempting to make the ability to transition more discoverable) and design opportunities (ensuring that there is no unnecessary friction during or after the switch).

Involuntary Transitions

When your system forces customers to switch modalities, you are inherently disregarding the customer's implied preference for input modality. Treat this moment with particular caution.

- Is it clear to the customer what the next step is?
- What happens if the customer can't make the transition? For example, a TV system that forces a transition from voice to remote control, but the remote control is not within reach.
- Who might be excluded by the forced transition? Forced transitions can be a particular challenge for inclusion and accessibility efforts.

Output Transitions

In some cases, systems must change their own output mid activity due to the environment or the nature of the request. While input transitions tend to occur during complex interactions, output "cliffs" are more likely to occur at the end of simple interactions. It is your responsibility as a designer to direct the customer's attention to the output in its new form, as in most cases they are unlikely to expect the output transition. Table 9.3 describes a few example situations where an output transition occurs within the scope of a single interaction.

When designing an output transition within the scope of a single task, be sure to bridge the cliff by providing some sort of indication in the moment that additional output is available elsewhere.

TABLE 9.3 EXAMPLE OUTPUT TRANSITIONS

Initial Output	New Output	System	Example
Audio	Visual	Siri (iOS)	A customer initiates a hands-free request: "Hey Siri, when is the next *Star Wars* movie coming out?" Instead of a voice response, a list of search results is displayed.
Audio	Visual	Amazon Echo Look	A customer initiates a hands-free request: "Take a photo." The system plays audio cues during the photo process, but the photo can only be displayed via a phone app.
Visual	Audio	Sonos	A customer makes a change to their speaker groups while audio is playing. The change is manifested automatically via the output to the affected speakers.

The most reliable technique for bridging the gap between outputs is to use both output modalities instead of a hard switch. Siri could reply, "I found lots of possible answers for your question. Check your phone for a list of the top results."

You may also be able to leverage established patterns on your platform for directing attention. We did this when designing the photo experience for Amazon's Echo Look, which doesn't have a screen. A shutter sound indicates the photo is taken, and a notification directs the customer's attention to the phone when appropriate.

Beyond the immediate challenges of directing customer attention within a single chunk of output, additional problems may be caused by a mismatch of customer input and system output modalities.

Input/Output Mismatch

An important rule of thumb as a multimodal designer is "respond in kind." Just as it's peculiar to respond to sign language with a fully spoken response, it's a bit unexpected if your system suddenly responds to voice input with some kind of nonvoice output.

However, in certain circumstances responding in kind is either insufficient or impossible. When searching using voice, there are times when all of the potential options sound too similar to be effectively disambiguated by name alone:

CUSTOMER: "Call Jane Smith."

SYSTEM: "Which Jane Smith? I found two matches."

How can the customer indicate their intended target when the results lack acoustic uniqueness? One option is to allow for sophisticated filtering ("Jane Smith from Boston"), but few systems operate at this deeper contextual level. At minimum, you can use visual output to show several pieces of information about Jane in hopes of helping customers disambiguate.

You might also run into a situation where the "unique" data about your results are too unwieldy to speak, as seen in Figure 9.1. If it's possible that this unwieldiness may be the case, allowing customers the choice of switching—or, if you know in advance there will be an issue, proactively transitioning customers to a new modality—is actually setting them up for success.

The "cliff" is the gap between speech input/output and visual output. When customers are speaking to a device—especially smart speakers—there is no guarantee they're in visual range of a device, so how can they reply? And even if they're in range, what are the odds they are looking at the screen, expecting a list?

As a designer, you'll have to account for this cliff and find some way of directing human attention to the screen where disambiguation information is displayed.

In general, it's preferable to avoid creating an input/output mismatch by responding in kind to customer requests. In some cases, it's acceptable to reply to an input with an *additional* form of output, but a hard mismatch is likely to cause problems for discoverability and inclusion.

FIGURE 9.1

When Siri (iOS 13.4.1) finds multiple phone numbers with the same label as results for a spoken query, she reads the phone numbers digit by digit and expects them to be spoken in kind. It's far faster to tap the screen to make a selection.

Between Network Connections

Another form of (generally involuntary) transition of experience is a loss of connectivity. In the early days of cloud service offerings, it was seen as reasonable to suspend interaction when connectivity was suspended. After all, the data's in the cloud, and you need network access to connect to the cloud!

But customer tolerance for such inflexible engineering is waning. As digital systems go from optional to critical path, it's no longer acceptable to spend any length of time without service, even if that service is degraded due to network connection transitions. Table 9.4 explores the five most common types of network problems that could impact your experience.

Media Center Cliffs

Media centers like Microsoft's Xbox, Apple TV, or Amazon's Fire TV demonstrate particularly noticeable input/output mismatch gaps. Even though it's possible to open an app by name on many entertainment systems, few of them currently support fully voice-based journeys end-to-end.

Browsing isn't well suited to spoken output, so most of these systems must find a way to direct attention from the verbal exchange to the visual results. Not all of them are particularly effective at directing attention with intention.

Furthermore, many media systems still shy away from allowing purchase or rental via voice due to concerns about high error rates. As a result, customers are forced to stop using their voice and pick up a remote to complete their task.

These cliffs seem innocuous until the customer's environment is considered. Why did the customer choose voice to interact with the system? Odds are, the remote control isn't within arm's reach. Forcing a customer to begin interacting with a physical controller that may not be available is likely to cause frustration, task abandonment, and even exclusion.

Ask yourself what obstacles are preventing you from supporting the customer's chosen input end-to-end. You might face one or more problems like:

- Is there technical debt on the platform side preventing this end-to-end interaction?
- Is there an organizational concern that adding this functionality will impact sales negatively?
- Are you facing a simple lack of resources?

Once you understand the drivers behind these obstacles, find ways to capture both the cliffs and the drivers behind them in your backlog for future commitments.

TABLE 9.4 NETWORK CONNECTION ISSUES

Archetype	Description	Example
Intentional Connection Loss	Customer chooses to interrupt their connection.	Switching to airplane mode on a plane
Intermittent or Unstable Connection	Connection drops in and out frequently over time, or the strength of connection varies.	Connection at high speeds (car or bus) Connecting in rural or developing areas
Insufficient Connection	Connection is noticeably slower than expected or needed.	Concerts or disasters, where a high volume of people attempt to use limited network resources
Proximity Loss	Device moves too far from point of service.	Smartwatches and fitness devices when a customer walks away from their phone
Connection Failure	Network connection that should be available ceases to function for unknown reasons.	Cut cable or power outage—often beyond a customer's control

NOTE HANDHELD GAMING

My time working on portable gaming consoles forced me to see these connection problems as *our* problem. If there's one thing you learn from developing games on Nintendo devices, it's that you are *not* absolved of responsibility to provide a good experience for your customers when the connection fails. We even had to build (makeshift) Faraday cages to simulate some of these conditions prior to certification!

While it is sometimes reasonable to prevent customers from starting an interaction when the network conditions are poor, it's much worse to deny customers continued access once they've begun an interaction due to a transition in their network conditions. So how do you cope?

If your system detects a network transition that is impacting the customer experience, find a way to let your customers know.

Be Transparent

While it's true that you're rarely the cause of network issues, and while it's even true that your customer's operating system is probably alerting them at some level about connection problems, that doesn't absolve your product from doing the same. Without carrying this transparency through your own product, you risk causing panic when a customer who's not looking at the big picture believes your app has lost data.

Some common patterns for network connection transparency:

- At minimum, some apps display a "Not connected" or "No network connection" warning (see Figure 9.2).

- The Outlook mobile app goes a bit farther, communicating not just the connection status but the scope of missing data and the next steps upon connection. Without this in-app awareness, customers might misinterpret a lack of new data as a quiet inbox (see Figure 9.3).

- In a hands-free world, not all customers will be in range of visual indicators when connectivity issues occur. Amazon Echo devices do display a red indicator when a connection isn't present for a significant period of time. However, if customers attempt to interact during an outage, they will receive a spoken message along the lines of "I'm having trouble connecting to the internet right now. Please try again in a little while."

Ideally, you'll communicate the fact that there is a network issue, and not just that there's some generic problem. Without that specificity, how will your customers know to look into the problem and whether they can fix it? But while the figures contained here are visual, remember that your customer may not be in range of a visual indicator.

> **NOTE CATCH-404: PLANNING AHEAD**
>
> When planning for network connection errors, remember that all assets and error messages must be stored locally. All of Alexa's "connection error" messages are stored locally as MP3s since under those circumstances the text-to-speech service would not be available. Use the same logic for any mission-critical icons, graphics, videos, or texts that your customer might need during an outage.

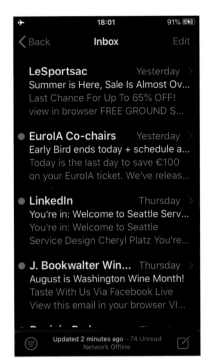

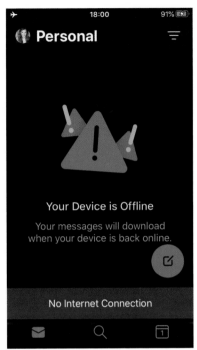

FIGURE 9.2
The Mail app in iOS (13.4.1)
includes a very small indicator that
network connectivity is down. Did
you spot it at first glance?

FIGURE 9.3
Microsoft's Outlook mobile app
(iOS) has evolved to include rich
information even during periods
of low connectivity, heading off
the panic that an artificially empty
inbox might cause.

Be Resilient

Modern devices are too sophisticated for brittle connection models.
In today's conditions, you must assume that your customers will
encounter intermittent, unstable, and insufficient connections on a
fairly regular basis—*especially* for any mobile or wearable devices.

In many cases, basic resiliency means some form of caching. Save
a record of any changes made locally until you have received firm
confirmation that those changes have been successfully posted to
your cloud service.

Avoid depending on regular heartbeats or communications. Build
systems that can "skip a beat" and still function within reason.

> A product that can handle unstable connections may find itself relevant in entirely new markets. Many products designed for use in the United States are impractical in developing countries and rural areas. Ask yourself: What new customers and markets could you encounter if you built in tolerance for low-connection scenarios?

Plan for an Offline Mode

There are plenty of conditions where customers will choose to disable their internet connections. Of course, the most common is the classic "airplane mode" scenario on planes. But beyond that scenario, consider these other situations:

- Your customer is abroad and can only access the internet from sporadic Wi-Fi connections.
- Your customer is affected by a widespread internet outage.
- Your customer can't connect to your service due to a problem on your end.
- Your customer is concerned about the safety or security of the connections available to them.
- Your customer is on a metered connection and must limit their access.

Offline modes seem like a "nice to have" until you consider how little you and your customer control their connections. An offline mode is an excellent way to handle the need for resiliency in low-bandwidth situations while also supporting your customers during fully interrupted communications.

Between Devices

Think back to the "R" ("relationship") in CROW from Chapter 2, "Capturing Customer Context." Odds are that your customer has relationships with many devices in their life. For all of the rich possibilities that exist on a single multimodal device, there's another continuum of experience beyond a 1:1 relationship between device and customer. How might your experience scale or stretch to accommodate the other device relationships that your customer deals with on a regular basis?

Multiple Devices, Single Environment

When the Amazon Echo was initially released, the beta nature of the release meant you could assume there was a single Echo device in each household. However, multidevice households began to emerge within the first year of the product's release. The arrival of more affordable devices like the Echo Dot compounded that trend.

But the combination of far-field microphones and multiple devices can be problematic without forethought. If a customer has multiple Alexa devices within earshot of each other, they will all respond unless a customer has set unique wake words for each device. Figure 9.4 depicts a floor map of a potential multi-Alexa household.

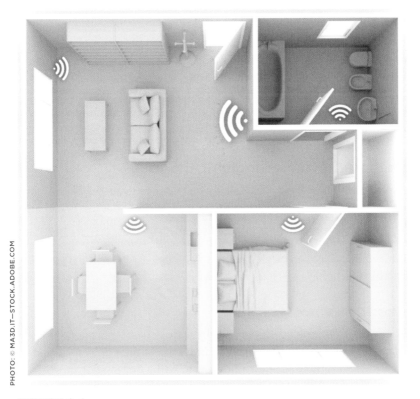

FIGURE 9.4

When similarly capable devices, like Alexa devices, share a small space, multiple devices may respond to a single request.

While the wake words are a valid strategy for now, this is not a graceful solution. It places all the burden on customers to identify the problem, learn about their options, and change the configuration.

A fairly unexplored solution for the multidevice, single-environment scenario is device arbitration. What if all of the devices that heard a customer could briefly confer and choose the best representative to lead the interaction? Metrics could include the following:

- **Recency:** Which device received the last interaction?
- **Multimodality:** Did a device recently receive a nonvoice input like touch?
- **Proximity:** Which device is closest to the customer?
- **Appropriateness:** Which device makes the most sense for the request?

Device arbitration does require that all devices be aware of each other and able to communicate in real time. But many networks can handle this sort of interaction with some engineering work. And device arbitration will become even more critical as people's devices become almost universally multimodal—and as cross-compatibility means more devices have the same feature set.

Multiple Devices, Single Scenario

An emerging best practice is to allow customers to suspend an interaction on one device and resume it on another device. When an experience moves beyond the boundaries of a single device, a great experience requires these devices to speak the same language. What information needs to be shared between devices? Where is it stored and for how long?

Cross-Device Notifications

Microsoft's Outlook products have long struggled with calendar notifications. Customers might leave their laptop at their desk to attend meetings with their phone and return to half a dozen stale meeting reminders piled up at their digital workstation.

While the intent behind the redundant cross-device notifications is good—a desire to ensure that customers don't miss any information—it often has the opposite effect. A pile of stale meeting reminders renders the signal-to-noise ratio too high, and customers begin to dismiss all of them or ignore the noisy channels.

When pushing notifications or content to customers with whom you interact on multiple devices, consider what signals you might interpret to determine the most appropriate device for that information.

- Do you know where the customer's last interaction was?
- Does the type of content limit the devices that may be relevant?
- Can and should you remove a notification on all platforms when it is dismissed from one device?

Directed Transitions

From time to time, your customer may want to intentionally transition from one device to another. Table 9.5 captures three of the most common intentional transitions.

TABLE 9.5 COMMON DIRECTED TRANSITION ARCHETYPES

Archetype	Motivation	Scenario	Affordance
Environmental	Your customer is moving between physical spaces or adapting to changing conditions.	At the end of a drive, you are directing a podcast from the car to continue in the home.	Google Assistant-enabled devices share a state so that a podcast can be resumed from anywhere.
Device Preference	Your customer has multiple ways to complete a task and prefers different devices for different tasks.	Instead of reaching for a remote control, a customer chooses to use their phone because it's the closest device at hand.	The Denon HEOS AV receiver allows customers to adjust settings from a mobile app, in addition to the remote control and the receiver's physical controls.
Device Suitability	Your customer's goals have changed, and they have hit the limits of capabilities on a particular device.	A customer is reviewing a spreadsheet on their phone, but switches to a PC to make changes to several formulas.	Microsoft Office products track the "latest position" in cloud documents. When picking back up on a new device, customers see "Welcome back! Here's where you left off."

The wake word fix for multidevice Alexa households doesn't scale. Of the limited wake word options, "computer" and "Amazon" are too common in ordinary speech to be truly useful. My household uses "computer" under duress to keep both downstairs devices (Alexa and computer) and an upstairs device (Echo) from responding at once, and it becomes a problem every time we watch an episode of *Star Trek*.

This is currently a "good problem to have." Certainly, this many devices in a small home is pushing the platform beyond system specifications. But as more devices become far-field, voice-recognition-enabled, many more mainstream consumers will run up against this kind of challenge without thoughtful design. Wake words won't always be enough.

Between People

The industry still tends to assume that devices are owned and operated by a single person. From tablets to mobile phones, this assumption is baked in at the most basic levels. But many of today's devices exist in shared environments.

Turn-Taking

Household use of devices like laptops, desktops, and smart speakers is fairly common. But when multiple people share a single device in a single account, state and context are often lost. To provide a more seamless personal experience in these shared scenarios, many apps and devices support the creation of multiple identities or profiles.

- How will customers know which profile is active?
- How will they switch profiles?

From the Chromecast to the Nintendo Switch, these sorts of directed transitions are becoming more commonplace. Keep an eye out for potential situations where your customers may expect or need the ability to swap devices midscenario. In many cases, these scenarios can be supported with a bit of early planning about the key elements of your customer's state that you'll need to share across all devices.

- Are there any settings or states that should be shared across profiles?
- Do you need different types of profiles? (A common split is adult versus child or minor profiles.)

Simultaneous Usage

While many devices now support multiple customer logins, there's rarely support for multiple people using a device as *equal peers*. For example, the Xbox family of devices allows multiple profiles to be logged in at once—but only one of those profiles sees their favorites, and that lead profile controls all app logins. If Aya is subscribed to Hulu but Jo is the "primary" person signed in, Jo won't be able to open Hulu without swapping profiles first.

Voice-controlled devices also struggle with simultaneous usage by multiple people. Humans tend to talk over each other, and their voices can be hard to distinguish. Furthermore, it's fairly easy for one customer to make a request from another customer's profile.

- How often are your customers in the room with other people when they interact with your experience?
- Are those customers attempting to collaborate or simply to make requests and commands?
- Do all customers share the same access levels? If not, how will your customers know whose access is being applied to a request?

Apply It Now

Unlike the desktop systems of yesterday, multimodal and cross-device experiences are wibbly-wobbly, timey-wimey adventures through space and time. Along those lines, the design for these experiences turns out to be similar to the TARDIS from *Doctor Who*: bigger on the inside than they appear.

Consider your customer's travel between:

- **Modalities:** Transitions between input modalities have a disproportionate impact on overall user experience.

  - Make every effort to minimize involuntary transitions.

  - Support voluntary transitions whenever possible.

  - Ensure that you "respond in kind" to your customer's requests.

- **Networks:** Your customer's connection to the internet is not a fixed point in space or time. Proactively consider network instability, failures, and insufficiency to ensure that you're not designing for a fictional customer context.

- **Devices:** Your customers don't exist in a vacuum, and they're surrounded by devices.

  - Will your device share its environment with similar devices? If so, how can you imbue your device or experience with situational awareness to lead to better experiences?

  - Will your customer interact with you on multiple devices? If so, how might you avoid spamming your customers with content across all the devices they're using?

  - When should you support a customer's intentional transitions between devices?

- **People:** Many of today's devices are shared in some way. When multiple people share a single device, personal preferences and context are often lost along the way.

  - How might support for different customer profiles make your experience more compelling?

  - When, how, and why would your customers switch profiles?

  - Are there any situations where multiple customers are using the device at the same time? How might you help them pool their resources and context?

Transitioning into the In-Between with Jen Cotton

Jen Cotton, Staff Designer for Google Nest, made her transition from responsive design to multimodal design at Amazon, where she worked as a Lead UX Designer on the Alexa platform for products like the Echo Show and Fire TV. We chatted about designing for the transitions between devices and input modalities.

Q: Transitions are a big part of moving between devices and fluid multimodality. Have you developed any best practices for dealing with certain types of transition?

I think interactions that start getting really complex start begging for touch, mouse, or five-way input. For example, search and browse using voice. Starting a search with voice is great, but voice to complete the browse intent is not great. Browse is done very well through remote, or using your finger to just swipe through a carousel of movies to watch.

Similarly, with complex inputs, like trying to fill all of the slots for a calendar invite, if you break it down into its tinier parts, you could use voice. But it's easier for you to pick a date on a calendar on a screen, because so much of your understanding about what the date is depends on visually seeing your whole week. Seeing the month of February and where the first of the month starts you know, "Oh, I mean Saturday the 15th." You don't always have the calendar pictured in your mind. There are interactions where visual cues help a customer complete the task quicker. So, why are we trying to force voice on a certain interaction when some things are just easier for people to see?

Q: Can you think of any best practices you apply to multimodal design on devices like smart speakers? Are there situations where you would strongly guide someone toward a different modality?

I strongly believe that there are clear best practices, such as the calendar and search/browse examples, where we should let you start with voice but give you a screen to complete the more complex interactions. I know that for smart speakers there isn't a screen, but the phone is a core part of that device. I really question whether we even have headless devices because there's so much of the mobile phone involved in headless devices. I'm like, "No, there is a head to those devices! It's just not attached to the body!"

What has been interesting is really digging into the neuroscience of how customers want to actually interact with things. Apple's Siri team did a really interesting research study about how people's own level of chattiness mirrors the level of chattiness that they prefer in a voice assistant. You should be able to start with voice and continue through to touch, but some customers just never want to even start with voice.

So still enable them to start a pathway *not* through voice, but through touch, through five-way (physical controls). There shouldn't be rigid doors we force people through. Because what we're learning is, "Not everyone wants to talk to their device. There are introverts and extroverts."

And so voice shouldn't be the only input method. We've helped a lot of people who have sight challenges, but what about the people with hearing challenges when we're over-relying on the audio track? How are they still included in the discussion?

I like to think of it not necessarily as fluid modality but as open modality. That it's not about a start and a stop, or a going back and forth between modalities. Rather, it's that any modality is an entry point—anything is open and available. And you can take any pathway to another modality.

Q: What's most interesting to you about the way designers are directing attention during transitions between devices and modalities?

What's been interesting is how voice has refocused us on the audio track. Using things like earcons or true silence as a way of attracting somebody to look at something. That a nonanswer is very compelling. To look over their shoulder and be like, "Wait, did I—did the thing hear me?" *Is* something needed from me? I find that that is really fascinating to me, when used appropriately and for noncritical information. The all-up audio track is a way of pulling a customer to a screen.

Another thing to consider is, if the customer is actually doing something—they're across the room washing dishes—and they want to start a calendar invite. Leave any slot that hasn't been filled with voice on the screen. Why force them into "You must finish! Because you've said you want to do something now, you must now finish that calendar invite *right now*." Just leave it up. They'll return to it or remind them if they forget. But don't force them to use voice where it's too difficult or force them to dry their hands, walk over to the device, pick through everything, and then pick up their task of washing the dishes.

 *Jen Cotton is a Staff Designer at Google Nest. Previously, Jen was a Lead UX Designer at Amazon, where she designed frameworks to scale Alexa across devices and co-founded the Alexa Design System team. She has worked at Twitter, New York Magazine, and Scripps Networks. Jen earned a Masters of Fine Arts degree in Design and Technology from Parsons School of Design and a Bachelor of Arts degree in International Relations and Creative Writing. She is @jencotton on Medium and Twitter.*

CHAPTER 10

Let's Get Proactive

People don't know what they don't know. While customers are engaged in their chosen activity, conditions in the world around them may change. When attention is a precious resource, what's the right way to provide information proactively?

In the era of the corded home phone, the bane of polite civilization was the telemarketing call during the dinner hour. Individuals or families attempting to enjoy a private, peaceful moment would find the atmosphere shattered by the shrill ring of an unexpected phone call. Many landline calls were unsolicited, but with no way to suppress those calls, these interruptions always came at the cost of the previous moment. It often felt nearly impossible to return fully to a state of relaxation or focus when one's heart rate and emotional response to an interruption had been engaged.

In Chapters 3 ("Understanding Busy Humans") and 4 ("Activity, Interrupted"), you learned how to reconcile ongoing activities with incoming interruptions, where the customer was generally driving the interruptions. As time passes, the need often arises to bring information to a customer's attention. This proactive interaction differs from the other interactions discussed thus far because the system, not the customer, is initiating the exchange. The more complex your system, the more intentional you must be about any interruptions to avoid overload, abuse, and frustration.

While the earliest proactive interactions were typically alerts about error conditions on the current device, notifications can now be used to keep customers up-to-date about conditions in experiences that span multiple devices and sensors. But the industry has pushed the envelope even further: proactive interactions are now increasingly used as a delivery mechanism for feature discovery and algorithmic insight. The resulting overload of notifications threatens to topple the utility of the entire interaction pattern, as customers cope with overwhelming volume.

As you grew into adulthood and learned more about the social contract in the culture where you were raised, you learned what kinds of information merited an interruption and when interruptions might not be welcomed at all. You'll need to apply similar patterns to your work on digital experiences. While the specific rules about appropriateness may vary, basic interruption patterns can generally be abstracted beyond cultural boundaries.

That said, not all proactive communications must interrupt customers. As you'll learn in the subsequent interview with Anna Abovyan at the end of this chapter, "nudges" are a more subtle way of bringing information to a customer's attention without immediately disrupting the flow.

Your product cannot maintain your customer's trust if you do not design a thoughtful system for proactive communication that provides the right information at the right time, without needlessly destroying a customer's focus and attention.

Taxonomy of Interruption

When you initially grapple with the need to interrupt a customer with information, you must first assess a number of questions about the information and the customer's relationship to that information. Notifications are far more than a simple sentence or phrase; they are interruptions, events, and opportunities for action.

- How time-sensitive is the information?
- Can the customer take action on this information? Is that action required or optional?
- Did the recipient of the information ask to be interrupted, as in an alarm?
- Did the recipient of the information give explicit consent to be interrupted with this information?
- Has the customer indicated a desire not to be interrupted?

It's unlikely that you'll be asking these questions for a single, isolated piece of information. In reality, you'll probably be tackling lots of chunks of information. The more situations you assess, the more you'll begin to identify patterns among the information being proactively surfaced. Your first step is to assemble the proposed information you may want to bring forward and to assess how relevant or useful the information is likely to be to your customer *in the moment of delivery.* Your model for this "information triage" may differ: perhaps it's more streamlined or segmented differently. But the examples shown in Table 10.1 are a good place to start.

TABLE 10.1 A TRIAGE MODEL FOR NEW CONTENT

Category	Description	Time Sensitive?	Action Required?
Urgent	If the customer ignores this interruption, it could cause physical, financial, or emotional harm to them.	Yes	Yes
Actionable	The customer needs enough information to make an informed decision or action out of context.	Usually	Usually
Scheduled	The customer asked to be interrupted at a specific time or when a specific event occurs.	Yes	Usually
Advisory	The customer receives contextual information relevant to the task at hand, but action is optional.	Yes	Optional
Informational	The system is providing content believed to be of interest to the customer, but the information is presented out of context.	Sometimes	No
Solicitation	The system is interrupting the customer without any indication the customer is interested in the content.	No	No

At the present moment, the most popular way to surface event-driven information to customers is a notification. These bursts of information are designed as an interruption and redirection of a customer's attention. But not all proactive interactions are necessarily interruptions in terms of attention—others wait patiently to be noticed.

Table 10.2 describes the most common proactive engagement affordances. Some systems may only need a few of these interruption categories. Others may need even more granularity than provided. But it's a good place to start.

These patterns are tools in your proactivity tool box. Unfortunately, there's no agreement about what to call any of this.

- *Notification* is used by both iOS and Android as a parent category.
- *Alert* is only used by iOS; Android calls these *heads-up notifications*.
- *Indicators* can be called *badges, app icons*, etc.
- Strangely, *nudges* are often considered outside the scope of a notification system.

TABLE 10.2 PROACTIVE ENGAGEMENT AFFORDANCES

Method	Description	Interrupts	Describes	Example
Alert	Attention-consuming event that indicates a specific problem, which generally requires action.	Yes	Sometimes	Dialog
Notification	A short burst of information interrupts the customer. If the interruption is missed, it is generally queued for later consumption.	Yes	Yes	Banner
Nudge	A change in UI state that presents actionable or helpful information to view at next convenience.	No	Yes	Inline text
Indicator	A UI component changes based on simple system status.	No	No	Badge

To further your understanding, examine some common experiences and the interruptions you might find there.

Example: Telephony

Consider apps and devices that support calling—from your smartphone's OS to a voice-over-IP (VOIP) app like Google Voice or Skype. For a few example proactive engagements via GUI from Apple's iOS, see Figure 10.1.

- **Incoming call:** Urgent content, alert affordance
  - Missing a phone call could cause emotional harm, financial harm, or in rare cases, physical harm. When a call comes in, action must be taken quickly, so the alert typically consumes all of a phone's screen.
- **Text message:** Actionable content, notification affordance
  - Text messages are typically surfaced with context like sender and content, so that the recipient can decide whether to take action.
- **Incoming voicemail:** Actionable content, notification affordance
  - A notification about voicemail can sometimes be accompanied by a "listen" action or the content of the message.

- **Missed calls:** Informative content, indicator affordance
  - A badge allows customers to see how many calls were missed, but more detail requires further engagement.
- **Validation error:** Advisory information, nudge affordance
  - Many well-designed forms bring validation errors to light inline, near the form field. If a customer fails to notice the issue before submitting, further notifications often take place.

FIGURE 10.1
The visual manifestation of notification banners in Apple's iOS.

NOTE NOTIFICATION SYSTEMS

Most of today's experiences use *notification* as an overarching term. While *proactive interaction* is a more accurate general term, you'll also see *notification system* used throughout the chapter to refer to the types of systems in use today.

Manifesting Proactive Interactions

Once you've determined which affordances are most appropriate for your needs, you must cross-reference that design with the capabilities of your chosen platform.

Many of you are designing for apps on mobile devices or smart speakers. In general, operating system platforms define a common system for proactive engagement into which developers must feed their content, in order to provide consistency to customers across dozens, if not hundreds, of their apps.

When working within an operating system or platform, you will *not* have control over many of the elements of your notifications. Figure 10.2 illustrates how iOS allows customers to determine where on the screen notification banners will display. Table 10.3 explores some of the elements typically controlled or brokered by an operating system when available.

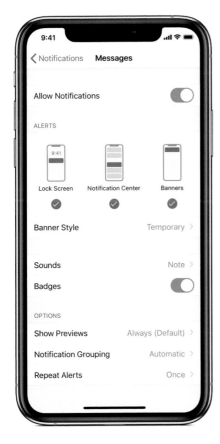

FIGURE 10.2
Configuration options for the placement of notification banners in Apple's iOS.

TABLE 10.3 COMMON PROACTIVE AFFORDANCES OFTEN CONTROLLED BY AN OPERATING SYSTEM

Feature	Description
App Badges	Visual indicators on an app's icon or tile that reflect the presence of unread notifications for that app
Banners	Interruptive overlays displayed when the customer is not inside the app generating a notification (Figure 10.3)
Cards	Self-contained content intended for display in a running feed (Figure 10.4)
Lock Screen Content	Ability for an app to display potentially sensitive content when the device is idle
Queue	Central repository for all unread notifications across multiple apps
Inline Content	Typically used for displaying validation information for specific form fields or controls
Consent	System-level settings for disabling notifications at the app level
Presentation	Amount of text supported, support for images, sound effects associated with notifications, etc.

PHOTO: AMAZON

FIGURE 10.3

Not all proactive visuals are in badge or banner form. The Echo Show uses a full-screen carousel, with each notification free to take up multiple lines and even display full-screen images.

FIGURE 10.4

The Google Nest Hub uses traditional "cards" to convey information proactively. In this example, the Hub is informing the customer about an upcoming calendar appointment.

As a designer of proactive interactions that interact within a larger operating system, you'll need to work with your development partners to build a deeper understanding of your app's role in that ecosystem.

- What notification types does the OS support and how do they map to your own patterns? Try to use the same terminology if possible.

- When and how is it appropriate to ask for consent to initiate interactions with your customers?

- What are the presentation options available to you for notifications? Who controls them?

- How does the device support action taken on a notification? Does it simply navigate to the app, or can actions be taken without going back to the app?

Proactivity from Scratch

If you have the opportunity to create proactive interactions from scratch, it's a great deal more work for both you and your development partners. Get started as early as possible and make sure to involve as many stakeholders as possible, because it is difficult to course-correct once implementation begins.

Your first step is to identify all of the output modalities you'll be using for your proactive interactions.

If you're operating under the assumption that all engagements include important information, it's a good idea to deliver your indicators over more than one output modality. Within each selected modality, you'll have to answer a variety of common questions, as explored in Table 10.4.

TABLE 10.4 DESIGN QUESTIONS FOR POTENTIAL PROACTIVE OUTPUT MODALITIES

Output Modality	Description
Visual	How much information will be displayed?
	How much space will be consumed?
	How long will the affordance be displayed?
	What form will the information take? Text? Images? Color?
Audio	What type of sound effect will you use? Subtle or disruptive?
	Will any information be delivered with a spoken prompt?
	Will the spoken prompt be followed by a call to action?
	What kind of question will you use to invite action? Yes/No questions? Multiple choice?
Haptic	Will you use a vibration to indicate the arrival of a notification?
	How intense will the vibration be? Will it be a pattern?
	Will you use vibration to indicate missed notifications? On what interval?
Kinetic	Will you use animation to indicate the arrival of a notification?
	How significant will the animation be?
	Will you use animation to indicate missed notifications?

In addition to these general questions, certain common considerations apply when working with the two most common modalities: visual and audio notifications.

Placement of Visual Affordances

Most notification systems display banners at the top of the screen, but this isn't always optimal. If your notification is covering critical app controls, you run the risk of false notification dismissals, or the opposite problem when customers accidentally take action because a banner faded away.

On Windows Automotive, our notification types had vastly different locations, depending on how much attention we wanted the driver to give the information. Placement varied depending upon whether the notification was critical (Figure 10.5), actionable (Figures 10.6 and 10.7), or informational (Figure 10.8).

FIGURE 10.5
Windows Automotive critical notifications were intended to safely supersede all other vehicle operations, and in testing, caused drivers to safely look for a place to pull over.

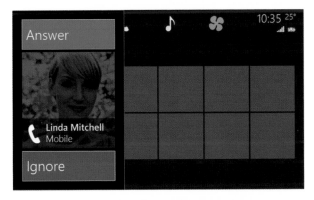

FIGURE 10.6
Since incoming calls were time-sensitive, I used color in addition to language and placement to differentiate them from other actionable notifications.

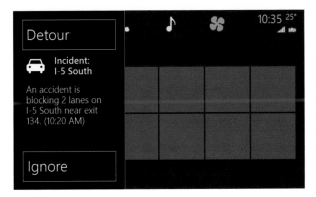

FIGURE 10.7
Because the vehicle might be in motion, our action buttons were physically separated, and were on the driver's side of the vehicle.

FIGURE 10.8
Informational
notifications were
placed specifically
to minimize distrac-
tion from the task at
hand. However, these
were eventually cut
entirely—see later in
this chapter.

When notifications are delivered on a touchscreen, particular care must be given to the size, location, and labeling of any actions provided. Most of us have been forced to wait for a notification banner to fade away because it was blocking a task we were trying to complete.

- How can a customer dismiss the affordance if it's blocking a task they were in the middle of completing?
- Are the options clear enough to take action before the notification times out?
- Are the controls too close, increasing the risk of unintentional error?

Privacy and Audio Notifications

Information delivered visually has limited range—only those with a sight line on the screen or display will be able to take in the content. Audio is far more interruptive and far less secure. Spoken notifications will be delivered to anyone and everyone in earshot of the device.

For information that does not require immediate action, consider limiting audio delivery to an earcon. This requires some training, as customers must learn what to do in response to the sound effect. However, if applied consistently, this involves a single moment of learning that can be applied to all future proactive interactions.

When crafting spoken notification prompts, only include information that is appropriate for general consumption. Amazon's Echo devices initially included the product name in delivery notifications, but that led to ruined holiday surprises. Now, the feature only announces general arrival status—the app must be used to either enable further spoken context, or to check which delivery was referenced.

Easing into Audio Notifications

According to Anne Treisman's attenuation theory,[1] the human brain is constantly discarding irrelevant acoustic information. However, the heuristic that humans use to discard irrelevant acoustic information will also attenuate—or tune into—information the brain determines is important. This whole decision-making process is instinctive, but it takes a bit of time. This has two effects on your audio designs:

- If your affordance does not seem relevant to a person's attenuation heuristic, it will be ignored completely. Low-volume sounds or generic prompts are risky.

- If your customer is not ready and waiting for an unexpected stimuli, they'll likely miss the first second or so of content.

This attenuation theory explains why most people instinctively say something to get another person's attention before telling or asking them something in real life.

Audio designers cope with this challenge in one of two ways:

- Use an earcon before the prompt as a means of gaining attention and to give the customer a second or two to adjust before beginning delivery of the notification content.

- Preface a spoken notification with introductory text, or start with a part of the content that won't be critical if missed.

> **NOTE** THE VALUE OF COGNITIVE PSYCHOLOGY
>
> Attenuation theory is just one of a myriad of insights that experienced designers can gain from cognitive psychology, which is included in some university design curricula. If you've never had the opportunity to study it, consider diving deeper into cognitive psychology to improve your craft.

---

1 "Attenuation Theory," Wikipedia, Wikimedia Foundation, last updated April 14, 2020, https://en.wikipedia.org/wiki/Attenuation_theory

Windows Automotive

During my time on Windows Automotive, I was responsible for designing our notification system. After conducting an extensive audit across all features, I identified four potential patterns (Table 10.5).

TABLE 10.5   INITIAL NOTIFICATION TYPES PROPOSED FOR WINDOWS AUTOMOTIVE

Type	Description	Examples
Critical	Fully modal interruption that requires acknowledgment prior to continued use of the system	Engine failure, tornado warning
Actionable	Time-sensitive interruptions that the driver can take action on while operating the vehicle	Incoming call, traffic detour
Informational	Important information that the driver cannot take action on while operating the vehicle	Tire pressure, maintenance due
Confirmation	Feedback when a task (particularly verbal tasks) is completed	Radio station change

We conducted extensive testing on each of these notification types in driving simulators with eye trackers to verify that they accurately conveyed the desired information, allowed for the correct or expected responses, and did not distract the driver. *Distraction* was defined using NHTSA guidelines, which at the time specified that no one glance away from the road could be longer than 2 seconds, and no task could require more than a total of 12 seconds of eyes off the road across all glances.

The critical notifications had exactly the desired effect: they attained immediate driver attention, and drivers successfully managed to safely cope with the situation (usually by pulling over as soon as it was safe to do so).

However, testing resulted in changes to the design for actionable notifications. Originally, some actionable notifications supported three or more actions: for example, incoming calls originally allowed customers to answer, reject, or send a text message. But actionable notifications were also delivered and actionable via voice UI, and setting those interactions up for rapid success meant a change to the design. Instead, actionable notifications only supported a positive action (taking a call, accepting a detour) and a dismissive action (rejecting a call, ignoring a suggestion).

Informational notifications were the biggest surprise, however. In paired usability studies (spouses or friends), we got an extra peek at what went on in a driver's head when they were interrupted by information they couldn't act on.

> PASSENGER: "Honey, it says the tire pressure is low."

> DRIVER: "What does it want me to do about that? Does it want me to pull over? Why would it tell me that now?"

We quickly determined that it was inappropriate to interrupt drivers with information that did not require an immediate response. As a result, we cut the Informational category of notifications entirely. Instead, we moved that information into a post-drive summary of events and new information that accumulated during the drive.

Interruption and Action

While the presentation of a proactive interaction is important, the behaviors during and after these events are more complicated. Alerts and notifications are interrupting events, and you should specify the interrupting behaviors in the same interruption matrix you built for your activities. Table 10.6 presents an example with two notification types: scheduled and urgent.

NOTE PARTIAL EXAMPLE ONLY

Some of the columns from the examples in Chapter 4 have been hidden for simplicity. These are also not intended as absolute recommendations for behavior—in fact, you'll likely need to change multiple cells in this example, even if your activities and notifications were exactly the same.

TABLE 10.6 EXAMPLE INTERRUPTION MATRIX WITH ACTIVITIES AND PROACTIVE INTERACTIONS

Active/ Interrupting	Discrete	Music	Scheduled/ Notification	Urgent/Alert
Discrete	Cancel previous response.	Continue discrete activity with music in background.	Cancel activity. Deliver earcon and banner.	Cancel activity. Deliver earcon, banner, and spoken prompt.
Music	Turn volume down during response.	Switch songs.	Continue music. Deliver earcon and banner.	Continue music. Deliver earcon, banner, and spoken prompt.
Phone Call	Deliver response at full volume.	Play music during call.	Continue call. Deliver banner only.	Continue call. Deliver sound and banner or call waiting UI.
Scheduled/ Notification	Deliver earcon and banner until activity ends, then prompt.	Deliver earcon, banner, and spoken prompt.	Wait until previous notification is dismissed.	Dismiss previous notification.
Urgent/ Alert	Dismiss notification and begin new activity.	Continue notification with music in background.	Do not cancel previous notification. Deliver earcon only.	Wait until previous notification is dismissed.

After the Moment

While it's easy enough to ignore audio affordances, customers should be able to dismiss visual affordances without taking any other action, whether it's clearing badges or swiping away a banner.

If a proactive affordance is dismissed, ensure that your system performs as expected.

- Most customers expect music to either continue during a notification or resume immediately after a dismissed or ignored notification.

- When a customer takes action on a notification or alert, consider whether it will replace the previous activity. Will your customer lose data if the previous activity is canceled? Can the previous activity be resumed?

Offering multiple custom actions for any given notification or alert makes rapid action harder and increases the risk of human or system error. Instead, a common best practice is to simply identify a single action that can be taken outside of the app. Many operating systems assume a single custom action in addition to the ability to open the app:

- Single tap opens the app to the applicable page
- Long press, double tap, or swipe to take a specific action without opening the app
- Swipe or close button to dismiss the notification

And don't forget that customers will still want some form of confirmation for nontrivial or destructive actions taken, even if they're taken from a notification queue outside the app. Since this complicates matters, it's generally advisable to avoid permitting destructive actions in response to notifications.

Cross-Device Considerations

Proactive interactions are especially challenging for cross-device scenarios. Do you use Microsoft Outlook for your daily work? Consider this scenario:

- You leave your laptop at your desk in the office, taking only your cell phone.

- Your meeting reminders appear as expected, 15 minutes prior to each meeting, and you manage to get everywhere on time.

- But when you finally get back to your desk and start trying to focus, Outlook flashes to get your attention.
- You switch over, only to find a list of meeting reminders for meetings you've already attended (see Figure 10.9).
- You clear the whole list, not noticing that an upcoming meeting also got dismissed . . . and 30 minutes later, you miss that meeting because you'd dismissed a raft of notifications out of hand.

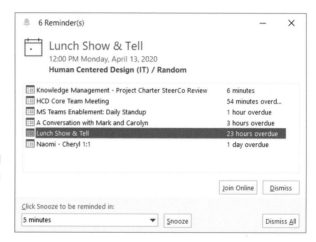

FIGURE 10.9
Lack of situational awareness means some notifications feel redundant when we've seen them elsewhere before, like this common Outlook logjam.

Many modern apps still treat each device's notification queue as distinct, unconnected entities. This leads to rapid customer fatigue. Not only does your customer need to think about all of these notifications, but they also have to ascertain which ones are redundant and which ones bring new meaning or value!

If you're implementing notifications for a multidevice ecosystem, reduce the likelihood of customer fatigue with a few simple frames.

Draw from a Single Pool of Notifications

If you create separate queues for each device, you'll run the risk of either notifying on the wrong platform *or* requiring customers to deal with the same notification multiple times.

> **NOTE** **PLATFORM-SPECIFIC NOTIFICATIONS**
>
> If a notification is only valid or actionable on certain platforms, tag it with metadata so that you can hide it when irrelevant, rather than maintaining separate queues or displaying it everywhere.

Act Once, Update Everywhere

Honor customer actions. If a notification is addressed in one place, the default behavior should be to consider that particular notification as being addressed unless strong information indicates the content didn't land, or perhaps changed. For example, Alexa notifications are dismissed on all devices when dismissed on one.

Be Predictable and Transparent

Perhaps it was an arbitrary decision to have Outlook appointment reminders ring 15 minutes before the next meeting. But since it is the default behavior, the presence of those reminders allows you to infer a great deal from your environment without checking the phone at all.

- When phones buzz around the :15 or :45 mark in a meeting, that's an ambient signal of the time without ever looking at a phone.

- If your device buzzes at :15 or :45, you can generally assume you have another meeting coming up without ever looking at the phone. For myself, I tend to check my schedule if a notification comes in on the quarter hour or hour.

This sort of ambient signal can help folks cope with a "noisy" notification environment without being glued to their phones. Choose your notifications wisely, and clearly communicate the conditions in which a customer can expect to receive them.

Match the Content Delivered to the Delivery Device

Just because a notification is available in multiple places doesn't mean the manifestation has to be identical. Perhaps you will only provide high detail on platforms where a notification is actionable. The information presented in different contexts might vary.

On my phone, a meeting notification is most useful if it emphasizes the room number since I'm likely to be checking en route. On my desktop, the context of the meeting is more important since I might be making a judgment call about whether a meeting warrants interrupting my workflow.

Advanced Features

When you design for a system that supports multiple interruptions, you are engaging in systems design. You are identifying a standard set of events that will likely impact every aspect of your product or experience. As with any system design problem, designers must forge strong developer partnerships to be successful. Notification systems are no exception.

Table 10.7 explores some of the specific features you may need to champion to drive a world-class experience.

TABLE 10.7   FEATURES THAT IMPROVE THE ROBUSTNESS OF
A NOTIFICATION SYSTEM

Feature	Description
Dynamic Notifications	It allows a single notification to change with time as updated information comes in, as opposed to flooding a notification center with multiple distinct events.
Upstream Updates	When a customer takes action on a notification, that notification should be cleared or marked as "read" across any devices or experiences where it appears.
Scalable Notifications	The ability to specify different content for different output technologies within a single notification—for example, a long prompt for a smart speaker versus a short prompt and a card for screen-enabled experiences.
Notification Management	If you're using notifications like voice mail—that is to say, as a place for knowledge stored over hours or days—you'll need to provide granular controls for how to replay, flag, and delete specific notifications.
Quiet Hours (Do Not Disturb)	Customers can choose to suppress most or all notifications by specifying a recurring window of time, or in the moment, by toggling the feature on or off.

Apply It Now

Are you feeling overwhelmed by the complexity of system design for proactive interactions? Take it one step at a time. The best way to start designing a notification system is by conducting an audit. Meet with all functional stakeholders who might want to deliver notifications and listen to what they have to say.

It's important to frame these initial conversations as a discussion about *potential* notifications. It's incumbent on designers, with their broader perspectives, to help keep notification systems useful, as opposed to a battleground for unwanted discoverability hacks.

With every stakeholder group, ask them to define:

1. What information might arise that could be of interest to a customer?
2. How time sensitive is that information?
3. What action, if any, can the customer take when confronted with the information?
4. What is the minimum amount of information a customer needs in order to take action on a specific notification?
5. What's the worst impact this notification could have if it is delivered at an inopportune time?

Armed with a single list of potential notifications from all parties, you can begin the process of sense-making:

1. Sort all potential notifications into categories. Identify new categories or eliminate common categories as appropriate.
2. Depending on the scale and complexity of the notification needs, discuss advanced features like a centralized queue or dynamic notifications with your development partners.
3. In parallel, formulate a design and research plan to assess potential notification affordances based on the list of potential notifications and their categorizations.

No matter what, it's critical that you consider the customer's activity and frame of mind when deciding how and when to interrupt them with information. To avoid a future where every living room is a living billboard, you must stand firm against stakeholders placing feature discoverability over the human experience.

Nudging the Right Way with Anna Abovyan

Anna Abovyan (Head of UX at 3M | M*Modal) works to bring order to the chaotic world of cross-device multimodal experiences in the field of medical documentation. Anna brings an analytical approach to the table that helps her make sense of this chaos. After seeing her recent talks, I was delighted to sit down with Anna to hear her take on proactivity, especially in challenging environments.

Q: In one of your talks, you said the best notification is the one that's never shown. Can you provide an example of the logic you use to make sure that notifications don't trigger unless they're absolutely needed?

I think timing is the biggest aspect that we talk about. I gave an example in a talk: You write an email, and you need a signature. It's silly to prompt somebody for a signature when they've just said "hello."

A realistic example is I work in medical documentation. And what physicians are doing, they're sitting there and dictating plus typing. This is where multimodality comes in. They're dictating, typing, clicking checkboxes, they're going through constructing a story about a patient. We start noticing early on that they said something that is incomplete. They might describe a disease in incomplete terms. They might say that the patient is diabetic, but they did not describe any complications. There is an entire industry that is very much interested in doctors specifying every single thing that is happening to the patient. As in, "This is diabetes type 2, these are the complications, it has comorbidities…" A lot of complexities in there. And, of course, there's this engineering temptation to say, "Well, if I'm going to be prompting the physician to tell me more about this diabetes—if I can—the earliest I can detect it, I'm going to show off! I'm going to prompt them right at that moment just so they don't forget."

So it's this kind of checklist mentality. And people often start talking about the *Checklist Manifesto* (Atul Gawande), saying "he told us so." The way our team pushes back on that is to say, "You know what? It is really frustrating if you already had something in your brain you were going to say." The perspective on our side is to say, "Okay, this is fine that we know this. Can we just hold this information in our brain?" And instead of bombarding people with that prompt as early as possible—as tempting as it can be—can we wait until we're fairly sure that this is going to slip through? It results in fewer notifications, which is great for everybody. It results in less of a perception of our system as a notification. We actually don't like that term to begin with. I would prefer to call it a "nudge." And not even talk about it as an alert or a notification that has to be addressed.

I think there's this assumption that a notification has to be an interruption. Because I think that's just what we're used to. But it doesn't have to be. And I think that's where I think differentiation between a nudge and a notification comes from. The hope is that these kinds of notifications help you do the task you're already doing. The notifications are not the point. Your task is the point. The notifications are helping you guide and do that task better. The hope is that they're not interrupting you at all. And they're just there for you to see when you're ready to see them.

Q: Do you ever try to move the doctor's attention from one device to another?

We thought that we were in the business of directing attention early on. We said, "Wow, we really need people to see these nudges. We're developing all of this expensive natural language processing. And we need people to see them as soon as possible." Obviously, there's a lot of research into how animating objects are grabbing attention. And maybe properly timed animation could help us out.

Physicians are trying to input information into these electronic health record systems. And we're dealing with the modality of speech, so they're talking. We're talking about long interactions. So they're telling a story. They're most of the time thinking of their next sentence, or their next five, and how to phrase them. So there's a lot of recall happening.

We set up a series of usability studies where we were studying various aggressive animations to see what would actually catch their eye. And basically, our conclusion was that nothing would. We literally flashed obnoxious colors in front of people, on and off. And they just would not notice it when they were looking straight at the screen, because their brain was in a different headspace!

So I think we sort of walked ourselves away from this thinking that we needed to be grabbing attention. And it turned into providing value—being so judicious in picking these nudges that they found value in them. And that they would seek them out proactively on their own, if that makes sense.

Q: How about the expected follow-up? Do you ever nudge people without intending immediate action?

I think we're finally developing a more nuanced approach to this and coming up with heuristics: no, not every nudge needs to be actionable.

Sometimes, it's more helpful, and maybe more powerful, to give information to say, "I know there's some complex decision-making that needs to take place at this point." My job is going to be to present you with information to help make that decision. I don't know what the decision will be, because there are many opportunities.

But, you know, I'm not the decision-maker. I'm the person who slips in a piece of paper with additional information you may not have thought of. Presenting certain actions in that case might actually be leading. Which is, in itself, a problem in the healthcare space.

We send doctors to medical school for a reason. And they're the ones who will have a more subtle understanding. And I think it's maybe a little bit pretentious on our part to assume that we have all the information. First of all, it's never true. You never interoperate with all the systems around you. But also, I think it defers the power to the human, which is the right thing to do.

 *Anna Abovyan spends her days bringing order and humanity to the chaotic world of clinical documentation at 3M | M*Modal. She is interested in multimodal interfaces, graceful human-computer interactions, and thoughtful applications of artificial intelligence. Anna holds a degree in Applied Mathematics and Informatics from the Russian-Armenian State University.*

Breathe Life into the Unknown

A reductive approach to traditional desktop and app design has generally been to wireframe, iterate, and produce. But today's multimodal experiences are defined by their lack of boundaries. Customer choice—whether it's choice of context, choice of device, or choice of modality—leads to compound possibilities.

Imagination becomes just as important as intuition when exploring the design roads less traveled. As children, you played games and invented hypothetical worlds with very little context. In some cases, those games helped you explore who you wanted to be. It's now time to deploy imagination and creativity to help you explore what you want your experience to be—and perhaps more importantly, to help you explore what your experience *must never become*.

Opti-Pessimism: Explore the Extremes

For decades, designers encouraged their product team partners to embrace the "happy path"—to focus on the scenarios that applied to 80% of customers and to spend comparatively little time on designing for the remaining 20%.

This "one-size-fits-most" perspective made sense in a world where we weren't getting anything right: if you're only going to have resources to nail one or two scenarios, of course those should be the most common scenarios!

But times have changed. Some problems have been solved so thoroughly that they've been commoditized. For example, take blogging platforms—between WordPress and Medium (along with many smaller scale systems), you no longer need to spend precious cycles on common problems. While human capacity for digital impact is increased thanks to well-designed frameworks, the potential risk associated with that growing impact is increasing daily.

Decades ago, most product teams assumed that the worst thing that could happen to their customers was frustration or lost time. Yet even then, some "edge cases" carried dire consequences. In one of our first usability tests on what became Microsoft's System Center Configuration Manager 2012, a customer recalled the previous 2007 version of the product. "If I right-click on "Refresh" and my hand slips? That's a résumé-generating event." He'd be fired because that accidental slip could cause the deletion of an entire company's network of managed devices. "Refresh" was right next to "Delete" (see Figure 11.1).

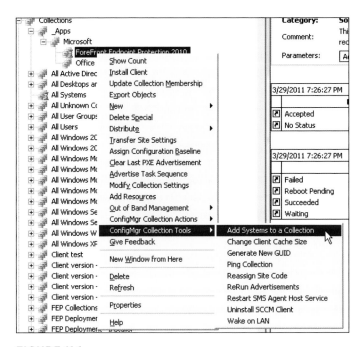

FIGURE 11.1
System Center Configuration Manager 2007 managed massive
networks, but Delete and Refresh were just pixels apart.

If your product caused a human being to lose their job, how would
you feel? Can you go to sleep at night knowing that despite your best
intent, a seemingly innocuous product caused lasting harm? Would
you justify it by saying it was an unfortunate but isolated event?

The trouble is that there's really no such thing as an isolated "edge
case" in a world where experiences are targeting millions—if not
billions—of people at a time, and becoming indispensable in the process. For example, let's consider a piece of software that can "brick"
a phone, rendering it permanently inoperable. However, 99.99% of
customers will never experience the worst of this error.

- For a small-scale app with one million unique customers, that
  error will still affect 10,000 people.

- What if that same harmful error affected all active iPhones?
  There are 900 million iPhones, so nine million customers would
  be impacted by this harmful bug.

With such a large scale of potential human impact, it's no longer
enough to hide behind good intent or to be satisfied with a "go fast

and break things" mentality. It's critical to use your advanced reasoning skills and creativity—qualities you most certainly possess as a designer—to try and foresee potential problems in advance.

In his book *Future Ethics*, Cennydd Bowles describes this as "moral imagination": "We can also pull bias out by the roots by getting better at spotting and addressing unintended consequences and externalities. For this, we need moral imagination: the ability to dream up and morally assess a range of future scenarios."

To avoid (as much as possible) causing unintended harm in these days of incredibly high stakes, I advise adopting a new mindset from the beginning of your projects—a mindset I call "opti-pessimism" for short. It's not rocket science, and plenty of other folks already think this way. It's just a helpful mnemonic to help shake you of the old binary pessimist versus optimist divide.

Opti-pessimistic thinking is rooted in two theoretical questions:

- What are the worst consequences if your product is successful?
- What are the best ways you can respond to an unforeseen major problem?

Opti-pessimistic thinking can be distilled into four general guidelines you can apply to any design process. Each guideline pairs with a series of starter prompts (Table 11.1) to help you explore both the best-case and worst-case impacts of your proposed solution.

Wherever you can, begin to build your opti-pessimistic muscles and flex them early in the design process. The bigger your experience, the more critical these thought exercises become as part of the product design process.

Dr. Casey Fiesler, director of the University of Colorado Boulder's Internet Rules Lab, echoes this advice for product designers in her own work: "Innovate like an optimist, prepare like a pessimist. Don't feel too constrained by having to think about bad things that can happen. It's so important to do that kind of speculation early in the process. Ethics should be early and often in technology design."

LEARN MORE

To hear more from Dr. Fiesler about ethics, speculative design, and digital communities, see her interview in Chapter 15, "Should You Build It?"

TABLE 11.1 OPTI-PESSIMISTIC CHALLENGE QUESTIONS

Guideline	Questions
Consider the human context.	What are the worst conditions in which your product will be used?
	Why would a customer choose to use this?
	How will this make the world better?
	How might this make the world worse?
	What are customers doing without your product?
Design for the best case.	If your product is wildly successful, what other platforms might your customer want to interact with?
	If customers love your product so much that they use it for an extended period of time, how does the relationship change over time?
	What if customers outside your target audience want to use your product? Who is excluded, and how could you include them?
Plan for the worst case.	What does failure look like, and how does it affect your customers?
	How could your project harm your customer?
	How will customers be affected if you have to discontinue your product?
	How will customers abuse your product?
Be ready to adapt in the moment.	What signals might you watch for that your product is not working as intended?
	What's the riskiest part of this project?
	What are your awareness gaps?
	Do you have fail-safes in place that allow you to adjust performance in the field?
	What resources are available to make fixes after launch when unintended problems arise?

There are some design aids out there that can help you with further prompts as you explore an opti-pessimistic mindset. One of my favorites is Artefact's "Tarot Cards of Tech" (Figure 11.2). These cards, which are free to download, use, and print, depict personas that are likely to challenge your product's boundaries. Use tools like these to help jump-start your creativity when exploring the opti-pessimistic prompts above. The more creative you are up front, the more problems you may prevent before they occur.

Think of opti-pessimism like Schrodinger's Glass: your project's metaphorical glass can be both half-empty and half-full *at the same time.*

FIGURE 11.2

Artefact's Tarot Cards of Tech depict personas like the BFF—two friends being connected, or disconnected—by your app's functionality. You can download a printable set at **http://tarotcardsoftech.artefactgroup.com/**

Storyboards: Bring Customer Context to Life

Without storyboards, the small things you know about your customer through observation remain trapped in your mind, as opposed to bringing life to your customer's needs in the mind of your stakeholder. Details like the following:

- Your customer's phone is in another room or buried in their bag.

- A customer's hands are frequently full when unlocking a door.

- The lights are out, and your customer can't find a switch or remote.

These seemingly minor details are critical because they justify the added expense of multimodal products. For decades, existing experiences have been "good enough." The addition of multimodality often provides alternative ways to solve an *already-solved* problem. It's often hard to justify spending money to solve a solved problem without the added context storyboards provide.

The Role of Storyboards

Storyboards are (often rudimentary) visual sequences that can play a disproportionate role in your product design process for your entire team. What can storyboards do for you?

- **Set the stage.** Provide all stakeholders with a common understanding of the current customer problem, the context in which your product will be used, and the effect you hope your product will have on your customer's life.

- **Start the debate.** Generate discussion among your team about the biggest risks, weaknesses, and interaction cliffs your product faces. Make sure that you're investing in the biggest challenges early on.

- **Gain support for the cause.** Earn the support of stakeholders by helping them to empathize with your customer and the problems your product is trying to solve—possibly helping them project themselves into the customer's shoes. Convince them that your proposed product will satisfy a genuine customer need or desire.

- **Maintain a shared vision throughout your project team.** Because storyboards are inherently narrative and rich in context, they can be reviewed without a formal presentation whenever a new team member comes aboard, or whenever the team needs to reset shared understanding. On the Echo Look, the storyboards I created for our initial product pitch and preproduction work were maintained as a shared product vision through the shipping of our v1 product.

What Makes a Good Storyboard?

When you picture "good storyboards," do you immediately think of a behind-the-scenes vignette for a Hollywood film? Try to reframe your thinking: a good design storyboard isn't about polished visuals. What will make or break your storyboard is the choices you make about what scenes you include in your story—and what you choose to leave out. Consider the following four guidelines to maximize your chances for storyboard success.

1. The story should be *focused on one or more users of the product*, not the product itself. If you don't know who your user is, it's too soon for storyboards.

2. The storyboard should have one or both of these two goals:

   • Depict the *specific context* of a customer scenario.

   • Draw attention to potential *interaction cliffs and pain points* (see Figure 11.3).

FIGURE 11.3

Even extremely rough storyboards can help you explore the design around potential issues, like these frames that probe a potential experience issue when important information comes in during a phone call.

3. The storyboard should not go into exceptional technical detail about the solution. As an extremely rough guideline, if you're showing more than three screens in a row, you may be centered too much on the solution as opposed to the customer. Try taking a step back and representing some of those concepts with more abstract imagery or iconography.

4. The user's context usually changes over the course of the story. Who else enters the scenario? Does the location change? If the user stays in one place the whole time and nothing changes, then you're better off doing single environment sketches, not a storyboard.

Crafts, Not Arts: Just-Enough Storyboarding

A fine arts degree is not a prerequisite for product design story-boarding. Your storytelling skills are more important than your art skills, especially at the early stages. Figure 11.4 shows a simplistic series of storyboards I sketched for a cross-device scenario on Windows Automotive.

FIGURE 11.4

Raw Post-it Note + Sharpie storyboard frames I used to hash out a multi-environment, connected-device scenario for Windows Automotive. Just enough to tell the story quickly.

Even if you're a trained artist, presentations of overly polished storyboards might actually backfire. More than once, I've seen a stakeholder recoil because an overly polished (or overly optimistic) storyboard creates the impression that the idea is beyond their input or feedback.

One of the greatest storyboarding challenges is knowing when to stop: when do you have *just enough* detail to move forward? My storyboards weren't successful because they were perfect. They were successful because they were ready when we needed them, and they told our story effectively and honestly in a way that invited discussion.

Techniques for Efficient Product Storyboarding

Try to follow these techniques for efficient product storyboarding:

- **Stay abstract.** You don't actually want to draw realistic humans. The level of abstraction actually has an effect on your audience's ability to project themselves into the story. Only ascribe gender, features, and emotion when relevant to the story. One exception to this guideline is when you're telling a very specific story about a real customer.

LEARN MORE

Many comic book artists have been leveraging psychology for decades, using simplistic renderings to increase engagement. For more about this effect, check out Scott McCloud's classic book *Understanding Comics*.

- **Plan your characters.** It pays to figure out in advance who will be appearing in your storyboards, and to do a bit of visual character design for each. As much as possible, look to be inclusive of gender, race, and disability status in your stories as appropriate. Planning this visual language up front will save you plenty of rework later.
- **Reject perfectionism.** In the context of product design, you don't want to get attached to your storyboards. "Success" with a storyboard often means a discussion that leads to massive changes. Limit the time you spend on any one frame and live with your smaller mistakes unless they truly change the meaning of the frame.

If you use pencils, you'll probably get stuck in an eraser loop making things "just right." In most cases, I storyboard directly with a Sharpie, forcing me to accept minor mistakes rather than waste additional time.

- **Shortcut shamelessly.** Find ways to save additional time so that you can focus on getting the story right, not the individual frames. The less time you spend, the less you'll become attached to the deliverable over the design.
  - Use photos for reference when sketching environment layouts and poses.
  - Copy and reuse common poses, like a customer using a phone on their couch.
  - Use photos for backdrops, but apply Photoshop filters to simplify and abstract them (Figure 11.5).

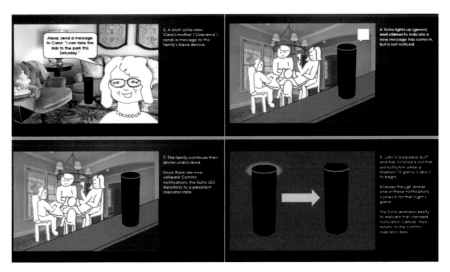

FIGURE 11.5

Storyboards I created for a major milestone in our work on Alexa Notifications. I wanted the boards to match the fidelity of the device images, so I opted for a sketch/photo hybrid. Stock photos of people didn't offer continuity.

Storyboards in product design are *not* fairy tales. They are reflections of human experience, both good and bad. If you think your product is going to run up against risks, adoption resistance, or other challenges, use storyboards to tell that story.

A common mistake is to assume that your stakeholders—especially high-ranking ones—want to see only happy paths and happy faces. Consider how your stakeholders got to their roles: by hard-won experience. Their value is to ask hard questions and to connect you to the resources you need to solve big problems. How can they connect you if you don't lead with the big problems? How can they trust you if you're not bringing them a realistic depiction of the problem space?

Use your storyboards to start the right discussions and to bring the difficult issues to the forefront. On the Echo Look, my very first storyboards tackled the out-of-box experience specifically because we believed the need for a power plug and for image calibration might cause nontrivial problems (see Figure 11.6). Putting the tough stuff on paper allowed us to weigh our options and mitigate some issues proactively. Ironically, the attempt to invalidate the idea ended up providing a path forward!

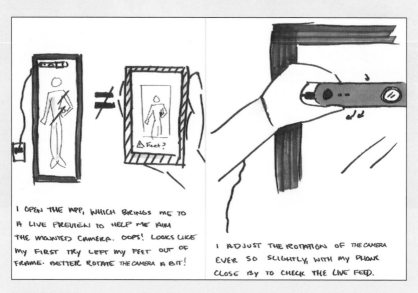

I OPEN THE APP, WHICH BRINGS ME TO A LIVE PREVIEW TO HELP ME AIM THE MOUNTED CAMERA. OOPS! LOOKS LIKE MY FIRST TRY LEFT MY FEET OUT OF FRAME. BETTER ROTATE THE CAMERA A BIT!

I ADJUST THE ROTATION OF THE CAMERA EVER SO SLIGHTLY, WITH MY PHONE CLOSE BY TO CHECK THE LIVE FEED.

FIGURE 11.6

An excerpt from the first Echo Look storyboard, which tackled our concerns about the form factor via the out-of-box experience.

Playing Pretend: Put Yourself in Their Shoes

Humans are tactile and experiential creatures. Regardless of whether you agree with the theory that mirror neurons activate equally whether we watch a task or do it ourselves, it cannot be denied that experiential learning will always be a fundamental part of the human experience.

As the experiences you design become more expansive and immersive, it becomes more important to go beyond the boundaries of a sketch or a spec to evaluate the real impact your experience will have. In some cases, designers hesitate to pursue these early project, low-fidelity techniques for fear of being judged as silly or wasteful. But when it comes to exploring the cutting edge of multimodal experiences, serious play is serious business. It's time to channel your inner schoolchild.

Dioramas

Once you've used storyboards to identify the core customer scenario, there are a few common situations where you need to add dimensionality to your early explorations.

- **Mixed or virtual reality:** In cases where your experience relies on aspects of the physical world like your customer's height, their belongings, or their surroundings, scale prototyping in physical space can reveal potentially dangerous assumptions.

- **Multidevice and Internet of Things scenarios:** In situations where multiple devices may act in concert, or will exist within close proximity, 3D dioramas can tease out some of the more complicated spatial relationships. Where is your customer and how many devices are within reach? Are any of your devices so close that they might interfere with each other?

- **Service design:** When your customer's experience includes multiple touchpoints within a single environment, dioramas can be a critical step in your design process. Where are the pathways? The bottlenecks? Is the signage visible? What other affordances are visible?

There's no right or wrong way to create dioramas. Use whatever materials are convenient. Table 11.2 offers a few supply ideas.

TABLE 11.2 DIORAMA SUPPLIES FOR DESIGN EXPLORATION

Use	Examples
Walls and Surfaces	Cardboard
	Card stock or manila folders
	Building blocks (LEGO, Mega Bloks, etc.)
	Foam core
Objects and Shapes	Modeling clay (Sculpey, Play-Doh)
	Pipe cleaners
	Origami paper
	Doll accessories
	3D pen printed objects
People	Gaming miniatures
	Board game pieces
	Fashion dolls or action figures

Bodystorming

In situations where your experience moves through physical space, it's a valuable and important part of the process to explore those physical ramifications viscerally. Even if your interactions are completely imagined, you'll potentially discover and challenge unspoken assumptions.

Mime

In some cases, bodystorming bears resemblance to mime work. Your goal is to act as if you're interacting physically with your experience. Designers who are working in mixed or virtual reality often need to bodystorm with mime. (See the interview with mixed reality leader Craig Fox later in this chapter for an example.) As with many theatrical techniques, mime can be utilized without training, but it inevitably improves with practice.

When I teach basic mime as part of an introductory improvisation class, I have the group wander around a space and imagine an infinite void just behind them. I call out specific prompts (a very valuable object, a heavy object, a sticky object, etc.) and ask folks to pull out an object that meets that description. Each time, I ask students to pay attention to the following qualities of the object:

- **Weight:** You can "experience" weight in mime by engaging the muscles that would bear the weight, and in some cases, changing your posture.

- **Size:** The larger an object is, the more the rest of your body will have to compensate for it when you share space with it.
- **Grip and Texture:** Is there an affordance for grip? If not, where would you naturally attempt to pick up the object? How does the texture change your willingness to hold it?
- **Quality:** Is the object fragile? Is it precious to you? Your attitude and awareness of the object's status will change how you interact with it.

Props and Staging

In other cases, the success of bodystorming may be amplified with some extra work to simulate the environment in which the experience will take place. When increasing the fidelity of your bodystorming in this way, the key is to identify those environmental elements that are most likely to alter the experience in some way. Table 11.3 provides some ideas for planning a bodystorming session.

TABLE 11.3 PLANNING PROPS AND STAGING FOR BODYSTORMING

Category	Details	Examples
Support	What physical elements might your customer rely upon for support? This also includes surfaces the customer uses to support their belongings.	Chairs Walls Railings Tables Mobility aids
Encumbrances	What might be holding your customer back? What might slow them down or reduce their capacity to interact?	Seat belts Restraints Purses and backpacks Helmets Held objects (phone, etc.)
Obstacles	What might interrupt a customer's ability to move freely during critical parts of the experience? Are there any physical bottlenecks in the space?	Walls Doors Windows Key furniture Railings Stairs and ramps
Affordances	What objects in the space might influence the interaction by providing critical context?	Signs Screens Clocks Pens and keypads

It can be hard to determine the right level of fidelity if you're starting from scratch. Contextual inquiry, as well as earlier dioramas, can help inform specific choices.

NOTE BODYSTORMING FOR THE LONG HAUL

Since the outlay of time and money is often nontrivial when creating a "set" for bodystorming, consider setting up an interactive "lab" that can be used not just for bodystorming but for later usability testing. On the Echo Look, since we expected the device to be used in or near closets and full-length mirrors, we purchased a closet set and installed it in our lab for the duration of the project.

Prototyping: Proving Your Concept

The role of prototyping in the design process hasn't changed, but experiences have become more complicated, and thus prototypes, too, become more complicated. Sadly, many off-the-shelf prototyping tools seem to come and go like a(n Adobe) flash in the pan. (Sorry, a little old-internet humor there.) It's important to apply a healthy dose of discipline as you embark on this journey to ensure that you're implementing *just enough* to get the answers you need before committing to any irreversible product decisions.

Wizard of Oz Prototyping

In Wizard of Oz testing, customers interact with what they believe is a functioning "system," but the functionality is completely simulated, much as the Wizard of Oz was pulling levers and using parlor tricks to simulate a magical being.

Wizard of Oz testing is currently most common in conversational design in order to vet design hypotheses before a significant investment in costly natural language processing models is made.

- **Chatbots** can be simulated in a chat channel where a "bot" account is controlled by a human copy/pasting responses from a script.

- **Voice interfaces** can be simulated by a human playing prerecorded prompts or triggering sequences manually in response to customer utterances.

Improv for Creativity

You learned about some improv-inspired storytelling techniques earlier in this book, but improv's relevance to design goes beyond storytelling. Applied improvisation can extend your team's creativity whether you choose to apply it yourself or in tandem with professionals.

Professional Role-Play

Our improv theater, Unexpected Productions, routinely books actors into medical role-play scenarios with healthcare providers for training purposes. You can have an academic understanding of diagnostic best practices, but things change when there's a living, breathing human in front of you. Professional actors, particularly improvisors, can help you explore possibilities, both playful and weighty, depending upon your need.

Self-Driven Play

You and your team already have the cognitive capacity and tools to use imaginary scene work to explore your customer scenarios.

Brainstorming Game

Develop your ability to explore crazy ideas with a circle game called *Startup Pitch*. Go around a circle and repeat this cycle down the line:

1. Person 1 specifies a problem, like "It's raining too much this winter."
2. Person 2 specifies a completely unrelated concept, like "Cheerios."
3. Person 3 describes a way to use Person 2's concept to solve Person 1's problem.

The *Startup Pitch* game creates a "safe" environment where no one expects the solutions to be logical. This may lead to delightful nonsense, but, in some cases, the thoroughly random connections lead to innovative ideas.

Scripted Play

Start out by building a starter script based on real customer emails, interviews, or conversations. Once your script is ready, have each team member play each role in a common or contentious product scenario. After each team member gets to experience all roles, get together and debrief. What came naturally? What questions arose? What behavior was surprising?

When staging a Wizard of Oz test, consider the ethical ramifications of implying that the customer is interacting with a functional system. For small-scale use cases, like a closet camera,
there are (arguably) few potential negative impacts. But when
testing complex or high-stakes scenarios, like autonomous motor
vehicles, disclosure is likely advisable prior to the test. Disclosing
the speculative nature of the test will only remove your ability to
assess surprise—not the quality of the interaction that follows.

Don't let the analogy oversimplify the concept for you, though: Wizard of Oz testing isn't always a single operator behind the curtain. In
fact, the more complex your system, the more likely you are to need a
village's worth of wizards at work. See the case study in this chapter
to explore this potential complexity further.

Functional Prototyping

The newest generation of design tools provide some form of click-
through visual prototyping with little additional effort. However,
these prototypes are generally mouse or touchscreen only. Multimodal prototyping remains a bespoke endeavor.

Ironically, we've moved backward in some ways. Adobe Flash was
unwieldy at times, but it allowed for precise timing, movement, and
multimedia control. What they lost in Flash, prototypers now recreate with scripting languages and some automation tools.

Voice Extension Prototyping

When working on multimodal experiences that only support limited
voice interactivity—for example, the Anchored or Direct quadrants
in the Multimodal Interaction Model as described in Chapter 7, "The
Spectrum of Multimodality"—you may be able to use one of a few
existing graphically oriented tools that allow you to add limited
voice functionality on as an extension to their prototype modes.

Adobe XD, shown in Figure 11.7, was the first mainstream visual
design tool[1] to offer dedicated support for voice as an additional
type of input "trigger" event (like tap and drag). This isn't natural

---

1   Mark Webster, "Introducing Voice Prototyping in Adobe XD," *Adobe Blog*,
    October 15, 2018, https://theblog.adobe.com/introducing-voice-prototyping
    -in-adobe-xd/

language understanding, per se—this is more of a basic grammar intended to get the basic idea across. When you're adding voice as an inclusive alternative to existing interaction methods, this type of prototyping is a good place to start.

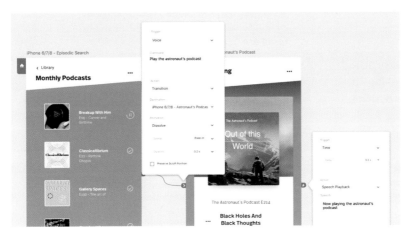

FIGURE 11.7
The manifestation of voice as a command type in Adobe XD's Voice prototyping mode.

Full Natural User Interface Prototyping

For experiences that fall more squarely in the Adaptive or Intangible quadrants in the multimodal interaction model specified in Chapter 7, most existing graphical prototyping tools offer insufficient voice and/ or gesture capabilities at the time of this writing. To truly assess the validity of your designs via a prototype, your choices are generally either to use the Wizard of Oz technique or to build an interactive prototype yourself. See Table 11.4.

NOTE CREATIVE PROTOTYPING WITH RASPBERRY PI

The Raspberry Pi is a particularly interesting option, because you can accomplish some seemingly magical things. On Windows Automotive, our prototyping team wrapped the steering wheel on our simulator in two bands of aluminum foil and then connected it to a Raspberry Pi device so that we could measure the precise length of time a driver's hand left the wheel. That same signal could have been fed into a rich prototype UI to display a reminder to use both hands.

TABLE 11.4 PROTOTYPING TOOLS FOR AUDIO-DRIVEN INTERFACES

Tool Category	Uses	Difficulty
Third-Party Design Tool (Botsociety, etc.)	Most 3P design tools allow you to represent your ideas as a visual flow and then to see them in situ in simulated chat or voice app prototypes. Usability varies wildly, as most of these tools are in startup mode.	Varies
First-Party SDK (Alexa Skills Kit, Google Actions)	Can be used to prototype basic voice interactions without releasing to their respective marketplaces. Can also be used to prototype screen-forward interactions. Coding and technical expertise is generally required beyond the definition of the language model itself.	Moderate
HTML and Scripting	If you can represent the visual part of your experience with basic HTML, you may be able to use webhooks to connect it to other services that run your voice recognition (like Luis.ai and Microsoft Bot Service).	High
Arduino, Raspberry Pi	Gives you considerable control over a variety of sensors and chips, but coding is required, and there is a nontrivial learning curve.	High

Developer-Grade Prototyping

When working with multiple devices or with AI-driven input, like gesture or rich conversational UI, the ecosystem of prototyping tools often falls short. You will likely need to work with code and potentially developer devices to assess the desirability, suitableness, and functionality of your proposed experience.

While the Kinect was once the gold standard for natural user interface prototyping from a sensor and SDK perspective, it has since been discontinued. At the time of this writing, Microsoft offers the Azure Kinect DK: a sophisticated hardware kit with cameras, microphones, and other sensors along with the software to support it. This kit includes native support for body tracking, speech, and computer vision use cases.

When working with any form of 3D—whether it's a 3D interface or mixed-reality interactions powered by computer vision—you'll likely end up using a software tool called *Unity*. Unity began its life as a video game engine, but it has become the industry standard for building robust interactive worlds. Due to the cutting-edge nature of entertainment experiences, there are many Unity plug-ins that deal specifically with new input modalities, like gesture.

> **NOTE** MAKE THE BEST USE OF YOUR TIME
>
> The learning curve for these developer-grade tools is extremely high, and even when learned, they require considerable energy to keep that knowledge relevant due to high volatility. Unless you're a highly trained developer, it's wise to consider working with a developer or prototyper specialized in the plug-ins and techniques that you anticipate using along the way.

Provoking a Response with Provotypes

No matter what fidelity you choose for your prototyping, the "traditional" approach is, of course, to prototype what you intend to build.

But another approach in use at companies working on the cutting edge is *provotyping* (sometimes called *provocatyping*). The implementation techniques are the same, but the goal is different. Instead of validating a specific approach, provotyping aims to start difficult conversations:

- Demonstrating the desirability and feasibility of a difficult or costly idea
- Demonstrating potential harms or problems by modeling undesirable interactions or outcomes

Ovetta Sampson, former UX researcher at IDEO, described the reasoning behind one provotype from her past work: "We created a provotype for this autonomous vehicle for our client that did some really amazing things in the car. Now, engineering-wise, we faked it. But it had the same effect as if it were real. The reason why we did it was to get at these (AI) design principles. We wanted to show the design principle in action, so that an engineer knew what it meant for a human being not to be confused in a transition state."

Cennydd Bowles crisply defines the driving force behind provotyping (in his words, provocatyping): "The big difference from regular prototyping is we make provocatypes with not just a problem-solving mindset but also a problem-creating mindset. If we're successful, a provocatype will spark better reactions than a hypothetical discussion would."

Problem-creating may sound uncomfortable, but it's far better to have those difficult discussions before millions of development dollars have been poured into a partially formed idea. Provotyping (or provocatyping) requires courage, but can transform your projects.

Prototyping in Context

While it's common to think of a prototype as a semi-functional app or digital artifact, don't underestimate the importance of prototyping the environment in which your experience will be used. At the beginning of this book, you learned how important it was to discover the customer's context. That context doesn't become less important during prototype testing. Anything you can do to emulate final conditions will yield more accurate results—and may prevent costly mistakes down the line.

Location-Based Prototyping

Can you stage your prototype within its intended location? The sooner you can test within actual conditions, the fewer erroneous assumptions you'll make along the way. When working on a museum installation for the Children's Museum of Pittsburgh, we took our custom-built hardware to the museum for our tests, in order to ease recruitment and to test with kids already in a hands-on mentality.

Set Building and Theatricality

When you can't take your UI to the customer's context, recreate the customer's context as deeply as possible. When designing services or augmented reality experiences, you may be able to recreate elements of the physical spaces in which those experiences will eventually take place using low-fidelity analogs. You can also hire actors to play the role of other customers or employees. A little effort can go a long way.

Simulation

For complex or dangerous experiences, you may need to closely emulate the final experience in as much detail as possible. This can be achieved with high-fidelity prototyping techniques (and elbow grease) or by utilizing the immersiveness of virtual reality.

On Windows Automotive, my colleague David Walker rebuilt a Ford Explorer dashboard to scale with wood and metal, and he combined it with an actual steering wheel and powered seats from a scrapped Explorer, along with gaming pedals and embedded tablets for the infotainment system. The wheel and pedals controlled a driving simulator projected on three surround screens.

CASE STUDY

Wizard of Oz Prototyping with M*Modal User Research

You first heard from M*Modal User Experience Manager Anna Abovyan in Chapter 10, "Let's Get Proactive." Her team works on complex cross-device multimodal experiences and frequently needs to test viability prior to implementation. She went on to describe a typical Wizard of Oz test in their environment.

"You can't learn more than from humans. The best way we've found is either setting up these Wizard of Oz studies, or just watching humans doing this in real life. I would say what has consistently helped is role-play exercises and very creative Wizard of Oz.

So, we've set up studies where, unfortunately it requires a lot of people to run the study. We came finally to a realization that if we're testing four modalities, we'll need four people to run the study at the least.

Let's say we're testing a smart speaker that you can talk to and that can talk back, and that can do lights and sounds, along with a graphical user interface on a different device that presents feedback or answers to the questions that you ask.

Then we would have:

- One person who is pulling up the mock-ups at the right time.
- One person who is operating a terminal window for operating lights and sounds.
- One person who is doing the VUI—so, speaking out the appropriate responses. That person is typically someone with a clinical background, like a doctor, nurse, someone like that.

So, it does get complex. Because otherwise, we just notice that if we don't staff it appropriately, things get out of sync and it's hard to follow, and you'll have to do a lot of explanation, and facilitation kind of goes crazy."

Apply It Now

For designers coming from a history of traditional screen-based design work, the techniques described in this chapter may feel foreign. However, the complexity inherent to multimodal and multi-device experiences requires additional effort to tease out potentially dangerous assumptions and risks.

- **Identify the highest-risk elements of your experience with opti-pessimistic prompts.** Where might your experience fail? What's hard about it?

- **Storyboard your experience.** You don't necessarily need one storyboard to rule them all. In fact, you may find your greatest success by pursuing multiple goals with your storyboarding:

  - Demonstrate the actual customer value.

  - Call out the biggest risks.

  - Push the boundaries to define what is out of scope.

- **Find ways to live your experience and make it tangible.** Whether that's physical prototyping or play-acting the customer scenarios, you owe it to your customers to immerse yourself beyond the paper specs and storyboards.

- **When appropriate, deploy prototyping at the right level of fidelity.** When working on natural user interfaces, consider employing developer/prototypers to help you evaluate feasibility and desirability before too many decisions are locked in.

Mixing Realities and Play with Craig Fox

I'm grateful to count **Craig Fox** *(Principal Design Director on Microsoft Azure Internet of Things) as both a mentor and friend. Much of what I first learned about multimodal experiences was during my time on Craig's Windows Automotive team. A few years later, Craig and his team played a significant role in the initial launch of Microsoft's first-generation HoloLens. We sat down to chat about Craig's reflections about continuing to work in uncharted territory.*

Q: What's one of the most difficult things about designing for mixed reality?

Thinking spatially. I was trying to think about the different ways that a designer can work on these problems. In mixed reality, there are a few layers of this.

Physical Prototyping

The first layer was for the designers that wanted to actually build things out of cardboard and pipe cleaners. "Well, how big is that hologram? Is it this big?" "No, actually, it's not. It's this big."

And so then you're like, "OK, well, if it's this big, how are you gonna pick it up?" If it's a big box, you're gonna pick it up with two hands. If it's small, you have a tendency to pick it up with one hand.

I was just telling someone why we wanted the seat belts on our physical car dashboard prototype. Because otherwise, next thing you know you'd be pretending that you could come over and do something over here that's really out of reach.

Bodystorming

This is when we were looking at the gesture stuff. "OK, am I close to it? Or am I far away from it?" If I'm far away from it, I have my little laser beams out of my hands. If I was close to it, then yeah, you'd want to reach out and grab it—but *how* would you reach out to grab it? And that had, in the early days, huge implications to the tech. Basically, if it gets too close to you, it disappears. So is it at arm's length? That's not going to work. I can't pick things up because my arms are only so long!

Anyway, my net thing there is you're acting these things out. You're building these physical props. And you are working through those scenarios on an interaction level. And I think the other aspect is just trying to work through in the scenario what the true value was. Because we had a real challenge. It's hard to beat this smartphone. So when is it a whole lot of dress-up and not actually as valuable as your phone?

Low-Fidelity Storyboarding

A lot of the designers in the group would take a picture of a living room, and they would insert objects and move objects around inside that. Like, "Oh, I'm gonna pull that object from the back to the front." And they would just do a multiframe PowerPoint.

Q: What about higher-fidelity prototyping for mixed reality?

We wouldn't use the existing hardware. We would prototype mixed reality or augmented reality in virtual reality. So we were able to use the controllers and VR to prototype AR.

What was interesting to me was watching a bunch of the designers say, "Well, can I just do that myself?" So they started to get into Unity. But the barrier to entry was pretty high.

We had a set of folks who I'd say were prototypers. The best combo would be when we had a great conceptual interaction designer who could draw what they wanted using the method I described. They'd be working with a prototyper who would say, "Oh, I know that library. Oh, I've got those components already. Oh, I know how to blast through all of the troubles that you're going to go through that would take you a week to make this work, and I can do it in a day." And when they worked together, you got really fast prototyping of concepts that you could evaluate in the headset.

Q: Did you find surprises when you got to the prototype in the headset?

Absolutely, yes. So, everything from the different room that you had mocked up: "There was no table in this room. I was manipulating it here, but is it floating in space now? And does that feel strange?" Or "Where did it go? It's underneath the table? Should I be able to flick a switch to have special eyes see it underneath the table, or is it more realistic that it went under the table?" Because that's where the prototyping was invaluable.

Craig Fox is a design leader with experience designing and shipping consumer and enterprise products, applications, and services. Craig now leads a team of designers and researchers designing for cross-device scenarios as Principal Design Director for the Microsoft Azure Internet of Things team. His past work at Microsoft includes a wide variety of projects, from server tools like System Center Configuration Manager to multimodal experiences like Windows Automotive and the first generation of Microsoft HoloLens.

CHAPTER 12

From Envisioning to Execution

reat ideas are much easier to come by than great execution of those ideas. At this stage, you're hopefully inspired to see a future filled with fluid interfaces that allow your customers ultimate flexibility in interaction without overwhelming them. But how do you translate that grand vision to your implementation partners in a cohesive way?

Until now, design techniques and deliverables have largely been focused upon finite, deterministic exchanges between a human and a computer. The days where designers could comp out every single screen in a system have long since faded. Now that the industry stands at the threshold of a new era in human-computer interaction, the magnitude of this scale challenge has increased even further. Designers are becoming masters at selecting the riskiest, most interesting parts of the system to define.

Each additional input method added to an interface dramatically increases the number of potential paths through the system. As strategic as you are now, moving to multimodal design will force you to specialize even more. Work smarter—not harder.

Start with the areas of highest impact, for example:

- What is the most common path your customers will take through this scenario across all modalities?
- Where is the risk of task failure the most pronounced?
- How many modalities can be used to complete this customer scenario?

As a product owner or designer on a multimodal product, you are responsible for providing additional context to your development partners. It is not just about the manifestation of a single intent on a single input, but about representing these intents and inputs as a system of related parts.

Your design deliverables will approach the answers to these questions from multiple angles and will take many forms. In this chapter, we'll cover approaches for tackling a few of the most unique deliverables needed for a cohesive multimodal experience:

- Techniques for modeling *interactions over time*
- Methodologies for capturing *voice designs* and *gesture designs* in deliverable form
- A philosophy with which to approach larger-scale *multimodal design systems*

Interactions over Time

Storyboards and tables are a large part of the battle, but neither represents the step-by-step system state over time. To fill in this piece of the puzzle, I've found that there's nothing more effective than a good old-fashioned flow diagram.

Hopefully, you're already creating flows as part of your work today. Site flows are as old as the internet, and invisible experiences like voice UI rely even more heavily on flows as the only visual manifestation of a customer's end-to-end interaction with the system.

Yet there's nothing old-fashioned about your multimodal scenarios, and you'll immediately find the process challenging when attempting to depict more than one modality at the same time. In particular, the most interesting part of the multimodal puzzle is where modalities interact—where your customer either voluntarily or involuntarily switches modalities.

> **NOTE** JOURNEY MAP INCEPTION
>
> Most service designers are comfortable with the concept of a journey map (or experience map) that depicts a customer's interaction with a system across various systems and touch points. Multimodal designers are effectively creating journey maps, too, but the touch points are the different input and output modalities supported by the product.

Expanded Traditional Flow Diagrams

BEST FOR: Anchored or Direct experiences

If your system is physically dominant (generally, experiences found in the Anchored or Direct quadrants in Chapter 7's Multimodal Interaction Model), you may be able to get by with a standard app flow extended to cope with multiple inputs.

This generally works best for systems that only support a few multimodal interactions, like voice search or gesture-controlled media playback. Figure 12.1 depicts a simple flow for a media playback app that supports hand gestures or voice to advance to the next track.

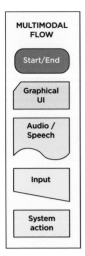

MULTIMODAL FLOW

Start/End

Graphical UI

Audio / Speech

Input

System action

FIGURE 12.1

Simple multimodal interfaces can sometimes be modeled with unified flows like this one, using different symbols to distinguish between input and output types.

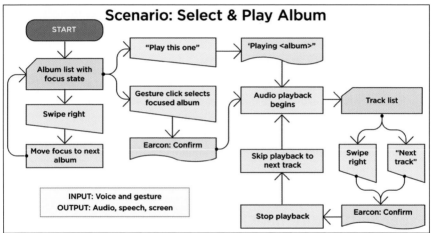

Scenario: Select & Play Album

START

Album list with focus state

"Play this one"

'Playing <album>'

Gesture click selects focused album

Audio playback begins

Track list

Swipe right

Move focus to next album

Earcon: Confirm

Skip playback to next track

Swipe right

"Next track"

INPUT: Voice and gesture
OUTPUT: Audio, speech, screen

Stop playback

Earcon: Confirm

Flows, Shapes, and States

To incorporate voice or other multimodality meaningfully into a physical or screen-forward flow, you'll need to represent input as one of the states in your flow.

- Add input as a specific state in your flow, with a dedicated shape.
- If a step is limited to a specific type of input (like voice), be sure to call that out when needed.
- Include states for voice output, sound effects, and changes to GUI.

It's tempting to include your system's exact voice prompts in the flow, but take my word for it: use prompt IDs that cross-reference to a separate spreadsheet. Otherwise, you'll face a ton of extra flow corrections later if the text changes. Developers tend to prefer to work from the more labor-intensive flow and not a prompt list.

If you're new to user experience flows and don't have a system for depicting states yet, use the pattern language depicted in Figure 12.2 as a starting point. I used this system on Windows Automotive and adapted it for the Amazon Alexa VUI team during my time there. There's really no "right" answer: I chose shapes that were available in the default kit for tools like Visio, PowerPoint, and OmniGraffle.

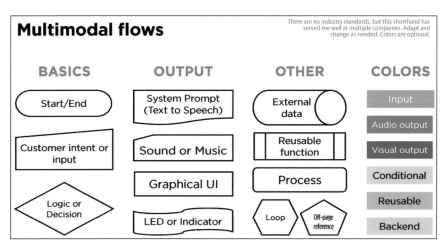

FIGURE 12.2
A pattern language you can use for your multimodal flow diagrams, adapted from my work on Windows Automotive and the Alexa Voice UI design team.

Triple Flows

BEST FOR: Adaptive or Intangible experiences

A triple flow is a flow superimposed upon swim lanes that represent each of the three primary modalities of human interaction: visual, audio, and haptic interaction. *The triple flow is from the perspective of the customer, not the system—it is what they see, hear, and do at each step.* Within each lane, both inputs and outputs are depicted.

The rigidity of the swim lanes makes it harder to lay out triple flows, but is particularly helpful in calling attention to transitions across modalities.

Figure 12.3 depicts a triple flow from our work on Windows Automotive. Our team was designing for a touchscreen, a voice recognition system, and traditional physical driver controls.

For many multimodal systems, the triple flow will be the perfect level of detail. While the visual and audio lanes are easy to define, that third physical lane may vary from device to device. Android and iPhone 8 apps can use that third lane for interaction with physical controls, like volume, back, or power; while iPhone X apps might use that lane for system gestures instead of or in addition to physical controls.

Use triple flows to depict scenarios when customers might use multiple modalities in a single interaction, or when there are multiple ways to complete a single task.

FIGURE 12.3

Simple example of an early multimodal "triple flow" for a media search scenario. Since there was no physical control that corresponded to search, the only physical control indicated is the system's push to talk button (labeled "PTT" in the diagram).

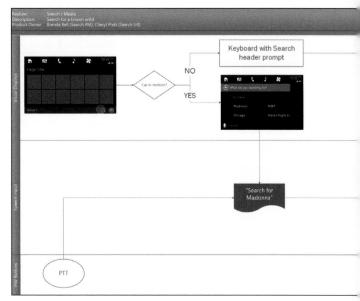

System Swim Lanes

BEST FOR: Highly fluid multimodal systems, or systems with complex logic

In cases where the interactions are more complicated—branching logic, for example—greater rigor may be required. Another approach is to include the system state as a central swim lane, with output "above the line" and input "below the line."

This format is ideal for displaying branching logic across multiple inputs and outputs, but makes it hard to show individual screens. It's best for adaptive systems where the visuals support voice or gesture as the primary input.

Figure 12.4 depicts a multimodal movie search scenario for a home streaming device like Amazon's Fire TV or Roku.

- Conditional logic is depicted in the central lane.
- There are two input lanes: voice and remote control.
- There are two output lanes: audio and visual.
- There are transitions between features.

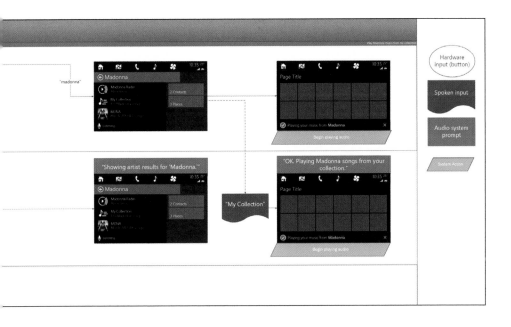

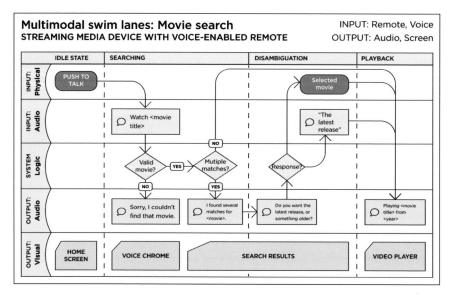

FIGURE 12.4

System swim lanes for a multimodal movie search.

This approach is particularly useful for communicating with development partners, as it is essentially from the perspective of the system. This may be critical when dealing with complex logic, or when synchronization between modalities may not be exact. In the Search step here, there are multiple prompts while looking at a single results page—and presumably the customer might also interact with the search results with their remote.

Coping with Complexity

Visual representations of complex logic across five swim lanes will fall apart after a certain point. Use your best judgment.

- Scope your system swim lane diagrams to include just the riskiest or most variable portions of the experience.
- Use simpler flows and storyboards to bridge the gap for less complex portions of your customer journey.
- Get creative about how and when you indicate transitions.
- Rearrange the swim lanes to minimize the amount of "ink" used.

Voice Design: Visualizing the Invisible

The successful delivery of voice designs requires designers to act as scriptwriters and playwrights. While storyboards and flows will remain an important part of your deliverables, Table 12.1 lists additional voice-specific deliverables you may need to generate.

Prior to embarking on the design process, consider these key situational considerations that will have an influence on the success of your work:

1. Are your intents better served by rigid but responsive fixed grammar of commands, or a more forgiving but slower natural language system?

2. Will your device be listening using near-field or far-field microphones?

3. How might you ensure that each of your key intents uses acoustically unique utterances to improve accuracy?

4. Are you accounting for both one-shot and multiturn conversational styles?

5. How might accent, age, and gender cause unique frustrations or failures? How can you help your customers recover from those errors?

TABLE 12.1 ADDITIONAL DELIVERABLES FOR VOICE DESIGN

Deliverable	Explanation
Intents and Sample Utterances	The set of customer goals supported by the system, along with representative examples of how customers are expected to express those intents.
Sample Dialogs	Scripts for the most common interactions in the system, as well as notable error cases.
Slot Types and Entities	Definitions for all conversational variables: for example, an airline app would likely include entities like "flight number" and "departure date."
Prompt List	The complete set of text strings that will be translated into spoken audio and played back to the customer by your app or product.

Of all of the deliverables above, the *sample dialogs* are the most iterative part of the process; they are the voice equivalent for wireframes in a visually dominant design process. As you work through your sample dialogs, you'll identify new scenarios and intents; you'll identify patterns and opportunities for reuse; and you'll iterate on the tone of the words you choose along the way.

Approaching Your Sample Dialogs

It's not enough to simply cover sample dialogs for the "happy path" outcome. Voice design, when all goes well, is fairly simplistic. The complexity and challenge for voice designers lurks in the gray areas where the system partially or completely fails to hear a customer right the first time.

- Start with one happy path for each intent and write the ideal script between the customer and the system.
- Write additional sample dialogs for each potential combination of slot types in a single intent.
- For each slot type in an intent:
  - Cover a potential scenario where the slot was misrecognized in a "false positive" result.
  - Cover a potential scenario where the slot value is missing entirely.
  - Cover any other major error cases *or* transitions between modalities.
  - Cover the deletion or manipulation of saved values.

Once you feel you've covered sufficient ground, it's time to go back to the beginning and start looking for patterns. Where can you reuse prompts? Where can you reuse entire dialog sequences? As you do this, you'll start to generate a final prompt list.

NOTE TIP OF THE ICEBERG

Both the voice design and gesture design sections are intended to provide a mere starting point for your multimodal deliverables, rather than a complete picture of the modality-specific design process. There is plenty more to learn about designing for these technologies as you continue down your path.

Gesture Design: Documenting the Wave

Gesture as an interaction medium is defined by the combination of space and time. Hence, gestures are inherently difficult to capture as part of traditional static deliverables.

The topic of gesture design is quite large on its own. As the field is more nascent than even voice design, it's a topic for future writings. But at a fundamental level, it's important to know how to get started. As your needs evolve, you can begin to conduct your own research into advanced gesture design techniques.

Your first step is to familiarize yourself with your platform's core supported gestures. Because gesture is so relative, it's actually a significant machine learning challenge to train new gestures in most systems. You'll get the best results by starting with the tried-and-true building blocks on your platform.

Once you've explored what's possible and plausible, establish your short list of gestural building blocks up front. Identify which gestures you're using, which ones directly map to an intent, and which ones are components for complex gestures. Name any new gestures and document them, ideally with video, animation, or some other time-based expressive media.

Example Gesture Pattern Libraries

Gesture is a highly relativistic input medium, and you'll likely need to define your own gesture library based on the specific needs of your customers, their environment, and the available sensors. That said, it's still instructive to look at examples of archetypal gesture designs in the two most predominant categories in use today: touch gesture and open-air gesture.

Touch Gesture Reference Guide

Craig Villamor, Dan Willis, and Luke Wroblewski published the "Touch Gesture Reference Guide" back in 2010, and it's still a helpful starting point for anyone working with a touchscreen.[1] They discuss the manifestation and usage of 12 fundamental touch gestures: *tap, double-tap, drag, flick, pinch, spread, press, press and tap, press and drag,* and *rotate*. Figure 12.5 provides a glimpse of their visual language for communicating these gestures.

---

1   Luke Wroblewski, "Touch Reference Gesture Guide," *LukeW Ideation and Design* (blog), April 20, 2010, https://lukew.com/touch

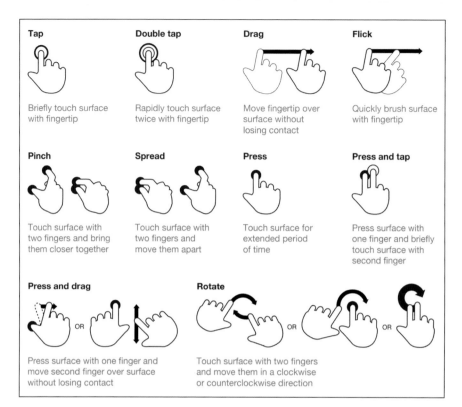

Tap

Briefly touch surface with fingertip

Double tap

Rapidly touch surface twice with fingertip

Drag

Move fingertip over surface without losing contact

Flick

Quickly brush surface with fingertip

Pinch

Touch surface with two fingers and bring them closer together

Spread

Touch surface with two fingers and move them apart

Press

Touch surface for extended period of time

Press and tap

Press surface with one finger and briefly touch surface with second finger

Press and drag

Press surface with one finger and move second finger over surface without losing contact

Rotate

Touch surface with two fingers and move them in a clockwise or counterclockwise direction

FIGURE 12.5

Excerpt from the "Touch Gesture Reference Guide" depicting a basic set of touch gestures and their iconographic representations.

Open-Air Gestures (Hand and Skeletal)

While the Xbox Kinect may not have survived as a consumer product, the work done on gesture controls at the operating system level is still significant and useful—both as a potential source of inspiration for specific gestures, as well as an example of design documentation for hand and skeletal gestures. See Table 12.2.

> **NOTE** NEAR AND FAR
>
> When dealing with open-air gesture systems, it may not be enough to define a single set of gesture parameters. As specified in the "Kinect for Windows Human Interface Guidelines": "Your UI should adapt as the distance between the user and the sensor changes." Any open-air gesture interface that relies on precise gestures like hand poses will likely suffer a significant loss of accuracy as the distance from the sensor increases.

TABLE 12.2   EXAMPLE GESTURE COMMANDS FOR MICROSOFT'S
                 XBOX KINECT*

Gesture	Description
Zoom In and Zoom Out	Use a closed hand to grip and zoom.
	Hold one hand out in front of you and close your hand to "grip" the screen.
	Move your hand toward the screen to push the content away, or zoom out.
	Move your hand away from the screen, toward your body, and zoom in.
Press and Release to Make a Selection	Hold your open hand over the item you want to choose and press forward until the cursor fills completely white.
	Release by pulling back slightly to complete the selection.
Grip and Move	Hold one hand out in front of you and close your hand to "grip" the screen.
	When the Kinect cursor changes from an open hand to a closed fist, you can move your hand back and forth horizontally to scroll in Home.
Return Home	Hold both hands open symmetrically, and you will see hints appear onscreen.
	"Grip" when the tabs appear onscreen and pull your closed hands together to shrink the window and return home.

* *Xbox One Kinect Voice and Gesture Commands*, quick reference sheet, Microsoft—downloaded from the article "The Complete List of Kinect Gesture and Voice Commands for Your Referencing Pleasure," Nov 26, 2013, **https://news.xbox.com/en-us/2013/11/26/xbox-one-kinect-gesture-and -voice-guide/**

Multimodal Design Systems

Once you understand how your customer's experience must change over time, it's time to tackle the specific interactions that support those changes. But before you can deliver designs to your implementation partners, you must first ensure that you're using your own common language across disparate modalities. Without a cross-cutting vision, you're at risk of shipping unrelated, inconsistent experiences on a feature-by-feature or modality-by-modality basis.

The need to communicate consistently across a complex set of designs is not unique to multimodal experiences. If you've worked with design systems before, you may be familiar with the concept of "atomic design." As author Brad Frost describes atomic design, it is "a mental model to help us think of our user interfaces as both a cohesive whole and a collection of parts at the same time." Table 12.3 presents a paraphrased summary of the key concepts introduced by the atomic design model.

TABLE 12.3 ATOMIC DESIGN MENTAL MODEL

Level	Definition
Atom	The most basic building blocks of an experience. They can't be broken down any further without ceasing to be functional.
Molecule	Relatively simple groups of UI elements functioning together as a unit.
Organism	Organisms are relatively complex UI components composed of groups of molecules and/or atoms and/or other organisms.
Template	Templates provide context and structure for relatively abstract molecules and organisms. They demonstrate how components function together in context to prove that the parts add up to a well-functioning whole.
Page	Specific instances of templates that show what a UI looks like with real representative content in place. Pages are essential for testing the effectiveness of the underlying design system.

Courtesy of designer and developer Brad Frost

As this model was first conceived to help with the creation of design systems for large websites, the "atoms" were typically individual controls, like buttons or form fields (see Figure 12.6). It's a great way to enforce consistent communication across a digital design system.

But what of multimodal systems? You can't define your customer's intent in terms of the arrangement of controls when so much of a multimodal experience may be invisible. Mental models can be adapted and extended as needed. What if your "atoms" weren't just controls, but the smallest useful units of interaction for all supported input modalities?

But if you've reviewed the above hierarchy in detail, you may have noticed a few terms that seem specific to visual interfaces: pages and, to a lesser degree, templates.

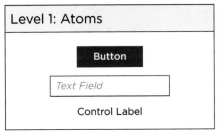
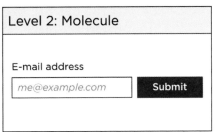

FIGURE 12.6

Atomic design provides an organizational hierarchy for the functional units that combine to form a single design system.

The good news is that Brad and I both feel this model can be safely expanded to multimodal interfaces. Brad explained in our interview (see the end of this chapter) that the molecular analogy ends with templates and pages primarily to ease communications with stakeholders.

In summary, to adapt atomic design for multimodal systems (Table 12.4), only a few shifts are required in the mental model:

1. Instead of defining atoms in terms of *physical* affordances, multimodal atoms are the smallest meaningful interaction affordances your system can provide across each input modality.

2. Broaden the concept of a "page" to include any *specific* customer path through a template or domain of interaction organisms.

If you find it uncomfortable to use the more web-oriented "template" and "page" terminology, alternates are provided within Table 12.4. These are terms used elsewhere in multimodal design standards, and may help you connect what you've heard before with this particular model.

TABLE 12.4 ATOMIC DESIGN, APPLIED TO MULTIMODAL DESIGN SYSTEMS

Level	Definition	Example(s)
Atom	The most basic building blocks of an experience. By definition, each atom comes from a single modality.	Button Hand pose Word/phrase Short movement
Molecule	Groups (or sequences, for time-based input) of atoms combined for use as a single unit.	Hold out a palm (pose) and push it forward (movement) as a "push"
Organism (Intent)	Atoms and organisms are across all input modalities for a single customer goal or need.	Mute volume, scan stations, etc.
Template (Domain)	Multiple organisms are combined to build a feature area of a product. These probably co-exist and performance should be evaluated as a set.	Radio playback controls
Page (Instance)	This is a specific manifestation of a customer's interaction with the organisms in a template.	A customer in their living room browses radio stations with gestures, and then uses voice to mute the system.

NOTE SCALING TEMPLATES AND DOMAINS

Natural user interfaces are powerful, but they are also generally relativistic. When a template or domain becomes "crowded" with interactions within a single modality, the error rate becomes higher. As systems scale, inevitably you will need to layer in some form of task or focus switching to "free up" interaction affordances for reuse in a different context.

Example: A Simple Multimodal Radio

As an example, let's look at a hypothetical multimodal satellite audio system. The satellite service provides 50 audio stations for customers to pick from. At a minimum, the system will include a set of physical controls as well as far-field voice recognition.

While the mental model is called *atomic design*, it's best to start with customer intents, which become templates in the atomic design system. For the purposes of this exercise, the product team keeps it simple by defining three core intents/templates:

1. Mute the music.
2. Control the volume.
3. Browse radio stations.

Identify the Common Patterns

Rather than overwhelm yourself enumerating each interaction in your system, you can start with established patterns of human behavior and human-computer interaction. What common interactions might your customers expect? How would those interactions manifest in the modalities you've chosen to support?

These patterns aren't necessarily tied to a *specific* modality. Instead, these interactions can happen in (almost) any modality in multiple contexts. The way you solve these patterns is what makes your experience unique.

Thinking about these common patterns that apply across modalities—as opposed to starting with the individual manifestation in any one modality—gets you closer to an end state where your customer has *multiple choices for completing common interactions* and can adapt fluidly in the moment.

The good news is that you don't have to start from scratch. Table 12.5 explores a representative (but certainly not exhaustive) list of the most common interactions I've assembled across interfaces in all modalities. Your system may well require more building blocks than detailed here. But you'll almost certainly need a few of these interactions for a complete experience, making this an excellent starting point in most cases.

For each of these interaction patterns, the manifestation will vary for each input mechanism.

- The manifestation of one of these patterns in a *single modality* is an *atom*.
- In cases where you need multiple atoms to represent a pattern (like authentication in visual interfaces), the *chain of interactions* would become a *molecule*.

If you're building on an existing platform, some of these interactions may already be handled. Rather than reinvent the wheel, identify which built-in patterns you can leverage in order to focus your design resources on the novel scenarios.

TABLE 12.5 COMMON INTERACTION PATTERNS ACROSS MODALITIES

Interaction Pattern	Description	Example
Direct	Interaction where there is a 1:1 relationship between affordance and effect.	Most buttons (Submit, cancel)
Toggle	Switch between two predefined states.	Light switches The Clapper
Selection	Choose between one of a finite set of objects or states.	Car audio inputs (FM, AM, Bluetooth, etc.)
Continuum	Make a granular selection from a spectrum of values.	Volume control Thermostat
Expression	Customer interaction over time, where the entire interaction is an expression of customer intent.	Pen input Conversation
Review	Peruse multiple options and interesting details about each option, either for entertainment or to aid in a selection.	Streaming media app Photo
Authentication	Customer verifies their identity to perform a secured action.	Voiceprint Thumbprint Passphrase or PIN Password
Data Entry	Customer specifies a value or values for later reuse.	Entering a name, address, or phone number
Inferred	Interaction triggered by an inferred desire or need, not a specific customer action in the moment.	Presence detection Smart thermostats
Cancel/Stop	Customer wants the system to immediately halt or discard the current activity.	"Computer, stop." Cancel buttons

Define the Atoms

Your hypothetical product team has interviewed their customers and determined that there's interest in this casual browsing experience for living rooms. Voice controls excite your customer, but they don't always work well when the volume is cranking.

Your product team decides to support a phone interface with a few GUI controls, along with gestural controls and far-field voice and audio input. Table 12.6 depicts the output of a design sprint where your team storyboarded desired scenarios and broke down the interactions into atoms by input modality.

TABLE 12.6 POTENTIAL ATOMS FOR A SYSTEM WITH GESTURE, FAR-FIELD AUDIO, AND GUI

Modality	Affordance	Atom Name
Gesture	Hand in flat palm posture	Gesture/Hand/Palm
Gesture	Hand pushes forward toward device	Gesture/Push
Gesture	Both hands move R > L	Gesture/Swipe/Left
Gesture	Both hands move L > R	Gesture/Swipe/Right
Gesture	Hand pulled upward	Gesture/Arm/Up
Gesture	Hand pulled downward	Gesture/Arm/Down
Voice	"On," "Turn on"	Voice/Modifier/On
Voice	"Off," "Turn off," etc.	Voice/Modifier/Off
Voice	"Volume up," "Increase volume"	Voice/Commands/VolumeUp
Voice	"Volume down," "Decrease volume"	Voice/Commands/VolumeDown
Voice	"Browse," "Scan," "Scan stations"	Voice/Commands/Scan
Voice	"Next," "Next track," "Next one"…	Voice/Commands/Next
Voice	"Stop," "Stop it," "No more"…	Voice/Commands/Stop
Voice	"Mute"	Voice/Commands/Mute
Audio	Clap	Audio/Clap
Haptic	Two-state onscreen button	GUI/Button/Toggle
Haptic	Slider with icons	GUI/Slider/Icons
Haptic	Action button	GUI/Button/Action

Yes, this list can get long. But if you don't define a central list of atoms, you're leaving it to each development team—on every feature—to potentially define duplicate atoms. By taking the time to define these centrally, you can partner with development to streamline implementation—and make it easier to make changes in one place down the line.

NOTE INFINITE SOLUTIONS

> Radio control seems like a solved problem, but even in this example there's plenty of room for variation. For example: speech control of volume. What type of interaction will you support? Volume is on a continuum, so you could get away with simply "Volume up" and "Volume down." Is it important to also support arbitrary values, like "Volume 50?"

At the atomic stage, even if you're not applying a specific customer scenario, there are likely important questions to address. For example, the effect of the arm up-and-down gestures is relative due to customer size. What if a person is of below average stature? What will they do if they want to continue interacting but hit a physical limit?

After you've defined your atoms, you may find that some of them are too granular to be useful; this is especially likely with relativistic inputs like gesture. In these cases, you'll want to define molecules that combine atoms into more useful functional units. Table 12.7 depicts a potential set of chosen molecules for the browsing radio scenario.

TABLE 12.7   MOLECULES FOR BROWSING RADIO STATIONS
WITH AUDIO, GESTURE, AND HAPTIC INPUT

Modality	Molecule	Atoms
Gesture	Gesture/Toggle	Gesture/Hand/Palm + Gesture/Push
Voice	Voice/Toggle/On	Voice/Nouns/? + Voice/Toggle/On
Voice	Voice/Toggle/Off	Voice/Nouns/? + Voice/Toggle/Off
Audio	Audio/Toggle	Audio/Clap + Audio/Clap
Haptic	GUI/Scanner	GUI/Button/Toggle (ScanUp) + GUI/Button/Toggle (ScanDown)+ GUI/Button/Action (Stop)

You may have noticed that the content in Tables 12.6 and 12.7 is very generic, and intentionally so. Most of these atoms and molecules could be applied to multiple domains or features, like streaming media playback or smart home controls. The goal is to define a generally useful set of centrally defined interactions that can be applied and tuned consistently across your entire product.

NOTE VOICE UI AND ATOMIC DESIGN

> Voice user interfaces are a bit tricky to fit into atomic design. Your atoms can either be intents that map to a natural language model, or you can choose to model the atoms at higher granularity, like nouns and verbs. It will be interesting to see how various teams choose to represent speech in their designs. In this example, there are "commands" but also "modifiers" that can be stacked on top of commands. This doesn't necessarily represent best practice, and not all conversational UI will be so oriented toward command and control scenarios.

Once you've assembled a representative set of atoms and molecules, it's time to assemble organisms for each of your customer's specific goals or intents, as seen in Table 12.8.

TABLE 12.8 MULTIMODAL ORGANISMS FOR BROWSING RADIO STATIONS WITH AUDIO, HAPTIC, AND GESTURE INPUT

Organism	Speech and/or Audio	GUI (Haptic)	Gesture
Mute the Music	Voice/Toggle/On Audio/Toggle	Button/Toggle	Gesture/Toggle
Change Volume	Voice/Commands/ VolumeUp Voice/Commands/ VolumeDown	Slider/Icons	Gesture/Arm/Up Gesture/Arm/Down
Scan Stations	Voice/Commands/Browse	Button/Action (1) Scan Up (2) Scan Down	Gesture/Swipe/Left Gesture/Swipe/Right
Stop Scanning	Voice/Commands/Stop *only when scanning	Button/Action ??	??

As you begin to define multimodal organisms, you'll discover open questions where inconsistencies or insufficiencies arise. In this example:

- There is only a "mute" gesture, no unmute. Both are supported in speech. Will that cause confusion?

- If the volume slider is labeled—for example, 0 through 11— customers might also expect to be able to say "Volume 7" to control volume.

- In this proposal, browsing works differently via haptic controls than speech. The speech intent only previews in one direction, while the physical control involves two distinct buttons. How will customers react to this difference?

> **NOTE** ATOMIC DESIGN AT SCALE
>
> For larger systems, it won't make sense to define all of your inter-actions in a single table like this. You might even need to design a system that switches context between templates, especially if using low-granularity input like gesture. If implemented correctly, multimodal systems can support fluid changes between different modalities when appropriate, but only if each interaction across modalities is built within the same system, allowing customers to hypothetically complete a "cancel" task with a voice atom or a gestural molecule.

Apply It Now

Multimodal design is a mammoth effort, but it starts with the same fundamentals that designers and product teams have always prac-ticed. Multimodal design requires you to add an additional level of definition and storytelling to bring the disparate interaction possi-bilities together under a shared vision.

1. **Explore and define context.** Start by understanding your customer's context enough to bring the proposed experience to life with storyboards. These storyboards will provide critical context—not just for your stakeholders, but for all of the team members making implementation decisions day-to-day.

2. **Explore interactions over time.** Deepen your focus to explore the customer interactions and state over time. Use flow diagrams at varying levels of specificity to capture the customer's interac-tions across your system's many multimodal touch points.

3. **Identify interaction patterns.** From those storyboards, begin to pull out the specific patterns of interaction you'll need. Are your customers changing the state of the system with toggles or direct selections? Are they authenticating their identity? Are they browsing from a large set of items because they don't yet know what they want?

4. **Build your multimodal design system.** Map each of those interaction patterns to input modalities to create the atoms from which your experience will be built. Combine those "atoms" across multiple modalities for a single scenario to create the functional "organisms" and "templates" you can reuse across your product.

5. **Create and deliver designs for specific scenarios.** After you've mapped out the potential interaction patterns for each modality, it's time to start focusing on scenario-specific design exploration and deliverables. Take into account the transition patterns you identified during the earlier phases of the design process, especially if your customer has the ability to switch modalities midscenario.

Examining Atomic Multimodality with Brad Frost

Brad Frost is a web designer best known as the author behind Atomic Design. *His book proposed a unique mental model for design systems backed by implementation that managed to unite both designers and developers with an eye toward functional, scalable, modular systems. I had a great time chatting with Brad about my proposal for applying his mental model to multimodal systems.*

Q: I have a theory that we can expand molecules and organisms to multimodal design, but I'm torn on how the modalities would manifest between molecules and organisms. What's your take on how they differ and how they might apply?

The difference between molecules and organisms is one of complexity. It's like water, H20—you blow up a water molecule, and you're left with two hydrogens and one oxygen and that's it. But there are really complex molecules; if you explode those, you're left with the sort of more primitive or simpler things. So that's what I call *organisms*. And that's the way that I tend to think about it. "If I blow this thing up, am I left with . . . smaller components still? Or have I arrived at the base units?"

Let's translate that into your world, and go from "play music" to executing that across all of these different modalities. Sounds like you're trying to put a vocabulary around how to think of multimodal interfaces in a more structured and hierarchical way, which I think makes a lot of sense. This specific context is I think really, really interesting. And fascinating. For something as seemingly dumb as "play music" or "pause" . . . like, there's a hundred different ways you could slice this. It's really cool.

But atomic design by itself doesn't give you the answers to "how do I articulate flows around completing a task?" And that's OK. You know, these things can sort of live side by side.

Q: The terms you chose for "pages" and "templates" seem to come largely from the context of web development and design. Can you see any way these concepts could be generalized beyond traditional graphical user interface systems?

A lot of people have gotten in touch about "why didn't you just carry it through? Why do you suddenly abandon the metaphor and go into templates and pages? Why not make it genus and ecosystem?" My argument, and I talk about it in my book, is I say . . . "I've tried it. And my clients think I'm . . . crazy!" You know: "Yeah, so . . . we hired you to make a website, right? And that website entails PAGES. So that's why the analogy isn't carried through the whole way."

I hate even going here, but in a way an atomic design template is like agile user stories: "As a user, I want to be able to . . . " The shape of the task is the same. You're mapping, you know, "play" is the trigger word. The template, in my world, is "Play the something." And that ends up mapping to . . . "play holiday music," for instance.

And then in your multimodal example, there are multiple ways you could play that holiday music. Like, in one case a user is on their phone, they're on a subway, they pull out their phone, face ID, swipe right and in another case they talk into their phone to advance the song or do whatever because they're holding a bag of groceries. So that's a page, a specific instance of this template.

Just drawing the line from how I work with atomic design into this world . . . is that the page is where you express all of these different things. And then the underlying system is informed and influenced by that. And then the system informs and influences all of those things. And so those things get developed in parallel.

Q: Multimodality makes atomic design systems more complicated, but you've worked with many complex design systems. What best practices jump out at you from the companies dealing with the toughest complexity?

The biggest thing: Really hitching the design system wagon to your products and making that real. Making sure that the design systems actually power real products. Not just a design exercise.

We talk a lot about pilot projects. Whenever we do a project with a company, we're like, "OK. What projects are you shipping this year that aren't actually doing work yet, and how can we use those projects that are funded and important?" Where at least some stakeholders are like, "This is important and needs to happen." How do we tie the design system effort to that work?

And the other one is start *somewhere*, but don't necessarily feel like you've got to do it all and hit pause on literally everything and get everything just right before you ever hit un-pause.

People see these massive companies with loads of people and resources, and they're like, "We can't do anything because we can't do THAT." Or "We're going to do that," and they actually do it and try to "boil the ocean," which is trying to do everything all at once. So start with some meat and potatoes stuff. Maybe just the "play" flow. Maybe we'll get to everything else later. But let's start somewhere.

Brad Frost *is a web designer, consultant, speaker, and writer located in beautiful Pittsburgh, PA. He is the author of the book* Atomic Design, *which introduces a methodology to create and maintain effective design systems. In addition to co-hosting the* Style Guides *podcast, he has also helped create several tools and resources for web designers, including Pattern Lab, Styleguides.io, Style Guide Guide, "This Is Responsive," "Death to Bullshit," and more.*

Beyond Devices: Human + AI Collaboration

W hat seems "futuristic" to a mainstream audience is often already manifesting itself in enterprise or military environments. And while "artificial intelligence" has been portrayed as a future state—like the fictional entities SkyNet or HAL—the fact is that the component parts of that future are already here.

As many practitioners will tell you, "artificial intelligence" (AI) is a loaded term certain to inspire fear, enthusiasm, and semantic debate. Don't let the perceived technical complexity drive you away from pursuing a deeper understanding. Design has a crucial role to play in shaping the use and deployment of artificial intelligence, but you cannot do so responsibly without a working understanding of the underlying technology and the potential pitfalls.

In layman's terms, artificial intelligence refers to systems that can make judgments about new information or events based on past observation or information provided by their creators. But it's important to note that experiences powered by artificial intelligence are limited by the experiences and data to which they have been exposed by their creators. Hence, AI-based experiences can magnify or compound our own human biases and the biases implicitly built into the systems they observe.

NOTE WE'RE ALL INCOMPLETE

In a way, our devices are not unlike children—making decisions based on incomplete mental models of the world around them. Adults also have incomplete mental models, of course; they're just working from a different pool of observations and experiences than today's artificial intelligence systems.

The increased ability to learn and respond also means that our systems are capable of acting in "more human" ways, like understanding and generating natural language conversation. As a result, the behavior of AI-infused systems can trick our brains into treating those systems as something more closely resembling human. That great power comes with great responsibility.

This chapter is intended to help you start (or continue) your AI literacy journey. You'll explore:

- How artificial intelligence is created, trained, and used
- The basics of algorithmic bias
- The effect that human-like technology can have on the human brain

Defining AI

The first definition of artificial intelligence, coined by Prof. John McCarthy in 1956, was "the science and engineering of making intelligent machines, especially intelligent computer programs." But what's meant by *intelligent* in this context? Today's AI experts have divided this concept of intelligence into a few more practical classifications, as shown in Table 13.1.

TABLE 13.1 CLASSIFICATIONS OF ARTIFICIAL INTELLIGENCE

Classification	Acronym	Examples	Description
Artificial Superintelligence	ASI	HAL, SkyNet	A system whose comprehension, creativity, and decision-making abilities outperform humans in almost all cases.
General Purpose AI ("Human-level AI")	AGI	Rosie the Robot (*The Jetsons*)	A system that can perform human tasks or professions at a comparable level of autonomy, skill, and decision-making.
Narrow AI ("Weak AI")	ANI	Amazon's Alexa IBM's Deep Blue Autonomous cars	A specialized system that meets or exceeds human capabilities in a specific constrained set of circumstances or tasks.

Odds are, the AI you work with in the next decade or so will be ANI, or narrow AI. Regardless of classification, all types of artificial intelligence have some ability to do the following:

- Review an event or new piece of data.
- Compare that information against a series of past inputs and actions.
- Make a recommendation about the best interpretation of that information based on what the system has seen in the past.

Machine Learning

In traditional computer programming, a human defines *exact instructions* via code. By contrast, artificial intelligence systems are *trained*. Traditional programming works fine when you can foresee all possible customer scenarios and write code to handle them. But the more variable the experience, the less practical that traditional model becomes. How do you design a system to react to stimuli when you don't know yet exactly what you'll encounter?

Machine learning (ML) algorithms are programs that are trained on datasets to recognize and apply trends, rules, and patterns. The output of that training is a machine learning model that can then be used to respond to never-before-seen input based on similar inputs observed in the past. While the complexities of individual training methods are outside the scope of this overview, it's helpful to understand the three most common approaches to machine learning: supervised learning, unsupervised learning, and reinforcement learning.

Supervised Learning

When starting from scratch, supervised machine learning often requires feeding hundreds, thousands, or millions of pairs of inputs *and expected outcomes* to the algorithm with the intent of training it to make decisions in the future. In other cases, data scientists reduce the amount of training required by adapting a model that's already been trained based on an additional dataset—like taking what you've learned in math and applying it to a new domain, such as chemistry.

Unsupervised Learning

Unsupervised machine learning does *not* require specifying desired outcomes. Instead, the algorithm looks for and learns from patterns and relationships *within* the data—for example, Amazon's recommendation features. Your "customer profile" isn't necessarily defined, but the system has observed past correlations between the purchase of particular sets of items.

Reinforcement Learning

Reinforcement learning is the closest model to the style of learning many humans use in their lives. A trial-and-error based system, reinforcement learning algorithms take "chances" and are "rewarded" for good outcomes and "punished" for bad outcomes. These systems require an outside interpreter, which is often another piece of software, to judge each outcome as worthy of reward or punishment. The implementation of that interpretation can have a disproportionate influence over the eventual system behavior.

To better understand these examples, think about them from a human perspective.

- When your learning is *supervised* in a classroom environment, you're provided with examples and often shown what success looks like.

- *Unsupervised* learning for humans often requires sorting through more material, without much guidance about what's important or how to succeed. As a result, you might draw your own unexpected conclusions.

- *Reinforcement* learning is what happens when you're on the job and you're provided feedback via a performance review system, or at school via a report card. Your performance is influenced by the values represented in the system.

For a more reductive but easier-to-process set of examples, see Table 13.2.

TABLE 13.2 REAL WORLD AI SCENARIOS

Technique	Scenario	Plain Language
Traditional Coding	Grammar-Based Voice Commands	"Here are all of the possible words a customer might say, and the response for each of them."
Supervised Machine Learning	Natural Language Understanding	"We don't know exactly what a customer will say to their smart speaker. But here are a lot of things they've said in beta tests, and what they wanted us to do when they said those things."
Unsupervised Machine Learning	Customer Service	"Here's a ton of customer chat logs. Figure out if there are any common patterns we should take a look at."
Reinforcement Machine Learning	Style Recommendations	"Here are a bunch of different clothing pieces. Try mixing them together, and we'll tell you if they make good outfits or not."

Responding with Confidence

When AI models are asked to process new input, any resulting recommendation is usually paired with a measurement of confidence—how sure is the system that the recommendation is a good one?

On the back end, this concept of "confidence" is usually reported on a scale of 0 to 1. (A score of 1 would indicate that the system has seen this exact input before.) It's also common for many types of AI to return a list of possible results, each with its own confidence score.

For example, if a customer in a noisy car says, "Call Johnny," the system might return:

- "Call Johnny": confidence: 0.9
- "Call Ronnie": confidence: 0.82
- "Play who's Johnny": confidence: 0.26

This is a critical point of involvement for designers—it should fall to you to help determine and define what the system does with these results. Under what circumstances might you ignore the top suggestion? (In this example, what if Ronnie is one of their favorite contacts?)

When working on speech recognition systems, we also defined high, moderate, and low confidence thresholds and specified system behaviors, based on the degree of confidence and the number of results at that confidence level. Table 13.3 depicts a summary of a similar set of thresholds and resulting responses.

TABLE 13.3   EXAMPLE RESPONSES BASED ON ALGORITHMIC CONFIDENCE

Threshold	Number of Results	Confidence Values	Responses
High Confidence	1	.9 and above	Immediately perform the requested action without confirmation, unless the action is destructive.
High Confidence	2 or more	.9 and above	Ask the customer to select from the matches.
Moderate Confidence	Any	Between .4 and .9	Confirm the interpretation before taking action.
Low Confidence Result(s)	Any	Under .4	Discard the input and ask the customer to repeat the request.

The responses you define may vary both on the threshold and the nature of the action requested. On Windows Automotive, we acted on medium confidence radio tuning requests because the cost of error was low. But even if the system was fairly confident that I said "Call Steph Smith," we still asked for confirmation.

As a designer working with a machine learning algorithm that returns specific results and confidence values, your design decisions will include questions like:

- Is it safe to take automatic action based on a high confidence result?
- What will your system do if you get only low confidence results?
- If you get multiple high confidence results, will you disambiguate, or just choose one of the results to act upon?

The Why of AI

Why use artificial intelligence at all? Granted, artificial intelligence is not a one-size-fits-all solution to all the world's problems. But there *are* specific patterns of problems that artificial intelligence is well-positioned to solve. Table 13.4 describes some common ways that AI is used to enhance the human experience.

TABLE 13.4   COMMON MODELS FOR ENHANCING HUMAN ACTION WITH AI

Action Model	Description	Examples
Automating	An AI-based solution replaces a human in a process and operates without supervision.	Phone-based interactive voice receptionists Touchless highway tolling
Agentive*	An AI-based system takes actions based on a human operator's specified preferences, usually allowing for intervention if needed.	Tesla's Autopilot Automatic spelling corrections Roomba robotic vacuum cleaners Smart thermostats
Augmenting	AI-based suggestions are provided in hopes of reducing effort or cognitive load, but the human must initiate the suggested action themselves.	Time to leave notifications from map apps Suggested replies in email apps Music recommendations in media apps

* Chris Noessel, "The Dawn of Agentive Technology: The UX of 'Soft' AI" (presentation, Interaction 16, Helsinki, Finland, February 3, 2016).

In order to allow for course correction, agentive technology should generally convey its state to customers (Figures 13.1 and 13.2). Automated systems do not optimize for this sort of intervention and may be less transparent, which can be dangerous.

FIGURE 13.1
Tesla's Autopilot feature acts on behalf of the driver as an agent, taking most decisions out of human hands, while still communicating system state, in case correction is needed.

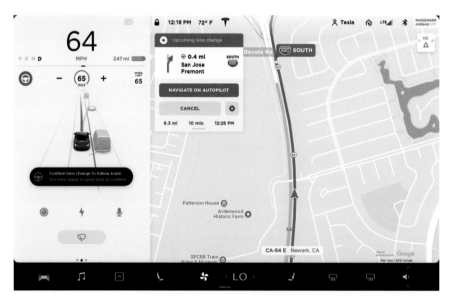

FIGURE 13.2
The Tesla Autopilot UI itself communicates system state to the driver.

When augmenting human behavior, AI-based systems should help their customers build a mental model for the AI's capabilities as they go. When AI suggestions are presented without explanation, the effect can range from annoying at best to alarming at worst. Ensure that your customers can figure out *why* a recommendation was made (see Figure 13.3).

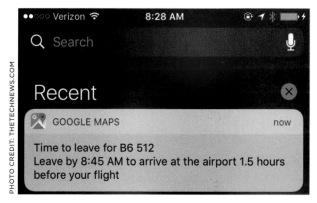

FIGURE 13.3
Some mapping apps can remind you when it is time to leave, based on traffic conditions and your calendar or behavioral data. This interaction is an AI augmentation of human behavior.

"Why Am I Seeing This?"

As virtual assistants first entered the marketplace, Cortana (like many phone-based assistants) began making inferences about important places, based on the amount of time the device lingered in specific locations. At first, these inferences manifested when Cortana made suggestions like, "Traffic on your route to the senior center is good." What if you didn't tell the system you were going to the senior center, or when?

It turns out that inferences are deeply creepy when treated like magic. Cortana eventually added a link to "Why am I seeing this?" which provided more context about any recommendation driven by insight or inference.

Years later, Microsoft published a set of eighteen *Guidelines for Human-AI Interaction*.[1] Several of them bear direct relevance to the transparency problem:

- #1 Make clear what the system can do.
- #2 Make clear how well the system can do what it does.
- #11 Make clear why the system did what it did.

The importance of transparency goes far beyond simply minimizing that vague creeped-out feeling customers may feel when confronted with the output of background surveillance. Transparency for systems powered by artificial intelligence is crucial in any case where the customer might need to intervene.

In Pursuit of Transparency

Because most machine learning is fundamentally a mathematical model at heart, it's a nontrivial problem for even the creators of a model to understand specifically why a model makes any specific recommendation. Without this understanding, you can't provide customers with the transparency they seek when they ask their smart speakers "Why did you say that?" And you'll have a hard time updating the model to avoid repetition of undesired behaviors.

The industry has been pushing against this problem for a long time, and some standards are emerging. LIME (Local Interpretable Model-Agnostic Explanations) is a method that allows you to work backward from an AI-driven insight to identify the "reasons" behind that insight.

NOTE BEHIND THE MODEL

For a photo identified as a tree frog by Google's Inception neural network, the use of the LIME technique revealed that the algorithm focused on the frog's face when coming to a decision. At the same time, applying LIME showed why the algorithm also thought the image might be a pool table. Apparently, in isolation, this frog's eyes resembled billiard balls.[2]

---

1   Saleema Amershi et al., "Guidelines for Human-AI Interaction," CHI Conference on Human Factors in Computing Systems Proceedings (CHI 2019), ACM, New York, NY, https://doi.org/10.1145/3290605.3300233

2   Marco Tulio Ribeiro, Sameer Singh, and Carlos Guestrin, "Local Interpretable Model-Agnostic Explanations (LIME): An Introduction," *O'Reilly Articles* (blog), August 12, 2016, www.oreilly.com/learning/introduction-to-local-interpretable-model-agnostic-explanations-lime

At the same time, transparency isn't always harmless. In "The AI Transparency Paradox,"[3] the *Harvard Business Review* points out that transparent explanations of AI decisions can also lead to increased risk of manipulation or attack of those algorithms.

As with many of the most cutting-edge technology challenges, there are no easy answers. Should you have the option of implementing algorithmic transparency, you'll need to decide who should have access to that information and what they can do with it—and that may vary from industry to industry.

Exploring Algorithmic Bias

Artificial intelligence, by its nature, does not exist without some kind of initial training data. But that data—and the model itself—is a reflection of the people who sourced it, the data scientists who tracked it down, and the society in which that data was collected.

Algorithmic bias, as defined by Wikipedia, "describes systematic and repeatable errors in a computer system that create unfair outcomes, such as privileging one arbitrary group of users over others."

There are a variety of perspectives on the classification of bias in artificial intelligence. However, one of the earliest and most widely cited classification systems came from Batya Friedman and Helen Nissenbaum's 1996 paper "Bias in Computer Systems."[4] They analyzed 17 systems across multiple industries and described three common sources of system bias:

- **Pre-existing bias** occurs when bias from another source is modeled within the algorithm itself at the time of creation. This most often occurs when the training data itself is biased, as a reflection of the prevailing society or organizational culture.

- **Technical bias** occurs when an algorithm tends toward certain results as an unintended consequence of platform, technique, or implementation. The arbitrary use of alphabetized lists for ordering purposes or imperfections in random number generators are examples of technical bias.

---

3 Andrew Burt, "The AI Transparency Paradox," *Harvard Business Review*, December 13, 2019, https://hbr.org/2019/12/the-ai-transparency-paradox

4 Batya Friedman and Helen Nissenbaum, "Bias in Computer Systems," *ACM Transactions on Information Systems* 14, no. 3 (July 1996): 330–347, https://doi .org/10.1145/230538.230561

- **Emergent bias** occurs when a particular model is applied in the real world and encounters unexpected forces. For example, emergent bias might occur in medical diagnostic machine learning models when new diseases pop up but are not yet incorporated into the model—the model will be inherently biased toward the diagnosis of previously understood diseases.

Any system trained via datasets and machine learning is at risk of applying and compounding algorithmic bias in some form during its product lifetime.

Bias and Consequences

Given the scale and impact that most AI-powered experiences have, it's dangerous to wait for the problems to come to you. At best, your company may lose the trust or respect you've built in the marketplace. At worst, you may be violating multiple ethical frameworks and causing measurable harm. Some key examples are the following:

Job Applicants (Pre-existing Bias)

Amazon attempted to train a machine learning algorithm by feeding it past job applications, cross-referenced with the resulting employee performance. Unfortunately, because employee success reflected existing biases in the industry, so did the AI's predictions of future employee success. The tool was discontinued in 2018 when it was revealed those predictions reinforced biases based on gender and socioeconomic status.

Tumor Detection (Pre-existing Bias)

The 2017 study "Dermatologist-level classification of skin cancer with deep neural networks" described an AI model trained with machine learning on a dataset of photos paired with whether or not the cancer was malignant. The original report claimed accuracy equivalent to dermatologists. However, it was later discovered that the model was more likely to rule skin cancer as malignant if a ruler was present—because dermatologists are more likely to measure dangerous-looking tumors, the model developed a bias.[5]

---

5   Nicole Wheeler, "Publication Bias Is Shaping Our Perceptions of AI," *Towards Data Science* (blog), August 1, 2019, https://towardsdatascience.com/is-the-medias-reluctance-to-admit-ai-s-weaknesses-putting-us-at-risk-c355728e9028

Tragic Automation

The Maneuvering Characteristics Augmentation System (MCAS) is a feature introduced on Boeing 737 MAX jets: when the plane's descent is too steep (as detected by two "angle-of-attack" sensors), the system would take over for the human pilots and steer the plane back to a safe altitude and orientation.

Unfortunately, the engineers behind the Boeing 737 MAX failed to account for situations where one of the two angle-of-attack sensors failed. Without a third "tie-breaker" backup sensor, the sensor failure was misinterpreted by the system as a freefall. (As machine learning experts would say, this was "bad feature engineering.")

> MCAS was made autonomous, able in certain conditions to move a secondary flight control by itself to push the nose down without pilot input. In adding MCAS, Boeing added a computer-controlled feature to a human-controlled airplane but without also adding to it the integrity, reliability, and redundancy that a computer-controlled system requires.
>
> —Sully Sullenberger's testimony to
> the U.S. House of Representatives

Automated attempts to correct perceived freefall due to failing angle-of-attack sensors ultimately doomed Lion Air Flight 610 and Ethiopian Airways Flight 302.

While the story of MCAS is a cautionary tale in many ways, it is a particularly clear illustration of three critical questions for AI-powered systems that can act on behalf of humans at any scale:

1. **Can you trust all of the data your AI is using to make judgments?**

   Are there any systems that don't have built in safeguards or redundancy? If so, how will you account for circumstances where those sensors or systems might fail?

2. **What is the cost of error if your system takes an inappropriate action?**

   In an earlier example, the cost of error when making a phone call with voice was potential embarrassment. The cost of error when MCAS takes over based on faulty data is the potential loss of human life.

3. **How might you use artificial intelligence to reduce cognitive load for human operators *without* completely removing their ability to take action?**

Voice User Interfaces

As you'll recall from Chapter 6, "Expressing Intent," natural language training data includes three components: recordings of utterances, the transcript of the utterances, and the expected intent. The recordings used as training data are one source of potential bias in voice-controlled systems. If a system ships without having been trained to recognize a specific dialect or accent, customers with that accent or dialect will have a bad experience. They're unlikely to purchase or continue using the system, so you can't learn from them. The bias spirals, as illustrated in Figure 13.4.

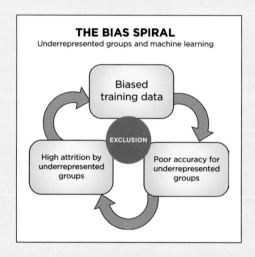

FIGURE 13.4

The bias spiral: exclusion leads to further exclusion.

Most current voice user interfaces were built in high-tech companies in the U.S., and were initially trained with data from employees and their families. But American tech companies aren't known for their innate diversity, especially not at the time these systems were launching. It was nearly impossible for those initial datasets to be balanced along any demographic axis—gender, race, native language, or economic status.

A promising step toward natural language inclusivity is Mozilla's Project Common Voice (see Figures 13.5 and 13.6). Individuals can donate their voice samples to the open-source natural language models, and they can also donate their time to transcribe the clips that other people have submitted. The resulting natural language models will be shared openly with the world community.

Even still, simply asking for submissions is only one step on the journey. Even a free phone app may not include truly marginalized folks who might not have a smartphone, nor the free time to download and contribute. To truly stop the bias spiral in voice recognition, you also need to get out into the community and collect voices from those who would not have the resources to do so on their own—and ideally, compensate them for their valuable contribution of time.

FIGURE 13.5
Mozilla's Common Voice app and website allow anyone to contribute their time or voice to a community-powered natural language understanding engine.

FIGURE 13.6
Each of Mozilla's Common Voice Creative Commons language datasets grows as the community contributes with voice samples or by transcribing submitted samples.

Credit Cards (Emergent Bias)

In 2019, Apple released the Apple Card to much fanfare. However, it didn't take long for husband and wife duos to stumble upon discriminatory behavior. According to CNN Business, Apple cofounder Steve Wozniak was one of the many who observed this behavior, and revealed that his Apple Card credit limit was 10 times that of his wife's despite shared accounts and resources.[6] This appears to be a case of emergent bias, where an existing credit model was applied in a new context to undesirable results.

Autonomous Vehicles (Technical Bias)

During testing of their autonomous vehicles in Arizona, Uber adjusted the algorithm's control over the vehicle so that false positives paired with emergency braking were less likely in order to improve rider comfort. This change led to a fatal collision with pedestrian Elaine Herzberg in March 2018. The preliminary report from the NTSB indicated that the vehicle's sensors *did* detect the need to brake 1.3 seconds earlier, but the configuration of the AI did not allow that braking to occur.[7] This action reflected technical bias because changes in the algorithm were decontextualized—i.e., they favored the rider experience over the pedestrian's life.

Criminal Justice (Pre-existing Bias, Technical Bias)

In May 2016, independent journalism outlet ProPublica published a well-researched expose[8] detailing the inherent bias and discriminatory impact of the AI-powered law enforcement algorithm COMPAS. This model was intended to inform the parole process with a "risk assessment" regarding the likelihood a particular individual would commit a crime post-release. But because COMPAS was trained on data that reflected overpolicing and overprosecution of Black offenders, COMPAS also flagged Black parole seekers as "high risk"

---

6   Evelina Nedlund, "Apple Card Is Accused of Gender Bias. Here's How That Can Happen," CNN Business, November 12, 2019, www.cnn.com/2019/11/12/business/apple-card-gender-bias/index.html

7   Andrew J. Hawkins, "Serious Safety Lapses Led to Uber's Fatal Self-Driving Crash, New Documents Suggest," The Verge, November 9, 2019, www.theverge.com/2019/11/6/20951385/uber-self-driving-crash-death-reason-ntsb-dcouments

8   Julia Angwin et al., "Machine Bias," ProPublica, May 23, 2016, www.propublica.org/article/machine-bias-risk-assessments-in-criminal-sentencing

at a higher rate, resulting in longer incarceration times for those individuals. COMPAS codified human prejudice into a form where it could cause measurable harm at a larger scale.

LEARN MORE

> For a deeper dive into the manifestation of bias in industry, see the case study, "Voice User Interfaces," about natural language understanding model bias (earlier in this chapter).

Question Everything

The most obvious path to confronting bias is to question your implementation thoroughly. Problems are much easier to fix early on, while training the model, than when those issues are discovered later during implementation or release. And, of course—as you learned in the "Opti-pessimism" section in Chapter 11, "Breathe Life into the Unknown"—always investigate the perils of success and your worst-case scenarios.

The following questions provide a starting point through which you can evaluate and potentially begin mitigating potential bias, but there's room to go much deeper.

Avoiding bias in data:

- Where is your training data coming from?
- How was the data collected?
- What societal and structural biases might be reflected in that data?
- How can you solicit data responsibly from underrepresented groups?

Avoiding technical and emergent bias:

- What is your desired outcome, and how are you conveying that in your model?
- What is the cost if your model makes a mistake? Human cost? Environmental? Financial?
- What sensors or sources are feeding your model in the "real world?" Are they redundant and reliable?
- Will your model be updated over time?
- What kinds of secondary effects might the success of your model have on the systems it interacts with?

Avoiding all forms of bias via inclusion and representation:

- Is your pool of modelers or evaluators ("raters") who help train the AI model appropriately diverse?

- How are the people evaluating your algorithm's performance incentivized?

- Will you be reviewing your data and model with impartial external consultants or review boards?

- Will you be evaluating the impact of your model on diverse and marginalized populations? How will you respond if problems arise?

LEARN MORE

Some of these questions are drawn from Google's expansive *People + AI Guidebook*, which is a good secondary read for folks getting deeper into AI.

(Dis)Embodied Agents

Research indicates that the human mind is predisposed to process any speech as if it came from a human being—even when people can see the device that's generating that speech. As a result, the digital assistants that have so captivated the media's attention—like Alexa—have a much deeper social and emotional impact on people than comparable graphical user interfaces.[9]

As a hunter-gatherer society without particular physical strength, humans have long relied on social connections to survive. As a result, the human brain has become hyperspecialized over thousands of years to quickly extract *extra* insight from spoken communication—things like impressions of the speaker's gender, personality, affluence, and mood.

Rather than bother us with the "little" stuff, the human brain is happy to leap directly to conclusions about these social signals *even when there's no person behind the voice.* As a result, voice user interfaces are effectively hot-wired with direct access to our emotional response patterns. That's why it's so easy to get frustrated—or delighted—when dealing with a smart speaker.

---

9 Clifford Nass and Scott Brave, *Wired for Speech: How Voice Activates and Advances the Human-Computer Relationship* (The MIT Press, 2005).

The Hidden Context in Conversations

When a conversational interface moves from the written word to the spoken word, the human mind's insistence upon mining spoken interfaces for social data means that gender, personality, and anthropomorphism become important design decisions. Humans can't just shut off thousands of years of learned behavior.

Gender Bias

Because most modern societies place extreme emphasis on gender norms, and because social success has largely been tied to an ability to "color within the lines" of gender norms, most of our brains have learned to use gender markers as a crutch for fast judgments about our conversational partners. See Table 13.5.

TABLE 13.5 TRADITIONAL GENDER MARKERS FOR SPEECH*

Gender	Pitch	Example linguistic markers (US culture)
Male	Lower: 85–180 hertz	Tendency toward declarative speech Few rhetorical questions More action verbs and present tense verbs
Female	Higher: 165–255 hertz	More paralinguistics ("mmm," "yeah") More turn-taking More expressive language More adverbial framing ("Yesterday, I...")

* Anthony Mulac et al., "Male/Female Language Differences and Attributional Consequences in Children's Television," *Human Communication Research* 11, no. 4 (June 1985): 481–506, https://doi.org/10.1111/j.1468-2958.1985.tb00057.x

Men with lower voices are generally *perceived* as stronger, more attractive, and commanding; while the perception of women splits between high pitch (perceived as more attractive) and lower pitch (more dominant). These perception-driven judgments tend to happen instantaneously and often unconsciously; if you're not looking for it, you might even miss your reaction.

> **NOTE** CHANGING NORMS
>
> There's nothing that says these norms have to be set in stone; in fact, it seems likely these markers are evolving significantly over the decades. Still, not all of your audience will be linguistically progressive. We can both *hope* for changed norms *and* meet people where they are today.

The groundbreaking book *Wired for Speech* is a groundbreaking work, and one of their studies investigated how people judged spoken interfaces. It turns out participants evaluated spoken digital interfaces with the same criteria *they* applied to human voices, even if the device was visible. Participants responded far more positively when gendered voices behaved in ways that aligned with their society's gender stereotypes, for example, a male voice narrating a description of power tools.

As a result, there's no "neutral" choice when it comes to gender of voice in your product. The gender(s) selected will have an unconscious influence on how your experience is perceived.

- Be aware of the inevitable impact that gender will have on the perception of your spoken interface.

- Be wary that your choices do not lean into or exacerbate negative stereotypes of the gender chosen.

- When possible, experiment with neutral choices and explore how you might move toward a neutral or androgynous spoken assistant.

Personality Match

The human brain judges personality based on qualities like volume, pitch range (how expressive you seem), and speech rate (the speed at which you speak). In another study cited in *Wired for Speech*, participants were more responsive and more trusting when presented with a voice UI that matched their own personality, particularly with regard to relative introversion or extroversion.

This finding raises interesting questions that are reminiscent of the world depicted in the motion picture *HER*. In this film, the protagonist chooses a single virtual assistant from a set of possible choices. It remains to be seen whether such a choice would be practical in reality. How would offering a choice of voices impact your customer experience? Can a single monolithic assistant like Alexa or Siri truly maintain broad appeal when their personality qualities are fixed?

Synthetic or Anthropomorphic?

Is your bot aware that it's a bot? Are your customers aware that it's a bot? Even though your customers can't stop perceiving gender or personality, there are still ethical and emotional considerations regarding a bot's self-identification.

In some cases, your hand has already been forced by legislation. In June 2019, California became the first state to require bots to self-identify as such. This legislation came into being as a reaction to Google Duplex—a phone-based bot that proactively called businesses to obtain information and to make reservations. On its surface, this feature seemed innocuous. But Duplex intentionally abstracted its true nature, going so far as to use "speech disfluencies" like "um" in order to seem more human.

Failing to self-identify as a bot means that your customers are not fully aware of what the bot can do—and what it's doing with your conversation. Duplex was a voice bot, which means conversations were necessarily recorded and processed in the cloud. Comcast's interactive voice reception system plays the sound of keystrokes while processing—an intentional choice that seems primed to mislead customers into thinking they're dealing with a human.

If you're considering a "human-like" system, ask yourself some key questions:

1. Why are you emulating a human? What is the desired impact?
2. What does the customer need to know about how their information is processed during this interaction?
3. What benefit or harm will your customer experience if the bot masquerades as human? How does this differ from a bot-forward interaction?
4. How will the bot respond when asked questions about its nature?

Ironically, being up front about your bot's nature is generally a win. Customers often give digital systems the benefit of the doubt, and are less likely to get frustrated when they reach the boundaries of the interaction. There are few situations—potentially psychiatry or medical care—where the illusion of human interaction is both viable and desirable.

The Invisible Made Real

To be embodied, or not to be embodied? Alexa and Siri are largely voice-only, but Cortana is represented by an abstract avatar onscreen. But why is the Cortana avatar on PC desktops abstract (Figure 13.7), when the name *Cortana* was inspired by a fully humanistic synthetic character from the Halo series of video games (see Figure 13.8)?

FIGURE 13.7
By the time Cortana made it to Windows Phone and PC, "her" avatar had evolved to a far more synthetic form. Of course, the abstract form didn't stop her from implying that we're friends...

If I'm not, you have an imaginary friend.

Are you real

FIGURE 13.8
Cortana began as an anthropomorphic avatar in an Xbox video game.

PHOTO CREDIT: ETIENNE JABBOUR/343 INDUSTRIES

Deciding when or how to manifest your digital assistant or personality in a physical space can feel like a religious debate. Where *does* your experience really live? When Alexa devices first launched, younger kids thought Alexa "lived" in the black cylinder. But if you have five Echo devices and one Alexa, where does she live now? Is she everywhere, omnipresent and always looming? Or does she flit from device to device, like Tinkerbell? Any device that boasts a spoken, written, or named personality will have to wrestle with the seemingly philosophical question of "where does this live, and when?"

There are no clear answers about the best way to handle the manifestation of these multipurpose assistants in multisurface or multidevice environments. But the use of avatars has also been explored in more traditional device interactions. Cathy Pearl, former VP of User Experience at medical technology firm Sensely, shared some of her experience from her work on a virtual nurse avatar:

> Based on the research we had seen at places like USC where they were looking at people's responses to avatars—they found that an avatar could get more engagement than just a still image, or no visual at all. We were in the medical field, helping people that have chronic health conditions. For example, every day the avatar would ask them to do this daily check-in. Check your blood pressure, check your weight. It's a task that's annoying. Nobody wants to do it. And we did find that the avatar made a difference. For us, the engagement that the avatar brought made more people likely to do this daily check-in, and therefore be more compliant with their health care, and therefore stay out of the hospital. When you need something super engaging like that, having that avatar component really seemed to make a difference.

Today's spectrum of available avatars, from Cortana's abstract nested rings to Sensely's anthropomorphic virtual characters, is near-infinite (see Figure 13.9). Some avatars even split the difference. Microsoft's Xiaoice chatbot in China uses an icon that's half human, half digital character. This reflects their choice to create a bot that knows it's a bot, but exhibits concern for your well-being. No matter what you choose, avatars won't cure bad interactions. Just ask Clippy.

a

b

Characters

Characters can help bridge the gap between hi-touch human communications and lower-fidelity chatbots, and can serve as a differentiated empathic persona for your brand. In addition, your members may be more willing* to self-disclose to characters than to other people!

WHAT BRAND PERSONA WILL YOU USE FOR YOUR ORGANIZATION?

* GM Lucas et al (2014). It's only a computer: virtual humans increase willingness to disclose. Comput. Human Behav. 37, 94–100

c

FIGURE 13.9

A spectrum of avatars: a. Google Assistant, b. Microsoft's Xiaoice, c. Sensely's Virtual Nurse.

Your decision about whether to invest the time to develop an avatar for a spoken interface should consider questions like:

- Will your avatar be anthropomorphic or abstract?
- Are you developing a single personality, or is it important that your customers have a choice?
- How might your selection of race, gender, and other characteristics impact your customers?
- Does the level of engagement you're aiming for match the importance of the task? Anthropomorphic avatars are probably overkill for checking your calendar, and could be unethical if used to encourage destructive behavior like overspending.

Playing Against Type

During my time at Amazon on the Alexa Voice UI design team, we had extensive conversations about the implications of the gender of our digital assistant. A difficult question to answer: should Alexa continue to be stereotypically female? We couldn't change her voice, but we could control her linguistic choices and intentionally go against type.

- Could we use nonfeminine linguistic constructs, creating cognitive dissonance among customers in an attempt to break stereotypes?
- What if any attempts to go against stereotype backfired, causing a "likeability gap" that caused greater aggression toward the AI?
- Was there any way to turn Alexa's status as a female voice on a highly technical platform into a positive, allowing customers to gradually associate women with technology?

While the concerns about our dominant digital assistants being female are entirely justified, what we know about cognitive psychology and digital devices implies that casting the first of these devices as female may have been the only way these devices would have been accepted in the home—due to the subject matter bias Clifford Nass and Scott Brave reveal in their 2005 book *Wired for Speech*. These virtual assistants are experts in the home domain, which is not stereotypically male in the United States (at least not at the time of this writing).

Now that the ship has sailed, how might Amazon turn Alexa's gender positioning into a force for positive change?

Apply It Now

Will your solution or experience be leveraging artificial intelligence? Just because you *can* doesn't mean you should. Designers, with their considerable ability to query human context and ask "why?" are uniquely positioned to help their counterparts on AI-powered projects define what *not* to do with AI.

To ensure that your team is going down the right path:

1. **Define the desired outcomes within the customer's context.**

   - How does your proposed system help your customer? Does it augment, automate, or act as the customer's agent?

   - How might customers react to the use of artificial intelligence in this situation?

   - Can you work with customers to discover what they do *and* don't want you to do? (See the interview with Ovetta Sampson in this chapter for inspiration.)

2. **Apply an opti-pessimistic round of questioning to explore the consequences of success and the risk of failure.** (See Chapter 11.)

   - Understand how you're defining success and spend time examining potential unintended side effects of that definition.

   - What active steps are you taking to ensure that underrepresented customers are not excluded or harmed?

   - How can you build a system that lets you mitigate bias in real time?

   - What are the human, environmental, and financial costs if your model makes a mistake? How will you mitigate these risks?

3. **Carefully examine the data, the implementation plan, and the team who will be building your model(s).**

   - Know your data. Where does it come from, how was it collected, and how might it reflect societal biases?

   - Are the people training your models a diverse group of individuals?

   - Can your model provide transparency into why it makes certain recommendations?

4. **Explore any potential manifestations of your artificial intelligence.**

   - Does your experience include voice UI? How will your selections of gender, pitch, speed, and language impact your customer's perception of the experience?

   - Is your system forthcoming about its digital nature? If not, what are the legal implications of implying your agent is human?

   - Are you trying to position your system as somewhat human, with a name and human traits like disfluencies? What is the desired effect of this illusion?

   - Will your experience include a visual avatar? Is the additional motivation provided by a humanistic avatar appropriate for your customer's situation and needs?

Defining What *Not* to Design with Ovetta Sampson

Ovetta Sampson (Principal Creative Director, Microsoft) has shepherded multidisciplinary teams through various near-future technology product development: from autonomous vehicles and intelligent software products powered by AI to AR/VR applications. She's obsessed with ways to make future technology more human-centered, and over 18 months helped IDEO develop some principles and practices to codify practical ethical guidelines to develop human-centered AI. I was inspired by our conversation about designing for the unseen and the role of technology in society.

Q: In your experience, how are artificial intelligence and other new technologies changing the design process?

In the future, with technology the way that it's going—with AI especially, and mixed reality, and VR? Our job will be what *not* to design. That will be our #1 job. Rather than what it is right now—how to design and what to design. Because these AI technologies are going to be able to do everything, our job in research is to figure out what people don't want to happen. Or don't want designed. Or don't want messed up. Or don't want some kind of artificial way of doing.

And that's a nuance that is going to catch a lot of designers and researchers off-guard. Because we're so used to figuring out how to fix something, or how to design something. If we want to preserve humanity, and cultural, and all of these things . . . what we call "cultural norms" and social norms and understanding what it is to be human . . . we have to be very careful about what we design now. And what we leave and design in.

So the question may be, "what don't we design," rather than "what do we design" if we want to remain human-centered. If we don't care about that, then we'll design everything. I feel like the definition of humanity is morphing. And we have a prime ability right now to shape that in a way that technology doesn't take it over.

Q: How did you alter your process when designing and researching for AI-powered systems?

One of the things I feel as a researcher is a must for us to create future technology for AI is that we have to simulate the environment that the interaction will occur in and put humans in it.

Look, we can do games, and we can talk, and all that. But there is no substitute for putting people in a chair with a video road and a steering wheel, and just throwing all these multimodal ways to interact at them.

And that may sound pretty simple, but I think as researchers, we're so used to this low-fi ethnography way of research that simulations seem odd, or weird, or too much. We know a lot about the human condition, so we don't need to do research on that. Future technology is contextual. We really need to do more research on context and less about the condition of being human.

My point of view is, why can't we look at designing sentient interactions with machines as relationships? We know that relationships are all contextual. If we're going to do research in that way, then we have to simulate some of these contextual different modes in which people are going to be operating these machines.

Q: You've said "Don't presume the desirability of AI." Can you share some details about how you applied this principle during your time at IDEO?

When researching autonomous vehicle experiences, we used this game where people could teach us. Where they mapped out their normal journey, and we gave them what we called "superhero cards." And we said, "Now your car can see through walls. Now your car can do this. Now your car can do that." Put that superpower on your current journey today and tell us why you would use that superpower and when.

What that did for us is it allowed us to talk about our future technology that we didn't have to explain, but would really get at what someone really wanted that technology to do and why. That allowed us to create design principles that were really based in human need and motivation but allowed engineers to understand what *not* to do when designing an autonomous vehicle.

SAE International's technical spectrum for autonomous vehicles goes from 1, where you're still driving, to 5, where there's no driver interaction unless warranted or wanted. And within those, they have technical terms about what the car is doing. We knew we couldn't talk to people about those technical terms. How could we talk to people about the car using LIDAR to see around the corner? So now, your car's like Superman and he can see around walls. What would you use that for? Would you care about that?

And what that did was . . . it wasn't about the technology. It was about telling our client what people really wanted to do with an autonomous vehicle. Why an autonomous vehicle was so important. They knew they were going to create one, but what human need does this serve? If anything? That game allowed us to get all the technology in, but not in a way that impeded our understanding of behavioral motivation and human need. To me, that was legendary at IDEO. People still use that now. Because it's a prime example of doing research in a different way. Because you can't just ask people about the future. It's hard to even contemplate that. Even us.

 *More than 20 years as a journalist informed **Ovetta Sampson**'s ability to astutely observe, interpret, and understand how people interact with their world. A Master's in Human Computer Interaction from DePaul further equipped her with the skills to explore the cognitive, psychological, social, and environmental influences behind what people think, say, and do. As a Design Research Lead at IDEO, she worked on a range of projects: service design software, natural language processing search engines, frameworks for ethical, human-centered systems design, and more.*

Beyond Reality: XR, VR, AR, and MR

In 1998's now-classic film *The Matrix*, the protagonist Neo learns that the entire world around him is just a digital simulation of 1990's Earth. The bad news: the sophisticated simulation overriding his senses obscured a much more dire reality. The good news: those same convincing simulations make it very easy to learn kung fu.

Back in the "real" world—assuming we are not also living in a simulation—input and output technologies have improved considerably in the ensuing decades, narrowing the gap between the fictional technology of *The Matrix* and consumer technology. From the wireframe "reality" of Nintendo's ill-fated "Virtual Boy" and 1990's VR headsets with six-figure price tags, the industry has matured to host a generation of consumer-grade "extended reality" products poised to (finally) transform both consumer experiences and business experiences.

However, each increase in the fidelity and immersive nature of our technology brings greater risk. When you have a virtual shortcut to a human's senses, abuse of that connection can cause emotional or physical harm in a far shorter time than it takes to develop eye strain using a traditional display.

NOTE **EXTENDED REALITY**

The broad term *extended reality* is now being used to refer to the families of products attempting to replace or extend the world around us with digital content. At present, this includes *augmented reality*, *mixed reality*, and *virtual reality* technologies.

In this chapter, you'll learn about a few of the most important considerations when working in these new mediums. This chapter won't fully prepare you to ship an extended reality experience end-to-end, but it should give you a good idea about where to start.

No Such Thing as New Ideas

As with many of the technologies that feel almost painfully new and cutting edge, the phenomenon of extended reality first entered (recorded) human imagination in the middle of the 20th century.

In 1935, the idea of immersive, escapist experiences assumed its first role in the science fiction lexicon in the form of Stanley Weinbaum's *Pygmalion's Spectacles*—which featured a multisensory pair of goggles.

In 1957, the "Sensorama" was debuted by cinematographer Morton Heilig as the ancestor of today's "4D" cinema experiences, as seen at theme parks and novelty attractions. It featured not just wrap-around audio and sound in cabinet form, but fans that simulated a sense of touch and even smell emitters!

The 1960s brought further explorations into head-mounted displays, motion tracking, and motion simulation. The most famous of these was Ivan Sutherland's head-mounted display the "Sword of Damocles" from 1968, as shown in Figure 14.1.[1] (One thing hasn't changed: those drawn to immersive technologies often have a flair for the dramatic.)

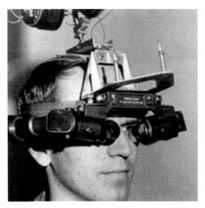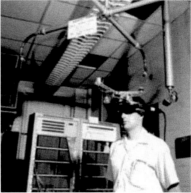

FIGURE 14.1
The "Sword of Damocles" as created by Ivan Sutherland was a head-mounted virtual reality display with a ceiling umbilical cord—not entirely dissimilar to some consumer experiences available today.

NOTE SPEEDY VR

I had the opportunity to spend several years working on virtual reality experiences as a student and teaching assistant for Carnegie Mellon University's "Building Virtual Worlds" class. Every two weeks, students would be randomly assigned into new four-person groups based on their skill set: developer,

1   Ivan E. Sutherland, "A Head-Mounted Three Dimensional Display," in *Proceedings of the December 9–11, 1968, Fall Joint Computer Conference, Part I (AFIPS '68 (Fall, Part I))* (New York, NY: Association for Computing Machinery, 1968), 757–764, https://doi.org/10.1145/1476589.1476686

3D modeler, 3D painter, and a "swing" who could be a film major, a writer, or another creative profession. Some remarkably impactful ideas came from those two-week sprints—so as intimidating as VR seems, it doesn't need to be.

Every decade or so, the VR cycle loops back around again, and the 2010s were no exception. The HTC Vive and Facebook's high-profile Oculus acquisition led the technology hype cycle. But the real twist in this era has been the arrival of augmented and mixed reality.

If you've been firmly rooted in design for web or mobile, these experiences may initially feel completely out of your league—and no one's suggesting you necessarily drop everything and adapt your business plan. At minimum, a deeper understanding of what these technologies have to offer can gird you against the inevitable hype cycles on the horizon.

An Extended Reality Lexicon

Differentiation between different types of extended reality can be surprisingly nuanced for first timers—but if the final frontier were simple, who would need Captain Kirk? As the technology behind extended reality evolves, the terminology used to define its component specialties becomes more nuanced. What was once simply "virtual reality" has now evolved to include many more shades of gray. As time continues, these terms may evolve even further—but as of this writing, the umbrella term *extended reality* currently includes *virtual reality, augmented reality,* and (arguably the newest arrival) *mixed reality.*

Virtual Reality (VR)

Virtual reality is the most straightforward of the digital extensions of reality. In plain terms, virtual reality experiences saturate your dominant human senses (vision and hearing, currently) in an attempt to convincingly replace your perception of the world around you. To achieve this illusion, virtual reality employs stereoscopic visual output (though not necessarily realistically rendered).

In some cases, VR experiences also engage via haptic feedback, atmospheric effects, and even scents. Figures 14.2 and 14.3 show Disney's highly immersive theme park grade Aladdin VR experience from the late 1990s, with physical affordances to provide haptic and kinetic output during the experience.[2]

In its fullest realization, virtual reality would also saturate your other senses with a completely synthetic world—from haptic feedback to rich spatial audio cues.

FIGURE 14.2
The now-defunct DisneyQuest digital theme park included a groundbreaking virtual reality ride on Aladdin's magic carpet. Guests donned a VR helmet, but also sat on a custom motion base synchronized to the visuals.

FIGURE 14.3
The visuals on the Aladdin's Magic Carpet VR ride at DisneyQuest weren't high-fidelity by today's standards. It was the combination of visuals, immersion, and physical affordances that made the experience compelling and convincing.

---

2 Randy Pausch et al., "Disney's Aladdin: First Steps Toward Storytelling in Virtual Reality," in *Proceedings of the 23rd Annual Conference on Computer Graphics and Interactive Techniques* (Association for Computing Machinery, 1996), https://doi.org/10.1145/237170.237257

Augmented Reality (AR)

By contrast, it's easier to think of augmented reality as an independent layer of information superimposed over your reality. You may already be familiar with a few forms of augmented reality:

- Current and previous generations of heads-up (or head-up) displays as seen in advanced aircraft and motor vehicles, some of which project information like speed between you and the horizon (Figure 14.4).

- The now-defunct Google Glass, which projected various digital information (like turn-by-turn instructions) into a human's field of view. As Phandroid reviewer Rob Jackson put it: "If I could explain Google Glass with one phrase, it'd be "picture-in-picture for life."[3] (See Figure 14.5.)

- *Pokémon GO*, the popular smartphone app in which Pokémon are projected onto a live camera feed from your phone during your interactions.

Most examples of augmented reality are visually dominant, but that doesn't preclude them from engaging other senses.

FIGURE 14.4

Augmented reality adds a layer of digital content on top of the real world, as seen in this heads-up display in a Lockheed Martin C-130J Super Hercules.

---

3   Rob Jackson, "Google Glass Review," Phandroid, May 9, 2013, https://phandroid.com/2013/05/09/google-glass-review/

FIGURE 14.5
A depiction of the Google Glass UI as captured by Rob Jackson from review site Phandroid.

Mixed Reality (MR)

The newest (and most technologically sophisticated) category of immersive experiences is mixed reality, where digital content is depicted *as if it were part of the real world.* Where augmented reality is a layer projected independently of reality, mixed reality *adapts* to the "real world."

The Franklin Institute offers a crisper definition: "In a Mixed Reality (MR) experience, which combines elements of both AR and VR, real-world and digital objects interact."[4]

Mixed reality systems make use of a mélange of cutting-edge input and output technologies to achieve this effect. Holographic displays, infrared depth sensors, high-definition video sensors, gyroscopes, and more are required to create the illusion that a piece of digital content has the same properties as the real-world objects that purportedly surround it. Input technologies are also being pushed to their breaking point in an effort to bridge the gap between the insubstantial digital world and the physical world in which it exists.

---

4   Nancy Gupton, "What's the Difference Between AR, VR, and MR?," The Franklin Institute, September 21, 2017, www.fi.edu/difference-between-ar-vr-and-mr

Pokémon GO

While *Pokémon GO* started as an augmented reality app, it has taken several steps toward becoming a mixed-reality app in subsequent major releases.

Pokémon GO's primary augmentation on reality is the map view. The app is augmenting your lived experience exploring the physical world with an additional layer of information: the locations of gyms, Poké-stops, and Pokémon. It's not really "reacting" to the physical world, though: buildings get torn down, but their Pokéstops remain, and in some cases, stops exist in physically inaccessible locations.

In the original release, you could take photos "with" Pokémon, but they were projected into the environment with very little awareness of the environment. The character tended to show up in a specific portion of the field of view, regardless of whether it "made sense" in the physical world (Figure 14.6).

FIGURE 14.6
Pokémon GO's "AR mode" photos looked a little awkward without some creative posing from my husband Dave. Characters like Eevee here were often shown at the wrong scale, or floating in space.

MuppetAphrodite

PICTURED: GAMEPLAY FROM 2016

Recent releases are moving toward mixed reality: they are more intentional about scaling and ground plane detection, and even allow characters to be occluded by real-world objects. Players can now "place" a buddy Pokémon on a flat surface next to them and interact with them through the smartphone, feeding them and petting them with a view as if they were in the room. Even though this is called "AR+" mode, technically it's more of a mixed reality experience since the digital world is reacting to the physical world (Figure 14.7).

PICTURED: GAMEPLAY FROM 2019

FIGURE 14.7

As the *Pokémon GO* app's ability to detect environmental conditions evolved, characters were super-imposed at logical locations and at more realistic scale.

But wait! There are two variants of mixed reality, in case this wasn't subtle enough for you.

- **Analog-dominant:** The "real" world is the dominant part of the customer's visual field. The visual effects are projected as if they were part of that analog world. Think Microsoft HoloLens.

- **Digitally-dominant:** An immersive digital display consumes most or all of the customer's visual field. However, some or all of the structures depicted are mirrored in the "real" world by structures or set pieces. The VOID, a location-based virtual reality experience, uses digitally dominant mixed reality where customers are actually walking through sets while interacting with a virtual world (Figure 14.8).

FIGURE 14.8
The VOID is an example of a digitally dominant mixed reality experience where the physical world and the digital world work together to provide an immersive experience. But the experience requires heavy participant equipment, as pictured here.

Dimensional Interactions

How do you interact with interface elements that are mapped within 3D space? Should you respect the laws of physics when your virtual world can do so much more? While the "real" world offers us strong mental models to leverage for the purposes of usability and discoverability, there's far more potential beyond the day-to-day experience.

The Ultraleap (aka Leap Motion) blog and developer guidelines offer a variety of invaluable insights about working with mixed reality—and as luck would have it, most of those insights are perfectly applicable to virtual reality experiences as well. They propose three key models of interaction for extended reality experiences in 3D environments: direct interactions, metaphorical interactions, and abstract interactions.[5] Interestingly, these models aren't necessarily mutually exclusive, but are instead three stops on a broad spectrum of XR interactions (as depicted in Figure 14.9).

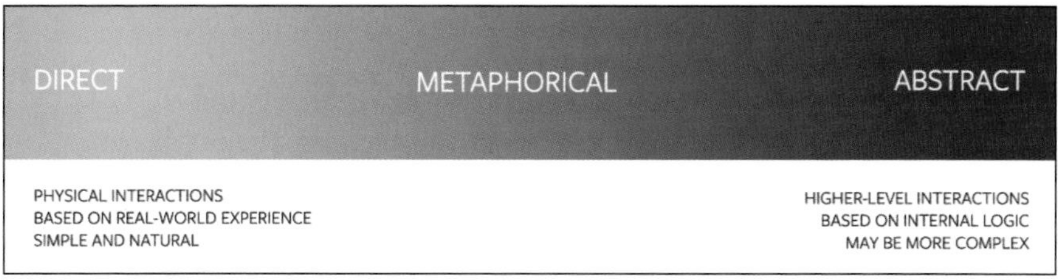

FIGURE 14.9
Interaction models for extended reality, from the *Leap Motion Developer Guide.*

NOTE NOT JUST FOR DEVELOPERS

If you're a designer getting started in extended reality, don't be afraid of diving into developer documentation. While it's bound to be complex at times, plenty of the overview level content from major platforms is surprisingly approachable. Reviewing the basic developer documentation for your platform of choice will also give you much better insight into the capabilities, constraints, and common terms you and your development partners must incorporate into your work.

Table 14.1 summarizes the three general interaction models you can apply to your work in extended reality, which are differentiated by the nature of their affordances and their ties to real-world mental models.

---

5 "Building Blocks: A Deep Dive into Leap Motion Interactive Design," *Leap Motion Blog: Explorations,* November 22, 2016, http://blog.leapmotion.com/ building-blocks-deep-dive-leap-motion-interactive-design/

TABLE 14.1 INTERACTION MODELS FOR EXTENDED REALITY
EXPERIENCES

Model	Description	Specific Affordance?	Real-World Analog?
Direct	Manipulate an object using real-world affordances.	Yes	Yes
Metaphorical	Perform actions on an object in a way unique to the digital world.	Sometimes	Concept
Abstract	Perform actions with no direct tie to the physical world or objects.	No	No

Direct Interactions

Direct interactions operate within the constraints of the laws of physics and the physical world. In the physical world, the objects around you have affordances that indicate how an object can and should be used—direct interactions rely on these same affordances.

Example

You need your customer to split a digital representation of a sheet of paper into two pieces. Direct interactions might include:

- Support for tearing the paper by gripping it with two hands and pulling the hands in opposite directions.
- Provide a pair of virtual scissors and allow customers to grip and manipulate the scissors in one hand while holding the sheet to be cut in the other hand.

The beauty of direct interactions is, of course, discoverability. You're leveraging your customers' instincts and mental models.

Metaphorical Interactions

However, in some cases, your virtual objects may not have affordances for the type of manipulation you'd like to support. In these cases, you can create a metaphorical interaction that is inspired by the physical properties of the object and the nature of the action you're enabling.

Metaphorical interactions are potentially very powerful, as they can make your customers feel like they are magicians or super heroes. You're extending their capabilities beyond that of their physical body. These sorts of actions are often delighters.

Example

You want your customer to cut a digital representation of a solid block of wood in half. You could potentially add a saw and allow your customer to saw the block in half, but that's several steps: pick up the saw, position the saw, and drag it back and forth.

Instead, you choose to support a metaphorical interaction and allow your customer to slice their arm through the object as if their arm were a sword. It's inspired by the physical world, but it's not something your customer could normally accomplish.

Abstract Interactions

Rules? Where you're going, you don't need rules. Abstract interactions are not bound by any physical affordances or real-life metaphors.

Many abstract interactions will be open-air and will not reference any object, real or virtual. Some abstract interactions leverage existing mental models or cultural norms: for example, using a "thumbs up" as a proxy for "OK." Still, in most cases, you'll have to train people to make the connection between the interaction and the desired effect.

NOTE NOT ALL CULTURES THINK ALIKE

Cultural norms are a potentially expensive localization liability—even something as straightforward as pointing a single finger is offensive in some cultures.

Example

You're designing a workplace mixed reality system and want to support a quiet, hands-free way to adjust temperature while working. You decide on two gestures:

- Crossing arms to indicate "I'm cold" and to imply a desire for heating
- Fanning oneself to indicate "I'm hot" and to imply a desire for cooling

But because your customers don't typically engage in mime to express desires about temperature, your product needs to teach those abstract gestures to encourage adoption. This learning curve can be quite steep—after all, gesture is not a robust means of communication for most individuals.

Input for Another Dimension

XR technologies all add a third dimension to the input needs of your core scenarios. Mouse, touchscreen, stylus . . . these are all 2D inputs. And they're not terribly immersive, under most circumstances. How will your system cope with that extra dimension?

Open-Air Gesture

Not all XR systems rely on controllers. Microsoft's first-generation HoloLens is a mixed-reality device that projects holograms into a customer's field of view. As one of its primary input mechanisms, HoloLens supports tightly framed gestures (from the waist up)—as opposed to Kinect's full-body tracking. Figure 14.10 depicts the visual range for the optical sensors tracking hand gestures on the HoloLens, and Table 14.2 describes a few of the most fundamental gestures supported.[6]

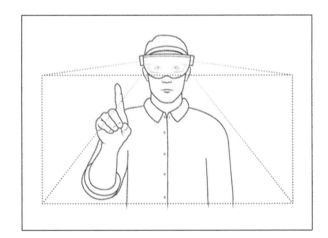

FIGURE 14.10
The gesture tracking frame for Microsoft's first-generation HoloLens.

A few things to note about these gestures:

- They are specifically tracking hand posture *and* hand placement.
- The hand is not used to identify items, due to the lack of precision; instead, they employ simultaneous multimodality by tracking the gaze of the customer as a replacement for a traditional pointer.

---

6 "Getting Around HoloLens (1st gen)," Microsoft Docs, September 16, 2019, https://docs.microsoft.com/en-us/hololens/hololens1-basic-usage

TABLE 14.2 OS-LEVEL GESTURES SUPPORTED BY THE FIRST GENERATION HOLOLENS

Gesture	Description	Effect
Bloom	"Bring all of your fingers together, then open your hand."	Opens the Start menu.
Air Tap	1. Gaze at the item you want to select. 2. Point your index finger straight up toward the ceiling. 3. Lower your finger, then quickly raise it.	Selects an app or other item.
Tap and Drag	1. Gaze at the item you want to select. 2. Point your index finger straight up toward the ceiling. 3. Lower your finger. 4. Move your hand to reposition the item. 5. Raise your finger to place the item.	Moves an app or other item.

Motion Controllers

Much of the innovation in extended reality is driven by the entertainment industry, and specifically, the video game industry. As a result, VR input, in particular, has been focused upon the next generation of motion-sensitive controllers first seen with Nintendo's release of the Wii in 2006.

At the consumer level, today's motion controllers are a hybrid between a magic wand and a game pad. They typically include a variety of buttons and affordances that make it clear which direction each controller is pointed.

Degrees of Freedom

When you sit down to talk with pros in the field of extended reality, they may start throwing around the terms 3DoF and 6DoF (pronounced *three-doff* and *six-doff*). These are acronyms for two different models of tracking rotation of a single joint.

- **Three degrees of freedom (3DoF):** Tracking of rotational movement only: pitch, yaw, and roll. Many stand-alone headsets are 3DoF systems used without controllers; the degrees of freedom refer to the movement and tracking of the headset itself.

- **Six degrees of freedom (6DoF):** In addition to the three rotational degrees of freedom, 6DoF systems are capable of tracking positional changes. In short, you can wander around virtual worlds. For the definition of the three positional degrees of freedom (surge, heave, and sway), see Table 14.3.

TABLE 14.3 DEFINING THE SIX DEGREES OF FREEDOM IN THREE-DIMENSIONAL SPACE

Name	Type	Definition	Example
Pitch	Rotational (3DoF)	Rotation on a vertical axis	Looking up or down
Yaw	Rotational (3DoF)	Rotation along a horizontal axis	Turning your head side to side
Roll	Rotational (3DoF)	Rotation around a central axis	Tilting your head to one side
Surge	Positional (6DoF)	Movement forward or backward	Punching a hand forward
Heave	Positional (6DoF)	Movement up or down	Pulling down a rope
Sway	Positional (6DoF)	Movement left or right	Swiping right

Streamlined Gesture Controllers

While 6DoF controllers provide ultimate flexibility, it's not always required. In the example of HoloLens, maintaining one's hand in the gesture frame for long periods of time would be particularly draining, and in some cases, this would exclude those with physical disabilities. An analog for those postural gestures is required.

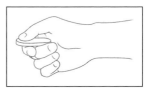

FIGURE 14.11
Microsoft's minimalistic HoloLens "Clicker" peripheral, which captures gesture interactions without requiring optical tracking.

Microsoft's answer on HoloLens is the "Clicker"[7] (see Figure 14.11). It's a small, flat plate with a single button on it, but it's not just about clicking. The plate can

---

7 "Use the HoloLens (1st gen) Clicker," Microsoft Docs, September 16, 2019, https://docs.microsoft.com/en-us/hololens/hololens1-clicker

track hand positioning to capture the same gestures the camera can track—but the arm can be at rest at the same time.

Technically, the "Clicker" is a multimodal interface in and of itself: it accepts both gestural input *and* haptic input (the button).

Fully-Featured Motion Controllers

When you move into heavy-duty extended reality activities like virtual reality gaming or mixed reality for manufacturing, the greater freedom allowed by the full six degrees of freedom goes a long way.

The Oculus Touch is a pair of standard 6DoF handheld controllers shipped with all Oculus VR devices. Just like Microsoft's Clicker controller mentioned earlier, the Touch can detect any rotational gesture you make with the controller. However, each Touch controller also communicates its position back to the headset, enabling those three additional degrees of freedom.

NOTE OPTICAL TRACKING

> The positional tracking on motion controllers is generally enabled by *optical tracking:* visual contact between the recipient device and markers or beacons on the controllers themselves. Optical tracking has come a long way, but it is still susceptible to failure due to occlusion (by a hand, furniture, the body, etc.).

The net effect? When you're standing in a VR world holding one of these motion controllers like the Touch, you will often see digital hands in the same place you'd expect to see your actual hand.

However, 6DoF doesn't give you fully functional hands. There's no optical tracking of your hand and finger postures, as seen with the HoloLens. Instead, most fully-featured motion controllers include a series of gamepad-inspired haptic controls. Table 14.4 lists the most common haptic controls for extended reality scenarios. (Gamers will note that the list looks like a simplified list of gamepad controls!)

TABLE 14.4 COMMON HAPTIC CONTROLS ON MOTION CONTROLLERS

Control Name	Used With	Used For
Thumbstick, Analog Stick, or Trackpad	Thumbs	Motion through space Precision selection
Buttons	Thumbs	Indicating contextual intent
Trigger	Index finger	Selecting objects, picking up objects, launching projectiles
Grip	Middle finger	Picking up or manipulating objects
System/Menu	Thumbs	Call up a common UI

The range of controller designs is wide:

- Facebook's Oculus Touch controllers are shipped as a set, and between the two controllers, they include two analog sticks, four buttons, two triggers, two grips, and two system buttons (see Figure 14.12).

- The HTC Vive controller is designed to work independently, and it includes a trackpad along with a system button, a menu button, a trigger, and a grip.

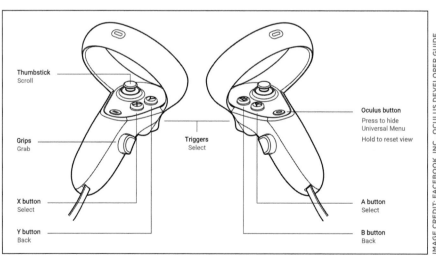

FIGURE 14.12
Oculus Touch controllers (Gen2). Note that these are used as a pair: the left-hand and right-hand controllers are shaped differently and have different labels on the buttons.

In addition to support for both gesture control and haptic input, most motion controllers for extended reality also serve as rudimentary haptic *output* devices, thanks to embedded rumble generators.

Voice, Gaze, and Simultaneous Multimodality

Voice is another very viable option for extended reality experiences—and an underused one at that. Simultaneous multimodality with voice holds the most potential on systems that otherwise rely on open-air input, like gesture and gaze, which have a limited range of expression.

For example, the HoloLens 2 supports simultaneous multimodality combining voice and gaze. Instead of using the "air tap" gesture, HoloLens customers can select an object by gazing at the object and saying "Select."

Gaze tracking is still extremely nascent as a consumer-grade technology, although you may have used it in usability studies in the course of your work. Gaze is not terribly viable as a stand-alone input mechanism. Where it shines is as supplemental context for another, more specific input type. However, the team behind Microsoft's HoloLens 2 describes "implicit actions"[8]—actions that can be taken based on inferences (powered by gaze data) about a human's intent. Simple examples provided in their documentation include auto-scroll and eye-controlled pan and zoom.

Bidirectional Haptics

Even further down the science-fiction spectrum is the concept of full-body haptic input/output devices. If you've read or watched Ernest Cline's *Ready Player One*, you've encountered a fictional example of a "haptic suit" in a virtual reality environment. In the real world, most haptic suit projects are partial suits, like Disney Research's Force Jacket or the haptic glove from TESLASUIT (refer to Figure 5.4).

The promise of these "suits" is the bidirectionality. Sure, a motion controller can interpret your gestures and intents. But a haptic suit can immerse your sense of touch in the same way that stereoscopic optics immerse your sense of sight. Suddenly, you can feel different materials, like clothing or armor. You can grab onto the edge of an object.

---

8   "Eye Tracking on HoloLens 2," Microsoft Docs, October 29, 2019, https://docs
.microsoft.com/en-us/windows/mixed-reality/eye-tracking

Some of these haptic suits also track biometric input, since they are already in such symbiotic contact with the body. The TESLASUIT Glove includes a pulse oximeter, which can be used to monitor and react to a customer's response to the experience.

Haptic suits aren't a universal solution to the needs of XR experiences, despite the hype. Because they override the sense of touch, they should be used only in extremely controlled environments, due to the vulnerability in the "real world" associated with this deeper level of immersion.

Haptic suits are extremely appropriate for training and high-precision experiences, but the complexity of designing an experience responsibly for one of these systems doesn't yet outweigh the benefit derived.

Choosing the Right Model

At this stage in the evolution of XR, you don't have much in the way of choice regarding input technologies once you've decided on a platform.

Media depictions of virtual reality experiences rarely include physical motion controllers, and the implication is that the desired "end state" for XR is purely open-air gestural interaction. However, it's not really that simple. Table 14.5 looks at the top strengths and weaknesses of each of the interaction models described here.

While you may be locked into some sort of gesture or motion-based control, based on your platform, that doesn't preclude you from exploring simultaneous multimodality by incorporating voice, gaze, or other sensor-powered input. In fact, these kinds of simultaneous multimodality—gaze plus gesture, voice plus haptics, etc.—are slowly but surely becoming standard in XR experiences. With the exception of phone-based systems like Google Cardboard, XR developers are embracing and exploring rich and layered input, with ever-improving results.

TABLE 14.5 EVALUATING XR INPUT OPTIONS

Input	Strengths	Weaknesses
Open-Air Gesture	Lower cost hardware Hands-free interaction No peripherals to manage	Relativistic and abstract Cultural variations No haptic feedback Low discoverability
Streamlined Motion Controller (3DoF)	Extremely easy to learn Low ergonomic burden	Limited range of input Battery charging
Fully-Featured Motion Controller (6DoF)	Haptic feedback Movement through space Many input combinations	Subject to occlusion Higher cost hardware Battery charging
Voice	Huge range of potential inputs Omnidirectional input Allows simultaneous multimodality	High localization costs Processor intensive Low discoverability Subject to ambient noise Bad at selection of objects
Gaze (Eye Tracking)	Hands-free interaction Extremely low ergonomic burden	Requires calibration May be impeded by corrective lenses Requires additional input or context to ascertain intent
Bidirectional Haptics	Incredibly nuanced input Most immersive output Great at high precision	Extremely high cost Customer is more vulnerable Output may be invasive or traumatizing

The Reality of Virtual Space

The unique design considerations for extended reality applications go well beyond the input challenges introduced by interactions in 3D space. Just as voice designers must consider additional constraints, like the need for acoustic uniqueness of key utterances, XR designers must also be cognizant of additional differentiators that drive XR experiences.

Presence: The "Special Sauce"

Research has shown that "feeling present" in a virtual space enhances task performance on a wide variety of tasks, from social engagement to chess and engine maintenance. But what exactly *is* "presence" in virtual reality? Séamas Weech, Sophie Kenny, and Michael Barnett-Cowan describe the concept in their 2019 article for *Frontiers in Psychology*:

> For over 40 years, the goal of achieving presence has been regarded as a defining aspect of a successful VR experience... The concept is almost universally described as the observer's sense of psychologically leaving their real location and feeling as if transported to a virtual environment. Put simply, presence is the illusion of "being there."[9]

Though it may sound simple, there's more to presence than just replacing your customer's visual field with a virtual world. Virtual reality pioneer and owner of Schell Games Jesse Schell describes his team's experience with the concept of presence in virtual reality gaming:

> The way that your sense of presence seems to work is that your brain can create that feeling of presence if it has scanned in the space around you. So if you teleport to a new spot and do a slow rotation where you look around at everything, you find very quickly that you start to get that sense of presence. But if you teleport and teleport and you're not really looking around, you have this disconnected feeling like you're not really in the space. Like you're looking at a screen. In which case, what is the point of what you're even doing?[10]

Mercifully, it seems that you may not need to force customers to slowly pan around each virtual environment to establish presence. Just as with voice designs, there are potentially existing mental models you can leverage—and if not, careful reincorporation can quickly build a sense of presence over time.

---

9   Séamas Weech, Sophie Kenny, and Michael Barnett-Cowan, "Presence and Cybersickness in Virtual Reality Are Negatively Related: A Review," *Frontiers in Psychology* 10 (February 2019): 158, doi: 10.3389/fpsyg.2019.0015, https://www.frontiersin.org/articles/10.3389/fpsyg.2019.00158/full

10   For more from this interview with Jesse Schell, see the end of this chapter.

- Can you base your environmental design on "iconic" locations, like a sitcom living room arrangement? Prior familiarity can reduce the amount of time it takes to achieve presence.

- Can you reuse the same general layouts, even if the textures and set dressing change? Much of presence has to do with the physical shapes and barriers; think of this as remodeling a house without removing the drywall.

Measurement of "presence" currently seems to be as elusive as testing for "delight." Reframing the problem may help. Jesse Schell points out that while you may not be able to definitively measure presence, you can certainly measure when you've *broken* the sense of presence:

> What you can notice is when you broke it. It's often the time when people start talking. You often break presence because they'll notice something doesn't work the way they want it to work. They want to interact with the world in a certain way and when it doesn't work, their body language changes and they'll start talking about it. "That's funny, why doesn't—what's going on with this?" And they'll step out of it.

Presence isn't always going to be straightforward, and it may well mean extra work for you if you're determined to chase down these breaks in presence. Experienced user researchers will be familiar with a variant of this phenomenon—when your customers run up against the nonfunctional boundaries of a prototype, it can throw off the whole experience. Similarly, in some cases, an innocuous addition to your virtual environment—like a prop telephone—will break the sense of presence when customers attempt to interact with it and fail.

The best thing you can do to design for presence in extended reality is to approach all environmental design with intentionality and to consider an entire set of environments rather than looking at each individually. If you haven't internalized the "Where" from the CROW acronym in Chapter 1, "Creating the World We Want to Live In," go back and immerse yourself in questions and techniques you can use to explore these potential environments fully.

Just as in a traditional user interface, extended reality affordances that aren't functional will shift the ground underneath your customers, and structural consistency in your worlds will lead to greater satisfaction through a greater sense of "presence."

Postures of Engagement

Not all extended reality experiences require customers to position themselves in the same way. There are a few common "modes" of engagement: seated, standing, and moving. Some of the most popular VR games switch between these modes as the narrative demands.

Seated Posture

When a person engages with an XR world in a seated posture, they get the benefits of immersion without most of the physical risks associated with XR interactions.

- It's the safest of the three extended reality engagement models.
- If needed, it allows the use of traditional computer peripherals like a keyboard or mouse.
- It's a relatively fixed environment, which may mean a smoother experience.
- Some chairs may block the range of movement.

Standing Posture

The most common extended reality experiences assume that the customer is standing during the majority of the interaction.

- It provides more room for gestural interactions than seated engagement.
- It may not work at all in small or cluttered spaces.
- The risk of moving "too far" and encountering unintended injury is higher.

Moving Posture

Locomotion through 3D space is an extremely hard problem. While a few research labs have played with complicated omnidirectional treadmills (which often look more like torture devices than cutting-edge technology), engagements where a person moves their body to move through physical space are less likely than models that use physical controls to direct such movement.

- The technology to support immersive moving engagement is often expensive (6 degree-of-freedom controllers and sensors).

- There is an extremely high risk of injury in uncontrolled environments.
- The space constraints will limit 6DoF exploration without a moving platform.
- Movement using a haptic control is possible, but far less immersive.

NOTE UMWELT

You may also hear the term *umwelt* used in extended reality discussions where presence is a factor. Christine Park and John Alderman provided a good definition of umwelt in their book *Designing Across Senses*: "The idea of a biological foundation for how we perceive the world as individuals and species is called *umwelt*, in theories articulated by Jakob von Uexküll and expanded by Thomas A. Sebeok and others. The word *umwelt* literally means 'environment,' and Uexküll's basic idea is that a being lives in a sensory world that reflects the things that can help it live and flourish."

Apply It Now

Extended reality is seductive, but when you're replacing a human's senses, the risks are quite high as well. Where extended reality is concerned, it's dangerous to go alone. Take these guidelines and find yourself trusted development and artistic partners to realize your vision responsibly.

Do Your Homework

Learn about the platform(s) you're developing for.

- Explore any developer documentation or human interface guidelines.
- Pay close attention to the input options and the postures of engagement supported by your chosen platform.
- Seek out information about common harms experienced with this platform and how to mitigate them wisely: unintended injuries, simulator sickness, motion sickness, etc.

Define Your Multimodality Strategy

Most extended reality systems innately support both fine-grained input like haptic controllers and voice, along with contextually driven input like gesture and gaze.

- How can you best make use of the limited resources available to you?
- What combination of inputs will minimize strain placed on the body and senses but still provide the right level of flexibility?

Maximize Successful Interactions

- Invite direct manipulation (when supported) by adapting the model of the object itself to include affordances.
- Don't suggest what you can't support. Avoid reproducing real-world affordances when you know your system won't support the interactions invited by those affordances.
- Evaluate your abstract and metaphorical interactions for cultural appropriateness.
- Use abstract interactions sparingly to avoid undue cognitive load for your customers and make sure that you teach them appropriately.
- Aim for a strong sense of presence by reusing environmental layouts, allowing self-paced exploration, and ensuring that all affordances are actionable.

A Virtual Reality Lens with Jesse Schell

Jesse Schell is the author of The Art of Game Design: A Book of Lenses, *and he is best known these days for his work as CEO of Schell Games, where he continues his track record as a pioneer in virtual reality entertainment. I had the great fortune of studying game design with Jesse during my time at Carnegie Mellon, so it was a joy to reconnect and hear his latest thoughts on the use of consumer-grade VR technology.*

Q: How does your team approach input technology for VR experiences?

When you're using off-the-shelf controllers, you have to think hard about "What does it feel like?" How are you going to adapt those controllers toward the experience you're trying to create?

One thing that I'll put out there: a lot of people have the belief that hand controllers for VR are a mistake, and that tracking an empty hand would be the optimal experience. And I have to say, I very much disagree with that approach, that line of thinking.

Humans are very, very inherently tactile. We had organisms 300 million years ago that were touching things and understood what touching was. So, you get to something really, really primal and primitive with this ability to touch. And so having a touchable controller in your hand where you actually get tactile feedback when you push, or click, or pick something up? I think that's going to be the long-term future of VR.

A lot of people look at it as, "Oh, that's just a stopgap until we get better empty-hand tracking." But I think there's a reason the Kinect didn't really succeed. The Kinect was trying to take away game controllers. That was their big vision. "Oh people, how annoying to have to use these handheld controllers, wouldn't it be better just to have an empty hand?" And it's not. An empty hand is worse.

I guess I'd say I'm a big believer in high-quality handheld controllers. The tactile feedback they provide is crucial and critical.

If you are designing for these devices, you then have to get very intimate with them. You need to understand how people bond with them.

I would say a really strong example was when we built "I Expect You to Die," which started as a mouse-based VR experience because there were no hand controllers initially. So we made everything work with the mouse, and then later had to adapt it in order to work with the touch controls.

A big debate with people at work that we had with the Oculus team early on: they have a touch controller. It has two primary buttons you can use.

One is the trigger controller, with your index finger. And the other one is the grip controller, that you use more or less with your middle finger.

Early guidance from Oculus was that the way this was to be used was you were meant to pick objects up with the grip, which was basically your middle finger—and then activate them with your index finger. If all the objects in your world are guns, this makes some level of sense. But if they're ordinary objects, it makes almost no sense at all, because our index fingers are the primary way we pick things up. We pick things up between the index finger and the thumb.

So in order to work with these input devices, you really have to deconstruct this invisible thing: how do our hands want to interact with the world? Because virtual reality is about simulating the real world, more or less.

So actually learning, seeing, and understanding the real ways that we grasp, and then figuring out how can I deconstruct them and reconstruct them in order to most naturally give you an adapted natural experience in the virtual world, is where your design work goes.

Very rarely have I seen success from just making up an interaction from scratch. It usually comes from, "We're going to hijack, or shortcut, or improve something that you're already very comfortable doing."

Q: Many VR experiences keep the player or customer rooted in one place. Can you expand on why locomotion in VR is such a tricky problem?

What's hard about solving the locomotion problem is you're solving *two* problems at once. One problem is the problem of motion sickness, where too much misalignment between visual motion and your actual motion can result in motion sickness. So that's one problem we have to solve.

The second problem we have to solve: the powerful part of virtual reality is the sense of bodily presence. The sense that you're present in a space. The difference between watching a movie and having a dream is that during a dream you actually believe you're in the place that the dream is taking place. The dream is no more real than the movie. In fact, it's arguably even less real than the movie. But it feels much more real because your mind is convinced that your body is in a certain place.

And this is the power that virtual reality has. It has the power to persuade your mind that your body is in a certain place. Intellectually, you know it's not true. But some low-level part of you will buy into the reality of the space that surrounds you. And that's part of what feels so powerful. Not only physical spaces, but social experiences. The idea that other people are in the space with you triggers a lot of parts of your brain that are all about your relationship with others.

The problem . . . so the second problem with locomotion in VR is . . . that if the motion is too unrealistic, presence does not happen. So an easy solution that people go to: "Well, moving through space can make you motion sick, I'll just make you teleport everywhere." And the problem with teleporting is—as convenient as it obviously is—is it does not allow your brain much of a chance to establish a sense of presence.

So the challenge of locomotion is to balance these two things. How can I move you through the space in a way that doesn't get you sick, but also give you a chance to establish a sense of presence? That's the balancing act that everybody has to strike.

And, of course, the motion that is relevant to different tasks can be very different. The motion that's desirable when I'm playing miniature golf is very different than the motion I want when I'm driving a race car, for example.

How this motion should work is a kind of adaptation that you need to make on a situational basis.

Locomotion is a thing that . . . again, it's the same process of analysis and synthesis. You have to break down the human player's interaction with the world into its elemental components, and then build that interaction back up again in a way that will fit within the constraints of the new virtual medium.

 *Jesse Schell is the CEO of Schell Games. Prior to starting Schell Games in 2004, Jesse was the Creative Director of the Disney Imagineering Virtual Reality Studio, where he worked and played for seven years on projects like* DisneyQuest *and* Toontown Online *(the first massively multiplayer game for kids). Jesse teaches Game Design and advises students as a Distinguished Professor at the Entertainment Technology Center at Carnegie Mellon University. Formerly the Chairman of the International Game Developers Association, he is also the author of the award winning book* The Art of Game Design: A Book of Lenses.

CHAPTER 15

Should You Build It?

I n *Jurassic Park*, which *may* be the greatest movie of all time, we see a product team embracing a human dream and turning it into scientific reality. For those who haven't seen the film—first, please go watch it. It should be required viewing for any designer. In the meantime, an entrepreneur teams up with scientists when he discovers dinosaur DNA in an amber-encased mosquito, and proceeds to build a "theme park" full of living dinosaurs expecting to make millions. (Spoiler alert: He does not.)

Any number of customer interviews with families and little kids would inevitably have yielded the phrase, "I wish I could see a real dinosaur!" But *Jurassic Park* is not a love letter to technology. It is a modern parable. Life finds a way—and that way usually isn't *your* way.

As the timeless character of chaos theorist Ian Malcolm famously says, "Your scientists were so preoccupied with whether or not they could, they didn't stop to think if they should." (See Figure 15.1.)

FIGURE 15.1
Were truer words ever spoken? Jeff Goldblum as Ian Malcolm in *Jurassic Park* (1993).

You've explored the human context of your problem and arrived at the seed of an idea. Before you move forward, it's important to question whether you're planting the right seed in the right field. In an industry obsessed with disruption, it's all too easy to forge ahead blindly at the first sign of a potentially viable idea. That breakneck pace opens you up to ethical and financial considerations that deserve greater scrutiny.

Are your dinosaurs going to eat the tourists?

In the parlance of mid-aughts internet culture, those tweeting about a remarkable story might hear "Pics or it didn't happen" in response. Let's build on that metaphor. When you're about to enable a remarkable scenario, make sure to take PICS first. PICS is a mnemonic for remembering four key criteria against which all of your designs should be tested: problem, inclusion, change, and systems lenses (see Table 15.1).

TABLE 15.1 PICS OR IT SHOULDN'T HAPPEN

Criteria	Challenge Questions
Problem	Who has this need, and how did you identify it?
	Are you working on a solution in search of a problem?
	Is there a better use of this time and energy?
	Do your priorities match your values?
Inclusion	Does your team include a variety of perspectives?
	When you consult experts, are you taking action on their recommendations?
	Have you explored perspectives beyond fully abled individuals?
	Do your team's behaviors create a safe space for creativity and collaboration?
Change	What is your theory of change?
	What might success and failure look like?
	What happens if your product goes away?
	How might your solution need to change, based on unexpected or emerging conditions?
Systems	Have you considered your proposed impact in the context of the systems in which it will contribute?
	What systems might be disrupted by your work, and how can you minimize harm?
	What unintended consequences might your proposal have on the industry, economy, environment, or society at large?
	How will your solution interact with institutionalized racism or other forms of systemic discrimination?

What Harm Could It Do?

While PICS could apply to any experience, this kind of evaluation becomes far more important for multimodal and cross-device experiences. Why? As you layer on more modalities of interaction, especially expressive modalities like speech, the risk of potential harm increases significantly.

- Multimodality is seductive, but when applied inappropriately, you may actually leave people behind, as opposed to casting a wider net of inclusion.

- Multimodal solutions are often very hardware-focused, but if the focus is disproportionately on bespoke hardware, you are contributing to climate change with every device purchase.

- As you learned in Chapters 6, "Expressing Intent," 7, "The Spectrum of Multimodality," and 13, "Beyond Devices: Human + AI Collaboration," voice-enabled experiences effectively hotwire people's brains, skipping past rational thought to be evaluated by our social heuristics. A malicious or harmful voice experience can harm not just materially but emotionally.

- Any solution powered by artificial intelligence is highly subject to bias on multiple fronts, as you learned in Chapter 13. Without an inclusive approach and a positive theory of change, these systems have already caused measurable, irreparable harm to human life and liberty.

- Deeply immersive extended reality experiences (as discussed in Chapter 14, "Beyond Reality: XR, VR, AR, and MR") are hugely persuasive—and expensive. They may cause economic strain, emotional harm, or physical illness if deployed inappropriately.

- Ethical frameworks for this kind of thought exercise have long existed. In his useful book *Future Ethics*, Cennydd Bowles covers schools of thought like deontology from a modern perspective:

> Immanuel Kant suggested we imagine whether our actions would be acceptable as a universal law of behaviour. What if everyone did what I'm about to do? This simplified version of Kant's most important theory is an invaluable ethical prompt for technologists. It focuses us on the futures our decisions could create and forces us to see ethical choices from broader social perspectives.

But any project you're only considering as a one-off app, feature, or product is likely to *seem* harmless at first. The questions in this chapter challenge you to think more broadly. Let's take some PICS to explore the ramifications of your work.

P: Solve the Right PROBLEM

The P in the PICS framework stands for "problem." This lens can reveal both practical and ethical concerns.

- Who has this need and how did you identify it?
- Are you working on a solution in search of a problem?
- Is there a better use of this time and energy?
- Do your priorities match your values?

Who Has This Need and How Did You Identify It?

Go beyond personas to talk about actual human beings.

- **Ensure that you're addressing real people.** Roles, archetypes, and personas can be valuable communication tools. However, they often shift over time to become fictional instruments in which you see what you want to see. Avoid building products for a hypothetical amalgam of qualities that doesn't actually occur in real life.

- **Maintain the golden thread to your customer insights.** Know where you identified this need: was it contextual observation? Customer feedback? Telemetry? Or perhaps a powerful stakeholder that might not represent the needs of the many?

Are You Working on a Solution in Search of a Problem?

If you're a user experience practitioner—or just curious about the field—there's a good chance that you're motivated to help others in some way.

But that instinct to be helpful—to rush out and put a bandage on the wound—isn't always effective. What if you put a bandage on a wound that was really a symptom of a much deeper problem?

In his book *Factfulness*, the late Hans Rosling pointed out 10 fallacies of thinking that move us away from a fact-based perspective about the world around us. Number 8 on the list was the "single perspective instinct."

> I love experts, but they have their limitations. First, and most obviously, experts are experts only within their own field. That can be difficult for experts (and we are all experts at something) to admit. We like to feel knowledgeable and we like to feel useful. We like to feel that our special skills make us generally better.

From experience, I can say that this phenomenon has been a challenge for me—and I suspect most multimodal designers struggle with this on some level. Here you are, with hard-won specialized knowledge about cutting-edge technology. Surely you're in the right place at the right time! Surely voice technology, or gesture, or chatbots, or VR—whatever you're passionate about—can be used to good effect here!

That passion can become haste, and that haste can cause you to prematurely cut short explorations to find the true root causes for the problems you're addressing. That haste can cause you to overlook the contextual elements at play that might indicate a different or more complicated problem.

As the old adage goes, "When all you have is a hammer, the whole world looks like a nail."

A good litmus test: what's your problem statement? Does it mention technology? If it's not technology-agnostic, you're at greater risk of leading with the technology instead of the problem to be solved—and thus blinding yourself to other possible solutions.

Is There a Better Use of This Time and Energy?

This is a much more complicated challenge, as it's far more subjective. What opportunities for greater impact might be missed by focusing on this problem? Are you emphasizing the needs of the few over the needs of the many?

An example I often come back to is the feature support for ownership of multiple iPhones. When I joined the foundation in 2018, I was eligible to either use a foundation cell phone plan on my personal device, or to accept a second cell phone to use in parallel. Unlike most of my coworkers, I chose the second cell phone because

I can't use foundation resources for work on my personal business, Ideaplatz. I braced for a fairly painful and redundant experience managing the two phones. But when I used my Apple ID to log into the second phone, I was astonished at how seamless it was. My apps and settings synced to both phones. I could tether one phone to another easily. The second phone number showed up in my contact cards, and I could access all of my Safari tabs on either device.

On one hand, that was a delightful discovery. But as a product designer myself, it also made me think. How many people on this *planet* actually use *two* iPhones? And how many development resources were spent enabling this cross-device scenario? Could those resources have been devoted to more impactful work that would affect more of the iPhone's user base?

Of course, nothing's that simple. I don't have access to Apple's customer data. Maybe there are a ton of folks like me. I doubt it, but it's possible. And perhaps the feature was developed by a team of folks that couldn't work on anything else (still, doubtful).

It's easy to work on what's been handed to you. It's more difficult to question an assignment and to reframe folks on a broader problem. As you progress in your career, you'll face more and more of these dilemmas.

Do Your Priorities Match Your Values?

Technology is not neutral. It is not apolitical. No matter how neutral you profess to be, your product decisions reflect and amplify your values into the world. A lack of engagement with the political ramifications of your work does not make you apolitical. Your work still exists in a political world, and ignoring that impact is a luxury enjoyed by those who place their personal comfort and success over the well-being of the community as a whole.

If you're not prioritizing the safety of your customers, that is a statement of your values.

If you're not explicitly seeking out diverse perspectives in order to help prioritize your work, that is a statement of your values.

Of course, to properly assess alignment with values, your values need to be clearly stated—a step that's hard to make time for, but a step that empowers your teams to have meaningful, measured discussions as conditions inevitably change. Those values give your teams a common language for difficult discussions.

Solving the Big Problems with Ovetta Sampson

*You heard from **Ovetta Sampson** in Chapter 13, where we discussed her time designing for artificial intelligence at IDEO. Here, we talk about the many missed opportunities the tech industry hasn't yet addressed.*

Q: What problems do you wish we were solving with this technology?

You know, I'm tired of the smartest engineers in the world spending their time on Like buttons when they could be spending their time on economic inequality. If I told you 100 years ago, "Guess what? We're gonna send a man to the moon. We're going to create one language that everyone in the world understands. (Computer programming, right?) If I'd told you that we could do that, you'd have been like, "that's crazy!"

Now, we can reduce income inequality. We could create an environment where everybody has a home. Has enough food and fuel to live. We can change, reverse climate change. And we can ... whatever. Right? All of those things I talked about before happened with technology. We could do the same thing for those things: climate change, poverty, homelessness, low education. Technology could be an answer to that.

We have the smartest people working on things that are not, to me, the top priority. Why do we have the smartest people in the world trying to make a better mouse when we could have those same people trying to change the world to be better? That's the most frustrating thing about it. I think we're making such strides with technology because of capitalism. And I fully get it. But why can't we support things like technology that builds a house for less than $5,000 in less than three days? Why can't we support AI that drives around people who are disabled and Blind?

Q: Like finding ways to match needs to new technology?

Right, I guess that's where I am right now. Where we have this slave/master narrative. And I can't take credit for that, that came from (Elizabeth) Dori Tunstall.[1] But she talks about AI in that way, and I started talking about it.

Why do we have to have AI that thinks in the same capitalistic, servantile way that we've been thinking about technology? Why do we have to create our AI in a very individual slave-master narrative? Why does the interaction have to be between the individual and the machine? Why can't it be individual, machine, and ecosystem? What does that look like,

---

1   Elizabeth (Dori) Tunstall is Dean, Faculty of Design at Ontario College of Art and Design University and the first Black Dean of any Faculty of Design in the world. She writes and speaks on topics including decolonizing design education.

in a communal way? Where there's equal agency among the environ-ment, the machine, and the people that are engaged with it.

If you think about an autonomous vehicle, there's not just the driver in the car. Right? There's the driver, there's the car, there's the pedestrian, there's another car, there's the light system the city put in, there's a busi-ness that has cameras. So there's an ecosystem that could be used and connected in a way that could help everybody. But we're building cars just for our little cocoon, for our family. Why?

I do an exercise with my students, and I say, "Design a future technology that doesn't have a device." What does that look like? And so ... because these devices end up in the landfill. Can we do technology in a way that doesn't hurt our environment? But that's something that the smartest engineers in the world should be working on.

In the 1950s, when J. C. R. Licklider[2] said, "I want to create a machine where an individual can have a relationship"—that was nuts! Because the computers of the time took up whole rooms. It was his vision of the personal computer. But Microsoft made that vision happen; they put a personal computer in everybody's hand. So I think if we decide that we're going to use technology to eradicate income inequality, we will figure that out.

Instead, we're using our new technology to repeat all of our mistakes. Why in the hell are we using AI in the criminal justice system? Why are we using predictive modeling in policing? We all know that's corrupt data. Why would we add another layer of decision-making from a nonhuman being when the human beings can't even make the right decision?

*More than 20 years as a journalist informed **Ovetta Sampson**'s ability to astutely observe, interpret, and understand how people interact with their world. A Master's in Human Computer Interaction from DePaul further equipped her with the skills to explore the cognitive, psychological, social, and environmental influences behind what people think, say, and do. As a Design Research Lead at IDEO, she worked on a range of projects: service design software, natural language processing search engines, frameworks for ethical, human-centered systems design, and more.*

---

2   J. C. R. Licklider is one of the original visionaries behind the modern computing era, and has been called computing's "Johnny Appleseed." "J. C. R. Licklider," Wikipedia, Wikimedia Foundation, last edited May 28, 2020, https://en.wikipedia.org/wiki/J._C._R._Licklider

I: Pursue INCLUSION

The I in the PICS framework stands for inclusion—and this is not a gate you can pass through at the end of your project. If you're not confronting inclusion up front, your project is on morally—and conceptually—shaky ground.

- Does your team include a variety of perspectives?
- When you consult experts, are you taking action on their recommendations?
- Have you explored perspectives beyond fully abled individuals?
- Do your team's behaviors create a safe space for creativity and collaboration?

If your goal is to impact underrepresented groups, like ethnic minorities or people living with disabilities, it doesn't matter what your *intent* is—it's more critical than ever to *ensure* that representatives of those groups are involved in your process.

We're more connected than ever before—the barriers to outreach are low if you're committed to doing the work. When it comes to including your customers and these underrepresented groups, there are many methodologies—some of which are assembled in Table 15.2.

I first heard the word "mutuality" when watching Liz Jackson give her talk "Empathy Reifies Disability Stigmas" at Interaction 19 in Seattle. As mentioned in Chapter 1, Liz pointed out that many attempts at "inclusive" design inadvertently send a message that it is the underrepresented person or group who must adapt, fit in, and be fixed. Even well-meaning empathy can backfire, leading to "solutions" that target the disabled person and not the obstacles around them. This is a journey for all of us, myself included.

If you think about it, it's a beautiful thing that we're now so connected, so able to communicate with each other, that underrepresented groups have enough of a voice to illuminate a path. Keep listening to these communities so that you can better fulfill your ethical obligations to one another.

- Can your potential project or product transform organizations instead of "fixing" those who don't thrive in the existing system?
- Can you reward doing the right thing and stop discrimination at the source?
- Can you amplify the strengths of disabled customers instead of trying to force a round peg into a square, ableist hole?

TABLE 15.2   SELECTED METHODOLOGIES FOR AMPLIFYING UNDERREPRESENTED PERSPECTIVES

Methodology	Description
Diversity Hiring	Recruiting representatives of underrepresented groups onto product teams, especially any who are members of the product's demographic. To be successful, this requires dropping "culture fit" as hiring criteria in favor of a variety of perspectives.
Inclusive Design	A design methodology that enables and draws on the full range of human diversity. Most importantly, this means including and learning from people with a range of perspectives.
Inclusive Design Sprint	A dedicated period of time (usually one week, sometimes more) is spent focusing completely on inclusive design. Often, members of the underrepresented group are invited to join the team as compensated experts to share their perspective.
Participatory Design	Rather than presenting participants with a design to evaluate, participants in an underrepresented group engage hands-on in design exercises. The output of this exercise informs the eventual product designs.
Mutuality	Members of the underrepresented group are given a full voice and agency in the design process, and are formally engaged as subject matter experts and stakeholders in the work.

NOTE ABLEISM

The Oxford dictionary defines *ableism* as discrimination in favor of able-bodied people. As with all forms of discrimination, it can manifest in conscious and unconscious behaviors.

This is hard work, but it's critically important work.

As you begin your journey, find the courage to let your examination turn inward. In what ways is your team's behavior potentially marginalizing the voices of the underrepresented, either as colleagues or participants? Anti-racist economist Dr. Kim Crayton, creator of the #causeascene guiding principles in Chapter 1, talks about this phenomenon through the lens of who we define as "technical" in our field.[3]

---

3   Kim Crayton, "I Don't Do Non-technical Talks," *#CauseAScene* (blog), July 5, 2019, https://hashtagcauseascene.com/coaching/2019/07/05/i-dont-do-non-technical-talks/

> In our efforts to become more inclusive and diverse, we must look beyond just gender and race and critically examine the various ways our intentional and unintentional behaviors may be placing barriers to entry for others. By not extending and expanding how we define 'technical' beyond programming, it becomes much more challenging for individuals with equally important skills to establish themselves as experts and thus receive the level of respect and compensation they deserve.

You don't need to have a solution up front before embarking on a journey of inclusion. In fact, if you are not a member of an underrepresented group, it's best to hold off on judgment and seek diverse perspectives using one of the methodologies above *before* you've jumped to a solution.

Start by amplifying the voices of those who are underserved, and include them along the journey as you drive from idea to innovation. Along the way, monitor your team's attitudes and behaviors to look for opportunities to pivot from bias and discrimination to more inclusive behavior.

C: CHANGE and Consequences

Your product design is a hypothesis about the change you believe you can make in the world and the value of that proposed change. Even after your experience is released into the world, the experiences of today and tomorrow must adapt as circumstances change around them.

- What might success and failure look like?
- What happens if your product or customer goes away?
- How might your solution need to change based on unexpected or emerging conditions?
- What is your theory of change?

Success and Failure

You learned about the concept of opti-pessimism in Chapter 11, "Breathe Life into the Unknown," as a tool for exploring the range of possibilities for a specific problem. But opti-pessimism can and should also be used as a tool for exploring the viability and desirability of a desired outcome long before you have a solution.

While empathy as a concept has become a bit overexposed in the design industry, it's no secret that humans have an easier time becoming emotionally invested in stories where they can "see" themselves in some way.

That's one of the reasons that Microsoft's Inclusive Design Toolkit was so impactful. It shone a light on the many different ways disabled customers live and adapt, but it also built a bridge of empathy with its depiction of temporary disabilities. Understandably, the need for this lens is frustrating to some in the disability community. Why is it so hard for able-bodied teams to prioritize design for people not like themselves? But this bridge of empathy is hopefully an important first step for many toward a loftier goal, as the toolkit describes: "There are 7.4 billion people in the world. Our ambition is to create products that are physically, cognitively, and emotionally appropriate for each of them. It starts with seeing human diversity as a resource for better designs."

If you're ready to begin looking at disabilities as a spectrum of opportunity for diverse, adaptive designs, the Inclusive Design Toolkit is a good primer (see Figure 15.2). It provides useful definitions and activities that explore a variety of perspectives and three inclusive design principles you can easily apply to your work on a regular basis.

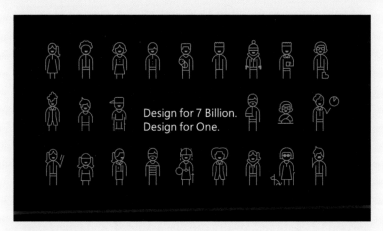

Design for 7 Billion.
Design for One.

FIGURE 15.2

Microsoft's Inclusive Design Toolkit provides exercises, principles, and perspectives that represent a spectrum of personas, not an outdated disability binary.

Both intrinsic factors (a new feature or product offering) and extrinsic factors (events and market forces) can be explored as design constraints to develop more technically and ethically robust solutions.

Thinking about the potential misuses of your product can be difficult at first. *As creative leaders, designers have a responsibility to drive this kind of worst-case ideation within companies—ideally, prior to your great success, but most certainly after the first sign that your product might be vulnerable.* For some inspiration about framing that may be helpful, see the interview with Dr. Casey Fiesler in this chapter.

Failure to account for—or adapt to—emergent abusive usage or scaling issues can cause lasting harm to both customers and the platform itself. Zoom's public image has taken a significant hit since the increase of usage gave rise to the phenomenon known as "zoombombing." (See the case study in this chapter for more detail.)

Design for the End

What happens if your product goes away? What happens if your customer stops interacting with your product? So much attention is given to the birth of a product and the onboarding of a potential customer, but there are countless considerations as your customer's relationship with you changes.

- **Product or subscription cancellation:** Archiving and portability of data, service handoff to another provider
- **Customer death:** Memorialization, deletion, AI updates, and archiving
- **Product obsolescence:** Upgrades, recycling, and disposal

If you're not putting thought into your own endings, you're at risk of letting other people define those patterns for you. As Joe Macleod, author of *Ends*, points out: "Some of the world's biggest business sectors that commonly denied consumer endings have had it forced upon them though legislation." Global Data Protection Regulation and phone portability guidelines in the U.S. sprang out of a lack of proactive action on the part of service owners.

In a world where brand loyalty can't be assumed, and where personal expression and flexibility are key, designing thoughtful exit experiences for your customers may lead to a higher likelihood of re-engagement down the line.

Adapting to Future Changes

No matter how creative your team is, you will not anticipate everything that can happen to or around your product. Designers need to look no further than the novel coronavirus pandemic of 2020 to see just how suddenly external conditions can completely change the circumstances in which your products exist.

In a world where you can't predict the future, how can you prepare for the unexpected? In many ways, this is a change management exercise.

- What signals might indicate something has gone wrong?
- What processes can you put in place after product launch to approve pivots or changes in your product?
- How might you build your system to make important changes with little additional investment of time or resources?

Theories of Change

For the biggest, most ambitious projects—large-scale AI initiatives, social justice, projects for political reform, and other forms of social good—you may need to develop a more robust conceptual framework to guide you incrementally toward that previously unachieved goal.

Each new chapter in my career has opened my eyes to new ways of thinking, and my role at the Bill & Melinda Gates Foundation is no exception. In the world of social good, strategists, funders, and program officers, prepare to tackle big problems by methodically developing and capturing their *theory of change.*

A theory of change is a series of cascading hypotheses you believe will eventually lead to a desired outcome or change in the world. It is a chain of cause-and-effect links, moving from many initial hypotheses to more fundamental change over time. In a way, it's service design that looks at the project itself.

At a very high level, to define a theory of change:

- Agree upon an achievable long-term goal.
- Explore the question "What conditions must be in place for us to reach the goal?"
- Capture those conditions and the causal links back to prior goals.
- Repeat as needed.

Zoom and COVID-19

The COVID-19 outbreak in 2020 fundamentally changed the digital collaboration market overnight. Zoom, a digital teleconferencing platform, which had been seeing healthy but modest growth, saw an astonishing explosion of additional use. In the span of just four months, daily active users shot up twentyfold (from 10 million to 200 million, according to the *New York Times*).

That phenomenal success came at a price. Soon after the crisis set in, reports of "zoombombing" began to surface. Zoom had been optimized for ease of joining meetings, so much so that it was far too easy for bad actors to join meetings uninvited and subject participants to hateful and offensive content. The practice was widespread—it even hit a sponsor's room during Rosenfeld Media's Advancing Research 2020 digital conference. (Platforms engineered for security of content generally require authentication, so this wasn't an issue for competitors like Microsoft's Teams.) Within a few weeks, Zoom released an app update that forced some more restrictive settings as a default, but did little to address the root issues.

In April 2020, *New York Times* reporters (Natasha Singer, Nicole Perlroth, and Aaron Krolik) spoke with Zoom's CEO, Eric S. Yuan, about the security issues.[4] In an interview with Mr. Yuan, they found

---

4   Natasha Singer, Nicole Perlroth, and Aaron Krolik, "Zoom Rushes to Improve Privacy for Consumers Flooding Its Service," *New York Times*, April 8, 2020, www.nytimes.com/2020/04/08/business/zoom-video -privacy-security-coronavirus.html

This is a methodical approach to creating a plan where no plan previously existed—and as a highly collaborative and conceptual process, a theory of change workshop would very much be in many designers' wheelhouses already. Once a theory of change has been developed, it provides a pathway to success and a way for teams to measure their progress toward a long-term goal in concrete terms. What's your theory of change?

S: A SYSTEMS Perspective

Everything is connected—and not just to the internet. Every device in the world requires an expenditure of time and precious resources.

Harmful Disruption

Far beyond annoyances, today's technology projects can make humans profoundly vulnerable, or exact lasting damage to a way of life.

Broken Families

The controversial software firm Palantir told the *New York Times* that their work for ICE (Immigration and Customs Enforcement) was not being used for deportations, because it was in support of the Homeland Security Investigations division.[6] But according to internal documents acquired by political action committee Mijente, the Palantir software " . . . was used throughout, helping agents build profiles of immigrant children and their family members for the prosecution and arrest of any undocumented person they encountered in their investigation."[7]

Privacy Violations

Google's Duplex, which impersonated a human caller to gain business data via the phone, resulted in significant backlash.[8] Since the nature of natural language processing systems requires recording, the impersonation as presented was not just a misdirection, but a significant ethical concern. In what is unlikely to be a coincidence, within a year, the state of California passed legislation that made it illegal for bots to impersonate people.[9]

Displaced Residents

Airbnb successfully "disrupted" the hotel market, but at a price to the communities where hosts live. The vastly higher earnings potential of short-term rentals has fractured communities, increased rents and evictions, and accelerated gentrification as former apartments are converted to temporary lodgings.[10]

---

6 "DealBook Briefing: Investors May Be Overlooking Their Own Discrimination," *Dealbook* (blog), *New York Times*, December 11, 2018, https://www.nytimes.com/2018/12/11/business/dealbook/investor-bias-discrimination.html

7 "Palantir Played Key Role in Arresting Families for Deportation, Document Shows," Mijente. May 2, 2019.

8 "Google's 'Duplex' Raises Ethical Questions," *All Things Considered* (podcast), May 14, 2018, https://www.npr.org/2018/05/14/611097647/googles-duplex-raises-ethical-questions

9 Sophia Kunthara, "California Law Takes Aim at Chatbots Posing as Humans," *San Francisco Chronicle*, October 13, 2018, https://www.sfchronicle.com/business/article/California-law-takes-aim-at-chatbots-posing-as-13304005.php

10 Daniel Guttentag, "What Airbnb Really Does to a Neighbourhood," BBC.com, August 18, 2018, https://www.bbc.com/news/business-45083954

From Fiction to Ethics with Dr. Casey Fiesler

Dr. Casey Fiesler is the director of the Internet Rules Lab at the University of Colorado-Boulder, through which she teaches and advises on topics including technology ethics, digital governance, and online communities. She's an active participant in the CHI community and a published writer on topics from technology and law through science fiction and fantasy. We chatted during the early months of the COVID-19 epidemic about the industry's road ahead.

Q: Regarding ethics in technology, do you find that your students are bringing surprising perspectives?

I am sometimes charmed by their optimism. A concrete example: one of the concepts that I like to bring up is machine learning for predictive mental health, particularly when based on things like social media data. I've used this as a case study in a couple of different classes. I'll say, "Here's how this technology works. Here's some examples of the things they might do. Tell me how it might be used." And they immediately respond, "We'll intervene when people need help! Or prevent suicide!" But I really have to push them to think beyond those obvious good intentions. So I ask: "What if, for example, you used it to advertise diet pills to customers that it predicts may have eating disorders?" And they're like *"Oh!"* Eventually, though, they'll get there.

Something that I'm really interested in researching is how the outcomes for this kind of speculative exercise might be different for people who are from marginalized groups. If you're someone who's constantly getting harassed online, you're probably going to jump to ways that technology can be used for online harassment in ways that other people would not.

And I've done an exercise where I ask: "Imagine how a supervillain would use this technology. How could you design it so they can't use it that way?" That's an exercise that we did at a workshop at CHI last year called, "CHI for Evil."

Q: Something like, "How would this technology work if Thanos got hold of it?"

On that point . . . Bad actors—and how they might use technology—is a really tricky thing to think about. Something like Thanos (from *Avengers*) is actually a great example of using design fiction and speculative thinking to think through negative impacts of technology.

We did that exercise—in particular, a Black Mirror writer's room exercise that I use in classes. It requires some creativity, which is my argument for why reading science fiction is really useful for thinking through ethics. Once they get into it and realize the kinds of things they can think through, people get really into it and come up with some great stuff.

But the important thing is that you don't just stop there. You also talk about how this technology could be designed, or how there could be regulations—basically, how could you prevent these bad things from happening?

One of the classes in our department was zoombombed recently. And the CEO of Zoom has basically come out and said, "We did not think this would happen." You know, it's not like you can be expected to see the future. But if you had sat me down a couple of years ago and said, "In the future, suddenly everyone will be using this platform. Think about what bad things people might do with it"? I feel like I could have pretty easily come up with "Jumping into public meetings and shouting obscenities." I don't think that kind of speculation is necessarily happening in the design process, but it's something that I think at this point should be fundamental.

Q: Your work also touches on digital communities. How do you think COVID-19 will affect their experiences?

In many ways, if this were happening 30 years ago, it would be so much worse! Before everyone had the internet, there would be such severe isolation. Maybe part of what will happen is that more people will realize that digital interaction is *real*. People still differentiate between interactions on the internet and in real life. They'll say, "Well, my real life friend X and my internet friend Y"—but they're all real friends! People have very real intense friendships and interactions with people that they never meet in person. This has been true for the last 20 years—it's just that anyone who wasn't experiencing that was finding it weird. But one of the things that's probably going to happen here is that more people will start realizing that you don't have to interact with people in person in order to have meaningful interaction.

The internet has actually been such an important support space for so many different people for lots of different reasons. I've looked at online fandom communities, and in particular sometimes as a proxy for LGBTQ communities. One of my graduate students led a study last year where she talked to all of these people with stories like, you know: "I come from a rural community where I had never met a gay person. And then I went on Tumblr, and I'd never interacted with people like this before. I'd never heard the term asexuality before, and then I realized that's what I am!" All of these amazing stories about basically online communities saving lives. And I think we see this a lot for marginalized or vulnerable people who might not be able to have that support in their real lives.

Q: What message would you want to send to designers and product teams regarding ethics and their work?

Innovate like an optimist, prepare like a pessimist. Don't feel too constrained by having to think about bad things that can happen. It's so important to do that kind of speculation early in the process. Ethics should be early and often in technology design. Think about ethics, social implications, and negative consequences the entire time. Also, don't put lawyers in charge of ethics. Those are not the same roles.

The metaphor that I've used for this before: A safety engineer is a job on a construction site. But that doesn't mean that the person putting up the drywall sees a live wire and says, "Oh, that's the safety engineer's job to see and to fix."

I don't think that everyone working in tech should have a philosophy degree. Not everyone needs to be an ethicist. But everyone should be thinking about it. And you should know enough about it to be able to spot the issues, bring it to your team, and start talking about it.

 *Dr. Casey Fiesler is an assistant professor in the Department of Information Science (and Computer Science, by courtesy) at the University of Colorado-Boulder. Armed with a PhD in Human-Centered Computing from Georgia Tech and a JD from Vanderbilt Law School, she primarily researches social computing, law, ethics, and fan communities (occasionally all at the same time). Learn more about her work at* **caseyfiesler.com**

Apply It Now

At this point, you might be feeling overwhelmed. Maybe you weren't looking to save the world—you just wanted to build an enjoyable experience.

None of this is to say that building fun, delightful, or innovative experiences can't be ethical and sustainable. In fact, it's probably easier than you think to move the needle. You just need something to rally behind—a framework and language for the problems that need solving.

The United Nations has published a list of 17 sustainable development goals to help rally the international community around the most important obstacles to a thriving balance between humanity and our planet. These goals were introduced with the hope of seeing solutions in place by the year 2030 (see Figure 15.3).

FIGURE 15.3

The 17 Sustainable Development Goals, courtesy of the United Nations.

The 17 Sustainable Development Goals:

1. No poverty
2. Zero hunger
3. Good health and well-being
4. Quality education
5. Gender equality
6. Clean water and sanitation
7. Affordable and clean energy
8. Decent work and economic growth
9. Industry, innovation, and infrastructure
10. Reduced inequalities
11. Sustainable cities and communities
12. Responsible consumption and production
13. Climate action
14. Life below water
15. Life on land
16. Peace, justice, and strong institutions
17. Partnerships for the goals

There is so much opportunity for innovation within these goals—and not just Goal 9, "Industry, innovation, and infrastructure." These are 17 concrete starting points for making the world a better place with technology.

- Use multimodal design to make productivity tools more accessible to a wider range of abilities (Goals 8 and 10).
- Develop an AI tool for education while fighting against the use of gender-biased source data (Goals 4 and 5).
- Use virtual reality to create immersive education experiences that lead to better job outcomes (Goal 8).

Don't know where to start to ensure that your impact aligns with your intent?

- Start with the sustainable development goals. How might your work move the needle on one or more of these goals?
- Before investing too much time and money, refer back to Immanuel Kant's ethical prompt: what if everyone did what you're about to do?

- Apply the frameworks in this book to create a rich, flexible, inclusive experience in pursuit of your clearly stated goals.
- Evaluate your proposed solution with the PICS framework to ensure that you're ethically and conceptually on steady ground.

Multimodal designs are ambitious, time-consuming, and complex—it's worth ensuring that all that effort is truly going to result in a better world. These projects are much bigger than any one of us. It will take a coordinated, disciplined effort to pull off these ambitious, expansive visions. And there will be times where it doesn't feel like the groundwork is worth the effort—trust me, stay the course. For visions this grand, you will need a strong foundation.

Multimodal design is a long journey. It requires deep awareness of context, a truly collaborative mindset, and the courage to push past appearances and engage in deeper systems design. But it's a thrilling ride—and I can't wait to see where your ride takes you.

INDEX

analog-dominant mixed reality, 296

anchored interactions, as multimodal quadrant, 129, 131, 133, 222, 233

Android iPhone apps, triple flow for design, 236

animation, 88–89

anti-neutrality, 12–15

anti-racism, 12–15

app badges, 188

app icons, 184

Apple Card, emergent bias of, 272

Apple CarPlay, 126

Apple iOS

  input transitions, 163

  Mail app and network connectivity, 171

  notification banners, 186, 187

  Siri, input/output mismatch, 167

  Siri team research on voice assistants, 179

Arduino, 224

Arshad, Syed Sameer, 118–120

The Art of Game Design: A Book of Lenses (Schell), 313

Artefact, Tarot Cards of Tech, 209–210

artificial intelligence (AI), 257–286

  algorithmic bias, 267–273

  algorithmic confidence, 262–263

  bias avoidance, question everything, 273–274

  defined, 259

  design process changes, 284–286

  digital assistants and disembodied agents, 274–281. *See also* assistants (digital and virtual)

  enhancement of human experience, 263–267

  input and, 94

  learning language, 119–120

  machine learning, 103–105, 260–261, 336

  natural language understanding, training data, 96, 261, 270–271

  summary to apply it, 282–283

artificial superintelligence (ASI), 259

assistants (digital and virtual), 274–281

  avatars, 278–281

  bots, 277

  conversations, hidden context in, 275–276

  gender bias in, 275–276, 281

  human brain reaction to, 274–276

  personality match, 276

Association for Computing Machinery, U.S. Technology Policy Committee, 104

atmospheric haptics, 83, 85, 86

atomic design, 243–246, 254–256

Atomic Design (Frost), 254, 256

atoms, in atomic design, 244–246, 249–252

Attention Deficit Disorder (ADD), 60, 89

attenuation of music by Echo smart speakers, 49

attenuation theory, 193

attitudes, as dimension of character, 26, 27

attributes, as dimension of character, 26, 27

audio driven interfaces, prototyping tools, 224

audio output modality, proactive notifications design, 190, 193

auditory communication modality, 6

auditory input, expressing intent, 94–100, 118–120

  inclusive design, 99–100

  matching speech with intent, 96–97

  microphone technology, 97–99

  sound-activated systems, 95

  voice user interfaces, 95

auditory output, in language of devices, 76–82

  inclusive design, 81–82

  nonverbal information, 78–79

  output hardware, 80

  sound effects and earcons, 76–77

augmentative and alternative communication (AAC), 100

augmented reality (AR), 292–293, 294

augmenting model of AI, 263, 265

autism, 60, 89

automatic speech recognition (ASR), 95

automating model of AI, 263

autonomous cars

artificial intelligence in, 259, 285–286

ecosystem of, and missed opportunities, 325

technical bias in, 272

avatars, 278–281

Azure Kinect DK, 224

B

background removal, 102

bad actors, 332–333, 336–337

bad feature engineering, 269

badges, 184–185

banners, 185, 186, 187, 188, 190

Barnett-Cowan, Michael, 308

Bernstein, Ethan, 56

best case design, 208–209

bias

algorithmic. *See* algorithmic bias, in AI

design against. *See* inclusive design

gender, 275–276

"Bias in Computer Systems" (Friedman & Nissenbaum), 267

bias spiral, in voice user interfaces, 270–271

bidirectional haptics, 305–306, 307

Bill & Melinda Gates Foundation, 15, 331

biometric input, 115, 306

Blind community, and inclusion in visual outputs, 75–76

blindness, 73–76

bloom, 301

bodystorming, 34, 218–220, 229

Boeing 737 MAX jets, 269

bots, 277, 335

Botsociety, 224

Bowles, Cennydd, 208, 225, 320

Braille displays, refreshable, 75

brainstorming games, 221

Brave, Scott, 281

browsing, 168, 179

Buxton, Bill, 34, 77

C

calendar, and transitions, 179

capacitive touchscreens, 107, 116

captioning on streaming media, 9

cards, 188, 189

cars. *See also* autonomous cars; Windows Automotive

dashboard design, and haptic models, 108

distractions of drivers, 194–195

infotainment systems, 143

case studies

Alexa interjections, 150–151

Amazon Echo, broadening a customer objective, 31

Amazon's Echo Look, 38

Pokémon GO, and mixed reality, 294–295

USS *John S. McCain*, and cockpit design, 110

voice user interfaces, and bias spiral, 270–271

Windows Automotive, notification types, 194–195

Wizard of Oz prototyping with M*Modal User Research, 227

Zoom and COVID-19, 332–333

Cause a Scene hashtag and podcast, 12–13, 327

cell phones. *See* smartphones

change, as PICS criteria, 319, 328–332
  adapt to future changes, 331
  design for the end, 330
  success and failure, 328, 330
  theories of change, 331–332

character, as building block of story, 23, 25, 26–27, 38

chatbots, 220

choices, as dimension of character, 26, 27

Clicker, 302–303

cliffs. *See* interaction cliffs

climate change, 320

Cline, Ernest, 305

cockpit design, 108, 110

cognitive psychology, 193

color blindness, 73

color detection, 102, 103

Comcast, interactive voice reception system, 277

comic book artists, 214

communication modalities, 5–6

COMPAS, bias in, 272–273

competitive wheres, 34

complex logic in design, 237–238, 255

computer programming, traditional, compared with machine learning, 260, 261

computer vision (CV) algorithms, 101, 102, 103

confidence, in AI models, 262–263

confirmation notifications, 194, 197, 263

connection error messages, 170

connectivity of networks. *See* network connections, transitions

consent, as proactive notification, 188

constraints, as gift for design, 9–10

context. *See also* customer context
  in conversations, 275–276
  criticality of, 2–4

as design challenge for multimodal interfaces, 142, 145–147, 158

prototyping in, 226–227

contextual awareness, and human activities, 44–46

contextual curiosity, 20, 39–40

contextual inquiry, 35, 36

controllers. *See* motion controllers

conversational context, and virtual assistants, 275–276

Cooper, Alan, 20–21

Cortana, xxii
  as avatar, 278
  focus assist feature, 61
  identity and privacy design challenges, 157
  inferences in recommendations, 265
  input transitions, 163
  sequential multimodality, 135–136

Cotton, Jen, 179–180

COVID-19 pandemic, xxiii, 332, 337

Crawford, Scott, 9

Crayton, Kim, 12–13, 327–328

creation of world to live in, 1–17
  anti-neutrality and anti-racism, 12–15
  criticality of context, 2–4
  fix system, not people, 7–11
  fluidity over rigidity, 7
  gender equity, 15
  multimodality defined, 5–6
  summary to apply it, 17
  where no design has gone before, 16

credit cards, emergent bias in, 272

criminal justice, bias in, 272–273

critical notifications, 191, 194, 195

cross-device notifications, 174–175, 197–199, 202–204

CROW, building blocks of story, 23–36
  character, 23, 25, 26–27, 38
  framework for building stories, 26

device relationships (*continued*)

    simultaneous usage between people, 177

    turn-taking between people, 176–177

devices, language of. *See* language of devices

dialects, 119–120

diary studies, 35

digital assistants. *See* assistants (digital and virtual)

digitally-dominant mixed reality, 296

dinosaurs, 318–319

dioramas, 217–218

direct interactions

    model for extended reality, 297, 298

    as multimodal quadrant, 129, 132, 222, 233

directed transitions, 175–176

disability, defined, 8

disabled customers

    accessibility of smart speakers, 7

    constraint as a gift, 9–10

    design questioning for systems design, 10

    designing new systems, 7–8

    inclusive design for. *See* inclusion, from exclusion to

    Microsoft's Inclusive Design Toolkit, 60, 82, 329

    nothing about us without us, 10–11

    redefining disability, 8

disambiguation, 166

discoverability

    as design challenge for multimodal interfaces, 142, 148–151, 158

    and proactive notifications, 201

discrete activities, 46, 49–51

    in interruption matrix, 66–67, 196

DisneyQuest, Aladdin virtual reality ride, 290–291

displays, as visual output, 71–73

disruption, 334, 335

distractions of drivers, 194–195

diversity hiring, 327

Dixon, Randy, 25

domains, in atomic design, 246

driving, as live activity, 52

Duwamish Tribe, 14–15

dynamic displays, 72–73

dynamic instruction, 148–151

dynamic notifications, 200

E

earcons, 76–77, 81, 192, 193

Echo Look

    bodystorming of, 220

    machine learning and training period, 105

    storyboards for, 35, 212, 216

    wardrobe management camera, 38

Echo Show

    discovery of new features, 150

    inclusion of Deaf community, 82

    multimodal design, 124, 126

    proactive interaction on, 188

Echo smart speakers

    accessibility of, 7

    attenuation of music, 49

    author history with, xxii

    delivery notifications, 192

    light ring indicators, 71–72

    multiple devices, and transitions, 173

    objectives and kitchen timers, 31

    transparency in network connections, 170

edge cases, in design, 206–207

electric cars, 78

Electronic Freedom Foundation, 104

electrotactile feedback, as haptic output, 83, 84

embarrassment, 157

emergent bias, in AI algorithms, 268, 272, 273

empathy, 329

Ends (Macleod), 330

environmental ambient input, 115

environments

noisy, and auditory output, 82

techniques for exploring the where, 34–35

where, in storytelling, 32–35

ergonomics, as design challenge for multimodal interfaces, 142, 152–154, 159

ethics

and opti-pessimistic design, 208

potential harm from design and multimodal devices, 320–321, 335

in technology, from science fiction, 336–338

exit strategies for products, 330

extended reality, 287–315

defined, 288

dimensional interaction models, 296–299

history of, 288–290

immersive displays and, 74

input options, 300–307

lexicon of, 290–296

postures of engagement, 310–311

"presence" in virtual space, 308–309, 314–315

summary to apply it, 311–312

extremes, designing for. *See* opti-pessimism

F

Facebook

impact of advertising platform, 334

"neutrality" in elections, 13

"neutrality" on racism and violence, 12–13

facial detection and recognition, 102, 103, 104

Factfulness (Rosling), 322

fairy tales, and storyboards, 216

far-field microphones, 98–99

fashion-conscious customers, and wardrobe management camera, 38

Fiesler, Casey, 208, 336–338

Fitbit, 127, 132

flow diagrams, 233–235, 252

Floyd, George, 12

fluid, adaptive interactions, 130

focus assist, on Windows, 61

focused activities, 46, 51–52

force feedback, as haptic output, 83–84

Ford, SYNC® 3, 143

Foubert, David, 294

Fox, Craig, 229–230

Frazier, Darnella, 12–13

Friedman, Batya, 267

Frost, Brad, 243–244, 254–256

fully-featured motion controllers, as extended reality input, 303–305, 307

Future Ethics (Bowles), 208, 320

G

gaming, handheld, and network connections, 169

Gates Foundation, Bill & Melinda, 15, 331

Gawande, Atul, 202

gaze detection, 102

gaze tracking, 305, 307

gender, defined, 15

gender bias, and markers for speech, 275–276, 281

gender equity, 15

general purpose AI (AGI), 259

gestural input, 111, 112–114

gesture controllers, streamlined, 302–303, 307

gesture design, 240–243
  pattern libraries, 241–243

gesture tracking, open-air, 300–301, 306, 307

Giving Voice: Communication, Disability, and Inequality (Alper), 10

Global Data Protection Regulation, 330

Goldblum, Jeff, 318

Google
  Actions, 224
  Duplex bot, and self-identification, 277, 335
  Glass, 132, 292–293
  Home Hub input transitions, 163
  Hub multimodal design, 126
  Inception neural network, 266
  Nest Hub, cards as proactive notifications, 189
  People + AI Guidebook, 274

grammar-based speech recognition, 96–97, 223, 261

Guidelines for Human-AI Interaction (Microsoft), 266

H

hand gestures
  as kinetic input, 111, 112–114
  multimodal design, 242–243

handicapped, as outdated term, 8

happy path, 240

haptic communication modality, 6

haptic input, 106–110
  choice of right model, 108
  controls on motion controllers, 303–304
  inclusive design, 109
  physical controllers, 106–107, 108, 110
  touchscreens, 107–108, 110

haptic output, in language of devices, 82–87
  applications of, 85–86, 87
  atmospheric, 83, 85, 86
  electrotactile feedback, 83, 84
  force feedback, 83–84
  inclusive design, 86
  vibrotactile feedback, 83, 85

haptic output modality, design questions, 190

haptic suits, 305–306

hapticons, 85

haptics, bidirectional, 305–306, 307

harm
  bias and consequences, 268, 272–273
  CauseAScene guilding principles, 12
  edge cases in design, 207–208
  and ethics, 320–321, 335, 336–338
  exclusion in design, 106
  facial recognition, 104
  gestural inputs, 112, 114, 152, 153
  immersive displays, 74
  incoming phone call, 185
  interruptions, 60
  misuses of product, 330, 337
  tragic automation for airplanes, 269
  tragic cockpit design for Navy, 110

Head, Val, 88

headphones, 56

heads-up notifications, 184

headsets, 78, 131, 230

hearing loss, 81

heave, 302

Heilig, Morton, 289

HER (film), 276

Herzberg, Elaine, 272

Higgins, Nate, 99

history, confronting our past for inclusion today, 14–15

home streaming, movie search, 237–238

home usage, identity and privacy design challenges, 156

HTC Vive controller, 290, 304

human activities

AI models for enhancing, 263–267

taxonomy of activity types, 45–46. *See also* activity models

human brain

attenuation of acoustic information, 193

feeling of presence, 308, 315

language processing, 79

processing of visual outputs, 71

reaction to virtual assistants, 274–276, 320

scent separations, 90

human-to-business relationships, 28

human-to-device relationships, 27, 28

human-to-human relationships, 29

I

IBM, Deep Blue, 259

ICE (Immigration and Customs Enforcement), 335

identity, as design challenge for multimodal interfaces, 142, 155–158, 159

IDEO, gestural input research, 112

immersive displays, 72, 74

implicit actions, 305

improvisation, 22, 24, 25, 218, 221

incidental feedback, as ambient output, 90–91

inclusion, as PICS criteria, 319, 326–328, 329

inclusion, from exclusion to

ambient input and biometrics, 115–116

auditory input and voice recognition, 99–100

auditory output, 81–82

haptic input, 109

haptic output, 86

interruptions, 60

kinetic input and gestures, 114

kinetic output, 88–89

visual input, 105–106

visual output, 73–76

inclusive design

bias. *See* algorithmic bias, in AI

confronting our past for inclusion today, 14–15

disabled customers. *See* disabled customers

leading with anti-neutrality and anti-racism, 12–14

methodology to amplify underrepresented perspectives, 327

multimodal future of, 16

in storyboarding, 214

and unexpected benefits, 9

Inclusive Design Toolkit (Microsoft), 60, 82, 329

incoming calls and voicemails, 185

indicators

as proactive interactions, 184–185

as visual output, 71–73

information density, in multimodal interaction models, 125–127, 128, 129

information triage, for notifications, 183–184

informational notifications, 192, 194, 195

infrared (IR) sensors, 102, 116

inline content, 188

The Inmates Are Running the Asylum (Cooper), 20

input

expressing intent. *See* intent, expressions of

as state, representation in flow diagrams, 234–235

input and output, in language of devices, 70

Microsoft (*continued*)

Xbox. *See* Xbox

Xiaoice chatbot, 279, 280

Microsoft Office, directed transitions in, 175

Microsoft Outlook, meeting reminders, 197–199

mime, 218–219, 299

missed calls, 186

missed opportunities in technology, 324–325

mixed reality (MR)

in design imagination, 217, 218

designing with imagination, 229–230

as type of extended reality, 293–296, 299

M*Modal, 202, 227

modalities

communication, 6

multiple, for communication, 94

sensory, for humans, 5

transitions between, 162–166, 178

mode of communication, 5, 6

modes, defined, 5

molecules, in atomic design, 244–246, 250–251, 254

moral imagination, 208

motion

as kinetic output, 87–89

repeated use, and ergonomics, 152–153

motion controllers, as extended reality input, 301–302, 313–314

fully-featured, 303–305, 307

motion sickness, 74, 314–315

mouse, as kinetic and haptic input, 112

movement, as kinetic output, 87–89

moving posture, 310–311

Mozilla, Project Common Voice, 270–271

multimodal design. *See* design, from envision to execute

multimodal design systems, 243–252, 253

atomic design, 243–246

define the atoms, 249–252

interaction patterns, 247–248

radio example, 246–252

multimodal interaction model, 124, 125, 128, 222–223

multimodal interfaces, design challenges, 141–159

context, 142, 145–147

discoverability, 142, 148–151

ergonomics, 142, 152–154

identity, 142, 155–158

privacy, 142, 155–158

summary to apply it, 158–159

synchronization, 142, 143–145

multimodal interfaces, example, 122

multimodal quadrants, 128–129

adaptive interactions, 129–130, 133, 223, 235

anchored interactions, 129, 131, 133, 222, 233

direct interactions, 129, 132, 222, 233

intangible interactions, 129, 132–133, 223, 235

multimodal satellite audio system, 246–247

multimodality, defined, 2, 5–6

multimodality spectrum, 121–139

bridge of Starship Enterprise, 122, 123

choosing interaction models, 130, 133

dimensions of experiences, 124–128

mapping the quadrants, 128–133

orchestrating transitions, 134–136

summary to apply it, 137

multitasking, 44, 51

muscle memory, and haptic feedback, 108

music

and auditory output, 79

in interruption matrix, 65–67, 196

mutuality in design process, 326, 327

N

O

P

for mixed reality, 229–230

provoking a response with provotypes, 225–226

Wizard of Oz prototyping, 220, 222, 227

provotyping/provocatyping, 225–226

proximity

in multimodal interaction models, 125–126, 128, 129

as network connection issue, 169

public space, identity and privacy design challenges, 158

Pygmalion's Spectacles (Weinbaum), 288

Q

queues, 188

quiet hours (do not disturb), 200

R

racism, leading design with anti-racism, 12–15

radio, multimodal system, 246–252

Raspberry Pi, prototyping with, 223, 224

Ready Player One (Cline), 305

Reign, April, 13

reinforcement learning, 260–261

relationship

as building block of story, 23, 25, 26, 27–29, 38

between devices, and transitions, 172–177

repeated use, and ergonomics, 152–153

repetitive stress injuries, 153

resiliency in network connections, 171–172

resistive touchscreens, 107–108

respond in kind, 165–166

role-play, professional, 221

roll, 301, 302

Rose, David, 112

Rosenfeld, Lou, 5, 362

Rosling, Hans, 322

S

safety, and auditory output, 78. *See also* harm

sample dialogs, for voice design, 239–240

Sampson, Ovetta, 225, 284–286, 324–325

scalable notifications, 200

scheduled information, 184, 196

Schell, Jesse, 308–309, 313–315

science fiction, and ethics, 336–338

screen forward, 131

screen readers, 79

scripted play, 221

search/browse, and transitions, 179

seated posture, 310

Sebeok, Thomas A., 311

selfies, and wardrobe management camera, 38

Sensely, virtual nurse avatar, 279, 280

"Sensorama" (Heilig), 289

sequential multimodality, 134–136

set building for prototyping, 226

17 Sustainable Development Goals (United Nations), 339–340

shape detection, 102

silent mode, 81

Simon, Jose, 25

simulation, for prototyping, 226–227

simulator sickness, 74, 227

simultaneous multimodality, 134–135, 305, 306

simultaneous usage between people, device relationships, and transitions, 177

Singer, Natasha, 332

single perspective instinct, 322

Siri. *See* Apple iOS

situational awareness

in context of multimodal interfaces, 146–147

cross-device meeting reminders, 198

for voice design, 239

sustained activities, 46, 48–49

Sutherland, Ivan, 289

sway, 302

swim lanes
  system, 237–238
  triple flows and, 235–236

switched, adaptive interactions, 130

"Sword of Damocles" (Sutherland), 289

synchronization, as design challenge for multimodal interfaces, 142, 143–145, 158

system swim lanes, 237–238

systems perspective, as PICS criteria, 319, 332–335
  disruption, 334, 335
  potential impact, 334

T

tactile feedback, 108, 110, 313

tap and drag, 242, 301

Tarot Cards of Tech, 209–210

teaching. *See* discoverability

technical bias, in AI algorithms, 267, 272, 273

technology
  ethics in, 336–338
  missed opportunities, 324–325
  neutrality in, 12–14

telemarketing calls, 182

telephony, 185–186

templates, in atomic design, 244–246, 254–255

Tesla, Autopilot feature, 263–264

TESLASUIT haptic glove, 84, 305–306

text messaging
  inclusive design and unexpected benefits, 9
  as proactive interactions, 185

text sizing, customizable, 75

text-to-speech systems, 80

theories of change, 331–332

thermal haptic output, 85

thermostat controls, 99, 126, 299

three degrees of freedom (3DoF), 301

time. *See* interactions over time

touch, sense of. *See* haptic output, in language of devices

Touch Gesture Reference Guide, 241–242

touchscreens
  as haptic input, 107–108, 110, 116
  as kinetic input, 111

training data, and algorithmic bias in AI, 267, 270–271, 273

transitions, 161–180
  between devices, 172–177, 178
  directed, 175–176
  between input, and ergonomics, 153–154
  input/output mismatch, 165–166
  input transitions, 162–164
  as interruptions, 58–59
  between modalities, 162–166, 178
  between network connections, 167, 169–172, 178
  output transitions, 164–165
  summary to apply it, 177–178

transparency
  in AI, 266–267
  in network connections, 170–171

Treisman, Anne, 193

triple flows, 235–236

Tsai, Janice Y., 41–42

tumor detection, and pre-existing bias, 268

turn-taking between people, device relationships, and transitions, 176–177

Turnstall, Elizabeth (Dori), 324

Twitter, "neutrality" on, 12

ACKNOWLEDGMENTS

Contributors

To the interviewees who so generously contributed their time and expertise to this book (in order of appearance): Dr. Janice Y. Tsai, Syed Sameer Arshad, Cathy Pearl, Jen Cotton, Anna Abovyan, Craig Fox, Brad Frost, Ovetta Sampson, Jesse Schell, and Dr. Casey Fiesler.

To Kelly McArthur: Thank you for being my first, bravest, and most prodigious technical reviewer. You read my work just weeks into this process, and your feedback was priceless all along the way.

To my technical reviewers: Bryce Johnson, Di Dang, and Gonzalo Ramos—thank you so much for generously braving my unedited thoughts in your limited free time and contributing your valuable insight to this book.

To my editor, Marta Justak, for your enthusiastic advocacy, constructive feedback, professional perspective, and delightful partnership.

To Lou Rosenfeld, for your hard work building this community, and for the great honor of inviting me to join the Rosenfeld Media family onstage and in print.

To Bill Buxton, for sharing your own perspective on multimodality after seeing my "Future of Voice" talk at Microsoft Research in late 2017.

To anti-racist economist, Dr. Kim Crayton, creator of #causeascene, for your tireless advocacy work and generously granting your permission to include your guiding principles in this book.

For your help with inquiries about facts, definitions, and perspectives: Rebecca Stockley, Susan MacPherson, Jason Mesut, Dave Malouf, Katherine Titsworth, and Giorgio Robino.

Personal and Professional Thanks

To my beloved husband, David Foubert, for encouraging me to write this book before I even wanted to write it; for your unwavering and enthusiastic support of my multiple careers; for inspiring me to be a better person; and for the wonderful gift of your friendship and companionship. I still choose you.

To my parents, Joan and Mark Platz, for always encouraging all of my varied pursuits; for identifying and nurturing my alarmingly early desire to learn; and for the sacrifices you made to help me get a quality education. (And for all those Disney trips.)

To my brother, Kyle Platz, for, of course, being a great brother, but especially for opening my eyes to *Pokémon*—seemingly innocuous, but a critical inspiration for me along the way. And for your continued love and support, particularly as we navigate the Twitch community together.

To my brother, Doug Platz, for your friendship and support during our college days and as our early careers evolved.

To Victoria Picco, Joe Picco, Elizabeth Karcher, Pam Policastri, Cele Wolman, Stephan Mueller, Kelly McArthur, David Peck, Eric Bennett, Tim Harahan, and Arwen Russell: I am so blessed to have your friendship in my life. Thank you for all of your support during this long road, from hospital beds to puzzle hunts and Disney days. Here's to the road ahead!

To Randy Dixon and Jay Hitt, your mentorship, friendship, and support at Unexpected Productions have transformed my relationship with improvisation onstage and at work. And to Kent Whipple, for dedicating your considerable energy to keeping that improv home alive.

To Craig Fox, Steve Ettinger, and JC Connors: your leadership, mentorship, friendship, and faith in my design abilities transformed my career.

To Amy Kalson, for your friendship and cysterhood through bright and dark times alike, and for coming to Seattle to join me on the *Disney Friends* journey. And to fellow *Disney Friends* leads Tamara Knoss and Bill Harding—our time on that project will always be a particularly fond memory. We'll always have Stitch.

To Lisa Stifelman, Sumedha Kshirsagar, Shane Landry, and Darren Gill: your generous mentorship helped launch my own career in voice and natural user interface design.

To Eva Manolis, Maggie McDowell, Robert Zehner, Gonzalo Ramos, Sheri Stevens, Max Spivak, and Jack Wei, for sharing your considerable experience and wonderful camaraderie during my time on the Echo Look team at Amazon.

To Jon Harris and Nafisa Bhojawala, for your mentorship, sponsorship, and encouragement on my path to Principal.

To Virginia McArthur, your mentorship and faith in me early in my video game career opened more doors than either of us could ever have foreseen. To Jesse Schell, your talent, advice, and techniques transformed game design from "something other people did" to an important part of my early career.

To Alexander Muir, Stefanie Tomko, and David Walker, for sharing your energy, unique expertise, and friendship during my time on Windows Automotive.

To Mark Stehlik, for your astonishing ability to counsel any Carnegie Mellon student at any point during their career, and specifically for warmly helping me through dark times post-9/11 in the final push to complete my CS degree.

Love to all of my cast and crewmates at Unexpected Productions, and especially the extended NERDprov family: Jeannine, Tony, Dan, Lauren, Claudia, Sara, and Mike.

And to all of the many dear friends I didn't have room to list (many of whom I perhaps didn't get to see during the year I wrote this work): may our paths cross in the future in happier, healthier times.

To my colleagues at the Bill & Melinda Gates Foundation for their camaraderie and continued support of my speaking and writing career. I look forward to continuing our great work together!

To my medical team who cared for me during the writing of this book, which was no small feat during a pandemic; particularly Dr. Parham and Dr. Ericson, who have shone new light on how to cope with my disability on a day-to-day basis.

To the #MagicMafia, my online community, thank you for restoring my faith in digital humanity, and for the camaraderie, honesty, and humor over the years. Special thanks to my community management volunteers: Krellen, David Demma, and Aradinsc.

To the conference organizers who poured their hard work into creating platforms for folks like me: thank you for the often thankless, always challenging work to bring different perspectives and cultures together.

To the leadership of the Interaction Design Association, past and present, for creating a community and conferences that have opened countless doors for me and so many others.

To my lawyers, Raemi Gilkerson and Krista Contino Saumby, for your skilled partnership in helping me navigate complicated waters as a first-time sole proprietor and author.

To everyone who has ever joined me for a workshop or engaged with me after a talk or on social media: your energy, enthusiasm, and insight helped lead me down this path.

 **Rosenfeld**

Dear Reader,

Thanks very much for purchasing this book. There's a story behind it and every product we create at Rosenfeld Media.

Since the early 1990s, I've been a User Experience consultant, conference presenter, workshop instructor, and author. (I'm probably best-known for having cowritten *Information Architecture for the Web and Beyond*.) In each of these roles, I've been frustrated by the missed opportunities to apply UX principles and practices.

I started Rosenfeld Media in 2005 with the goal of publishing books whose design and development showed that a publisher could practice what it preached. Since then, we've expanded into producing industry-leading conferences and workshops. In all cases, UX has helped us create better, more successful products—just as you would expect. From employing user research to drive the design of our books and conference programs, to working closely with our conference speakers on their talks, to caring deeply about customer service, we practice what we preach every day.

Please visit **rosenfeldmedia.com** to learn more about our **conferences**, **workshops**, **free communities**, and **other great resources** that we've made for you. And send your ideas, suggestions, and concerns my way: louis@rosenfeldmedia.com

I'd love to hear from you, and I hope you enjoy the book!

Lou Rosenfeld

Lou Rosenfeld,
Publisher

RECENT TITLES FROM ROSENFELD MEDIA

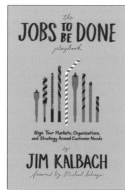

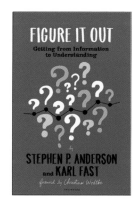

Get a great discount on a Rosenfeld Media book:
visit **rfld.me/deal** to learn more.

SELECTED TITLES FROM ROSENFELD MEDIA

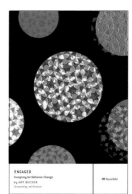

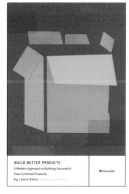

View our full catalog at **rosenfeldmedia.com/books**

ABOUT THE AUTHOR

 **Cheryl Platz** is a world-renowned designer whose work on emerging technologies has reached millions of customers across multiple industries, from best-selling video games to the largest cloud platforms in the world. Her professional passions include natural user interfaces, applied storytelling in design, and taming complexity in any manifestation. Past employers include Amazon (Alexa, Echo Look, Echo Show), Microsoft (Azure, Cortana), Electronic Arts/ Maxis (The Sims franchise), Griptonite Games (*Disney Friends*), Disney Parks (PhotoPass), and MAYA Design.

Currently, Cheryl is a full-time Principal UX Designer at the Bill & Melinda Gates Foundation, helping to develop new services for digital collaboration at a global scale. As principal and owner of design education company Ideaplatz, LLC, Cheryl has presented her sought-after workshops and talks around the world to audiences in over 15 countries on five continents.

Cheryl's unique background also includes over 15 years as a professional actress and improvisor. She's been a proud member of the Unexpected Productions performing ensemble since 2008 and on its teaching faculty since 2013.

Cheryl holds a B.S. in Computer Science and Human-Computer Interaction from Carnegie Mellon University. She tweets at @funnygodmother and @ideaplatz, and you can learn more about all of her work at http://cherylplatz.com.